D0553012

KT- 418- 747

199 501

The People's Game?

The People's Game?

Football, Finance and Society

Stephen Morrow

NORWICH CITY COLLEGE LIBRARY		
Stock No.	199501	
Class	796·3340691 MOR	
Cat.		Proc.	

© Stephen Morrow 2003

All rights reserved. No reproduction, copy or transmission of this
publication may be made without written permission.

No paragraph of this publication may be reproduced, copied or transmitted
save with written permission or in accordance with the provisions of the
Copyright, Designs and Patents Act 1988, or under the terms of any licence
permitting limited copying issued by the Copyright Licensing Agency, 90
Tottenham Court Road, London W1T 4LP.

Any person who does any unauthorized act in relation to this publication
may be liable to criminal prosecution and civil claims for damages.

The author has asserted his right to be identified as
the author of this work in accordance with the Copyright, Designs and
Patents Act 1988

Published by
PALGRAVE MACMILLAN
Houndmills, Basingstoke, Hampshire RG21 6XS and
175 Fifth Avenue, New York, N.Y. 10010
Companies and representatives throughout the world

PALGRAVE MACMILLAN is the global academic imprint of the Palgrave
Macmillan division of St. Martin's Press, LLC and of Palgrave Macmillan Ltd.
Macmillan® is a registered trademark in the United States, United Kingdom
and other countries. Palgrave is a registered trademark in the European
Union and other countries.

ISBN 0–333–94612–X

This book is printed on paper suitable for recycling and made from fully
managed and sustained forest sources.

A catalogue record for this book is available from the British Library.

A catalog record for this book is available from the Library of Congress.

10   9   8   7   6   5   4   3   2   1
12   11   10   09   08   07   06   05   04   03

Copy-edited and typeset by Povey–Edmondson
Tavistock and Rochdale, England

Printed and bound in Great Britain by
Creative Print & Design (Wales), Ebbw Vale

For Beth and Hugh and Caitlin too

Contents

List of Tables, Figures and Exhibits   viii

Foreword   x

Acknowledgements   xi

Introduction   1

1   Football's Changing Economics   4

2   Football Clubs: Businesses or Social Institutions?   43

3   Organizational Forms: Ownership and Governance   74

4   Where Business Meets Society: Learning From the
    Case Studies   128

5   Communicating the Business of Football   145

Conclusion   182

Appendix 1:   Football Business Coverage   185

Notes   194

References   208

Index   224

List of Tables, Figures and Exhibits

Tables

1.1	Scotland: concentrated sporting success	6
1.2	Scottish Premier League points differential	6
1.3	The Old Firm: League matches lost to other Scottish Premier League clubs	7
1.4	England: Concentrated sporting success	8
1.5	Italy: concentrated sporting success	9
1.6	Spain: concentrated sporting success	10
1.7	Germany: concentrated sporting success	10
1.8	France: concentrated sporting success	11
1.9	Netherlands: concentrated sporting success	12
1.10	Television rights fees	14
1.11	Broadcasting income as a percentage of turnover	15
1.12	Distribution of television income – the FA Premier League	15
1.13	Survivability of promotion	18
1.14	Ipswich Town: the cost of relegation	19
1.15	UEFA Champions' League revenue distribution 2001/02	23
1.16	Percentage split of the market pool	24
1.17	UEFA Champions' League market pool league table 2001/02	25
1.18	Domestic League television soccer audiences	29
1.19	Champions' League (Group Stage 1) television market share	30
2.1	Charitable donations	63
2.2	Club website disclosure index (January 2002)	64
3.1	Classification of football companies by ownership type, 1997	81
3.2	Ownership of Tottenham Hotspur plc	83
3.3	PSV share capital at 30 June 2001	94
3.4	Turnover PSV	99
3.5	Listed Danish clubs	103
3.6	Financial statements (extracts) – Brøndby	104

3.7   Ownership of Parken Sport and Entertainment   107
3.8   Profit and loss account (extracts) – Parken   107
3.9   Balance Sheet (extracts) – Parken   107
3.10   The importance of Borsa Italiana   116
3.11   The finances of Italian Serie A clubs   121
3.12   Financial performance of listed Italian clubs   125
4.1   Classification of football clubs by ownership type   132
5.1   Electronic availability of financial information   148
5.2   Youth development narrative disclosure   162
5.3   Newspapers surveyed   173
5.4   Reporting the business of football – items reported week
        beginning 15 January 2002   174

Figures

2.1   Spectator categories (detailed)   50
3.1   Spectator categories (simplified)   85
3.2   Organization structure at PSV Eindhoven   97
3.3   Movements in Parken share price   108
3.4   Juventus shareholder structure   118
3.5   The distribution of television and radio rights,
        season 1999/2000   122

Exhibits

1.1   Objectives – UEFA Champions' League   26
2.1   Social involvement (extracts from annual reports)   58
2.2   Social involvement (extracts from annual reports)   59
2.3   Social involvement (extracts from official club websites) 60
2.4   CCI narrative disclosure (1999/2000 annual reports)   65
4.1   Stakeholder conflict   130
4.2   Annual Charter Report – Tottenham Hotspur   143
5.1   Deferred income disclosure   156
5.2   Securitization disclosure   159
5.3   Sunderland plc annual results 2002   168
5.4   Reporting the proposed Rangers rights issue   180

Foreword

Hamish

Up at Tannadice
Framed in woodwork cool as ice
Keeping out the wolves in his particular way
A smile and a wave, a miraculous save they say
Out runs Hamish and the ball's in Invergowrie Bay

Up at Tannadice as they gently terrorise
Call the sentry, Oh Hamish give us a song
Raising the voices as high as the bridge is long
Nasser said hello and did you miss him while his voice was gone

I remember that time it was an evening game
A European tie in the howling rain
Gus Foy pointed to the side of the goal
And said
'There's Grace Kelly by Taylor Brothers coal'

In Tannadice

Up at Tannadice
Watching as the fortunes rise
Smiling when he hears 'Ah it's only a game,
Win lose or draw you get home to your bed just the same'
But Hamish stokes young mens dreams into a burning flame

'*Hamish*' from the album, *On Stolen Stationery*, by Michael Marra (Eclectic Records: 1991).

© BAT Music

The song celebrates both the testimonial of the legendary Dundee United goalkeeper, Hamish McAlpine, and the visit of Grace Kelly to Tannadice Park.

The song captures everything that football is about ... personality, success against the odds, hope, and community. It even manages to get a business dimension in too in the shape of the local merchants!

Acknowledgements

My thanks are due to all those who have assisted me in researching and writing this book. First, to representatives of clubs and supporters' organizations throughout Europe who kindly agreed to assist me with my research: Dan Hammer, Commercial Director and Flemming Østergaard, Chairman at FC København; Anders Larsen, FC København Fan Club; Daniel Levy, Chief Executive, Tottenham Hotspur; Joff Wild, Tottenham Hotspur Supporters' Trust; Harry van Raaij, Chairman, Fons Spooren, Director of Operations and Peter Foosen, Director of General Affairs at PSV Eindhoven; Jeff Slack, CEO Inter-Active at Inter Milan. I am also grateful for the warm welcome I received at these clubs. My thanks also to Brian Lomax of *Supporters Direct* and Antonio Merchesi of Deloitte & Touche, Milan, who agreed to be interviewed by me in connection with the research. I am grateful to FIFA and the CIES (Le Centre International d'Etude du Sport) in Neuchâtel for awarding me a Havelange scholarship, for this allowed me to fund this part of the research.

The book draws on published literature in a number of areas and I am grateful to all those authors referred to in the text. In particular I am indebted to my colleagues Raymond Boyle, Will Dinan and Philip Morris at the University of Stirling and Sean Hamil at Birkbeck College, with whom I have collaborated on different projects that have contributed to this book, to Francisco Serrano Domínguez from the University of Seville and to Marco Broekman from the University of Maastricht who provided me with literature and advice on football in the Netherlands.

Sincere thanks to Caroline Brand, Joyce Nicol, Alison Wilson and Claire Taylor who diligently transcribed my interview tapes, to Claire van Wengen and Dr Cyrille Guiat who provided invaluable translation assistance and to Jamie Corr for providing some valuable assistance with content analysis. My ongoing thanks to Barbara Kettlewell and Jacqui Baird from the Department of Sports Studies for their help and assistance throughout.

A very special debt is owed to my former colleague, Frank McMahon, for taking the time and trouble to read over earlier drafts of this book and for providing me with numerous insightful comments and suggestions.

Thanks also to my departmental colleagues Wray Vamplew, Grant Jarvie and Joe Bradley, as well as to Professor Pauline Weetman from the University of Strathclyde, Professor Rae Weston of Macquarie Graduate School of Management in New South Wales and John Moore of Bell Lawrie White, for helpful discussions and advice and to David Dale, Graeme Smith, Robin Sydserff, Mark Vettraino and my dad, Peter, for their comments and suggestions.

I am particularly grateful to Michael Marra for graciously allowing the words to his song *Hamish* to be used as a musical preface to the book. My sincere thanks also to Stephen Rutt and his colleagues at Palgrave Macmillan for their support throughout the duration of this project.

Finally, an enormous thank you to Jill for her love and support throughout the research and writing of this book, particularly in view of everything else that was going on at the time; to Caitlin for being Caitlin; and to Hugh and Beth for arriving in the middle of the writing and helping to keep things in some sort of perspective.

STEPHEN MORROW

The author and publishers are grateful to the following companies and organizations for the permission to reproduce their material:

Exhibit 5.3, Sunderland plc annual results 2002 (p. 168) is reproduced with the kind permission of Soccer Investor Ltd, London.

Figure 2.1, Spectator categories (detailed), p. 50 (reproduced from) and Figure 3.1, Spectator categories (simplified), p. 85 (adapted from) Giulianotti, R. (2002), 'Supporters, Followers, Fans and Flâneurs', *Journal of Sport and Social Issues*, vol. 26, no. 1, copyright © 2002 by Sage Publications, reprinted by permission of Sage Publications Inc.

Table 1.2 (p. 6) is based upon information reproduced by permission of Headline Book Publishing Limited.

Table 1.15, UEFA Champions' League revenue distribution 2001/02 (p. 23); Table 1.16, Percentage split of the market pool (p. 24) and Table 1.17, UEFA Champions' League market pool league table 2001/02 (p. 25), are based upon material reproduced with permission from the UEFA website; Exhibit 1.1, p. 26, Annexe VII, Paragraph 12 of the Regulations of the UEFA Champions' league 2002/03 is reproduced with the kind permission of UEFA.

Table 3.7, Ownership of Parken Sport and Entertainment (p. 107) and Figure 3.3, Movements in Parken share price (p. 108), are reproduced with the kind permission of the Copenhagen Stock Exchange.

Figure 3.5, The distribution of television and radio rights, season 1999/2000 (p. 122), is reproduced with the kind permission of Lega Calcio.

Tables 1.1, 1.3, 1.4, 1.5, 1.6, 1.7, 1.8, 1.9 (pp. 6–12) and Table 1.13 (p. 18) are based upon information location on the International Soccer Server (http://sunsite.tut.fi/rec/riku/soccer.html) reproduced with the kind permission of Riku Soininen.

Every effort has been made to contact all the copyright-holders, but if any have been inadvertently omitted the publishers will be pleased to make the necessary arrangements at the earliest opportunity.

Introduction

Of the many phrases used to describe football, one of the most powerful is its portrayal as 'the people's game'. The description conjures up many images: the game's majesty revealed in sweeping views of massive crowds at the Camp Nou or Wembley Stadium or the San Siro; cup winning sides parading triumphantly through crowded streets in their home town; convoys of supporter-filled cars, flags waving, horns blaring, celebrating their team's triumph; small boys playing kick-about among the tenements and housing schemes of Glasgow or Liverpool or Manchester ...

For many decades the national team was the pinnacle of footballing achievement. The World Cup remains the outstanding or premier football event. But the balance of power has now shifted from international football to club football. Clubs like Manchester United, Bayern Munich and Real Madrid have gained international status in their own right, initially through the advent of European club competitions, subsequently through developments in television and other technology, which enables European and domestic competitions to be conveniently exported. More fundamentally, clubs also provide an indispensable link to every aspect of football. As well as providing an infrastructure and opportunity for players of all ages to play football within a controlled competitive environment, they are also the focus through which fans channel their enthusiasm for the game. Clubs frequently are an enduring presence at the heart of communities; vital sources of local pride or esteem.

But football at club level has changed very markedly in the last decade or so. At several clubs there are players who are paid more in a day than some supporters will earn in a year. Several clubs have few if any players from the country in which they are based, far less the city or town in which they are located. Indeed clubs themselves are rarely clubs in the traditional sense of the word. Football clubs in some countries, most notably the UK, have traditionally been structured as companies. It is a more recent phenomenon for these companies to be owned by city financial institutions and media corporations. Indisputably major football clubs are now complex businesses; intrinsically concerned with matters of economics and finance.

1

Yet acceptance of football's economic base need not equate to a rejection of its social nature, to disregarding its importance as a social phenomenon. Certainly this book is about the business of football, about the relevance and significance of financial issues for football clubs. But finance and business do not exist in a social vacuum. Every day, directly and indirectly, people react to and are affected by financial and business information. For example, social outcomes like job security, house prices, mortgages, purchasing decisions, pension values and so on are all dependent on financial and business information. But football's social nature goes beyond this. Notwithstanding the increasing business orientation of football clubs, football continues to have social aspects that distinguish it from purely economic activity. Indeed it is the continued social and community significance of football that makes the study of the business of football so fascinating.

Key factors are durability and identity: for fans, supporting their clubs is about long-term commitment; for communities, clubs are a stable presence. People and communities will also change over time. What this book aims to provide is an insight into how changes in football and football clubs, both economic and social, have altered the relationships that exist between clubs and their changing communities. Football has changed – how far have people changed with it? Put another way, can the football business also be 'the people's game'?

The book is structured as follows. Chapter 1 focuses on the rapidly changing finances of club football in Europe. The revenues that have flowed into top-level football in the last decade or so are of a quite different magnitude to what has gone before. For example, the annual rights fee for broadcasting English First Division football in 1983 was £2.6m (Baimbridge *et al.*, 1996): 20 years on it is £367m (Dobson and Goddard, 2001, p. 437). This new-found prosperity has significant implications not only for clubs' business approaches and strategies, but also more fundamentally for our understanding of how leagues operate in terms of concepts like competitive balance and uncertainty of outcome. Clearly any discussion of how, and how well, leagues function, has both economic and social or societal dimensions. Chapter 2 focuses on the extent to which a conflict emerges between football clubs as businesses and football clubs as social institutions. The issue is explored by focusing on the relationships that exist between clubs and their stakeholders, with a particular emphasis on players, supporters and the wider community. How has football's business transformation altered these stakeholder relationships? Following on from this, Chapter 3 focuses on the organizational structure of clubs. Using case studies of clubs in Denmark,

England, Italy and the Netherlands it identifies aspects of their ownership, control and governance structures, both in the context of the particular country's system of corporate financing and governance and also its football culture and context. Themes and differences that emerge from the case studies are then identified and analysed in Chapter 4. The aim of this chapter is to identify examples of best practice, considering the extent to which these findings can inform our understanding of ownership and governance structures among other football clubs and of the interplay between the social and business dimensions of football. Finally, Chapter 5 focuses on the communication of financial information about clubs and the related issue of account-ability to interested groups. The chapter aims both to identify and analyse sources of financial information about football clubs as well as offering some points of guidance on the interpretation of that information.

Financial and social dimensions are inevitably and deliberately intertwined in this book. It is neither a book about the finances of football nor is it a book about the social nature of football. Rather it is an attempt to locate the middle ground where contemporary football clubs find themselves; an attempt to offer some insight into how those clubs interact with and affect their communities, both financially and socially.

1 Football's Changing Economics

The commercial development of football in the last decade or so has been much more swift, wide-ranging and dramatic than hitherto. While spectator income continues to be the major source of income for most clubs, other sources of income have become increasingly important; most prominently the huge expansion in television rights, but also commercial partnerships between clubs and non-football organizations and commercial exploitation of improved stadium infrastructure. As for most businesses these income sources are not risk free – for example, television rights income is in part dependent on wider economic factors like the buoyancy of the broadcasting market. It is arguable that conventional business risk is exacerbated by the fact that several of the sources are variable, being dependent on uncontrollable factors like sporting success or the competitiveness of the league in the country in which a club is obliged to participate. Taken together with the fixed nature of a club's major expense, players' wages, that are fixed contractually for a defined period and cannot be modified at short notice, it is clear that financial management in football clubs is particularly challenging.

However, after a decade of unparalleled growth, at the present time (December 2002), uncertainty surrounds football's economic environment: broadcasting markets are in decline, numerous clubs throughout Europe are in serious financial difficulties, breakaway leagues are proposed and players' wage restraint is high on the agenda. Football's uncertain environment extends beyond financial matters: uncertainties surround its legal and regulatory environment and consequently its social and cultural role (Brown, 2000a; Parrish, 2002). The structure and development of football in Europe is in a state of flux.

The aim of this chapter is to consider issues arising from the changing economics of the football business, within football's broader social and regulatory context. In particular, it aims to explore areas in which apparent conflicts exist between the social and business objectives of football's stakeholders and communities, a theme that runs throughout the book.

Competitive imbalance, certainty of outcome and concentrated sporting success

> It looks like being a two-horse race once again when the Danish Superliga kicks off tomorrow: Brøndby IF and FC København against the rest. That has certainly been the case over the last two seasons and with those clubs possessing the best organisation, finances and players, it is hard to see the champions coming from anywhere else.
>
> (Laudrup factor spurs København, *www.uefa.com*, 26 July 2002)

As has been well documented, professional sports leagues have what is termed peculiar economics (see, for example, Arnold and Beneviste, 1987; Dobson and Goddard, 2001; Neale, 1964; Sloane, 1971; Szymanski and Kuypers, 1999). This centres on the interdependence of the participants within a league and the importance of competitive balance and uncertainty of outcome therein. In simple terms clubs require someone to play against, while a strong league, attractive to spectators (and by extension to broadcasters), demands that the likely outcome of a match or the league itself is not virtually certain in advance. The theoretical literature suggests that market forces can maintain a reasonable degree of competitive balance among member teams (see, for example, Dobson and Goddard, 2001). But in practice football regulatory authorities have determined the market place, imposing restrictions on competitive behaviour such as transfer systems, redistribution mechanisms and restrictions on cross-ownership of clubs. At least in part, the authorities have been concerned with attempting directly to ensure competitive balance within a league, or indirectly through the redistribution of revenues among member clubs or between football stakeholders.

Where a league lacks competitive balance, evidence of increasingly concentrated sporting success would be expected. Scotland is often identified as a country in which the top league lacks uncertainty of outcome; sporting success being concentrated in two clubs, Celtic and Rangers, the so-called ' Old Firm'. For example, since its inception in 1975/76, the Scottish Premier League has been won by one of the Old Firm clubs in 23 out of 27 seasons, while no club outside the Old Firm has won the title since 1984/85. Table 1.1 sets out the recent history in terms of the concentration of sporting success within the Scottish Premier League.

Although ten clubs from a possible 25 have found themselves in one of the top five positions in the last five seasons, the continuing dominance of Celtic and Rangers is immediately apparent. Indeed, the last time these

Table 1.1   Scotland: Concentrated sporting success

League position	2001/02	2000/01	1999/2000	1998/99	1997/98
1	Celtic	Celtic	Rangers	Rangers	Celtic
2	Rangers	Rangers	Celtic	Celtic	Rangers
3	Livingston	Hibernian	Hearts	St. Johnstone	Hearts
4	Aberdeen	Kilmarnock	Motherwell	Kilmarnock	Kilmarnock
5	Hearts	Hearts	St Johnstone	Dundee	St Johnstone

Source: *International Soccer Servers* (http://sunsite.tut.fi/rec/riku/soccer.html)

clubs did not occupy the first two positions in the SPL was 1994/95, when Celtic finished in fourth place behind Rangers, Motherwell and Hibernian. Furthermore, increasingly the club finishing third is so far behind the other two clubs that it gives the appearance of a league within a league. Table 1.2 demonstrates that the points differential between the first two clubs and the other clubs has grown markedly over the most recent five year period.[1] One needs look no further than the bookmakers for confirmation of this fact. At the start of season 2002/03, while Ladbrokes were offering odds of 2/5 on Celtic retaining their Scottish Premier League title and 13/8 on Rangers becoming champions, the joint third favourites – Aberdeen, Heart of Midlothian and Livingston – were all priced at 250/1. A further indication of increasing concentration of sporting success is the marked decline in the number of matches that Celtic or Rangers lose against other Scottish teams during the course of a season; an indication of match uncertainty of outcome (see Table 1.3).[2]

Table 1.2   Scottish Premier League points differential

	2001/02	2000/01	1999/2000	1998/99	1997/98
Between champions and third placed team	45*	31	36	20	7
Between second and third placed team	27*	16	15	14	5

* From season 2001/02, the SPL split into top six and bottom six clubs for the last six games of the season. Hence the differential would be expected to grow as the best teams played among themselves rather than facing potentially easier games against weaker opposition.

Source: Rothmans (2002)

Table 1.3 The Old Firm: league matches lost to other Scottish Premier League clubs

	2001/02	2000/01	1999/2000	1998/99	1997/98
Celtic	1	1*	6	5	4
Rangers	1	5	2*	4	4

*One match lost after the Championship had been won

Source: *International Soccer Servers* (http://sunsite.tut.fi/rec/riku/soccer.html)

One expected consequence of (relative) certainty of outcome in a league is dwindling customer interest, both from spectators and from television audiences, and consequently dwindling revenues. Dobson and Goddard (2001, p. 427) suggest that the problem with leagues in a country like Scotland is one of critical size. In common with other small countries, they argue that Scotland suffers from a 'minimum efficient scale' problem, i.e. national populations are too small to sustain 16 or 18 teams able to employ players of sufficient talent to create a league with standards comparable to those of the big five countries (England, France, Germany, Italy and Spain) and capable of attracting commensurate spectator and television audiences. Consequently competition is highly unbalanced and television revenues are modest.

Paradoxically, until recently, the intense competition and rivalry that exists between Celtic and Rangers, have allowed both of these clubs to prosper financially.[3] Although this might appear to invalidate conventional economic theory on sporting competition, one rational explanation is that because these two clubs have the largest markets, in fact the competition between them generated sufficient interest to ensure high attendances and television interest. In other words, within an uncompetitive league of 10 or 12, there has been a competitive league of two. While the other clubs benefit to some extent from market interest in the Old Firm, the financial rewards they receive are not sufficiently large to allow them to compete fully in sporting terms.

However, football does not operate within a hermetic system – clubs may compete in European competition as well as in domestic leagues. The growing financial rewards available to top clubs in recent years – rewards largely fuelled by media rights – have focused attention on the conflict that exists between promoting intra-league competitive balance and providing a financial structure that allows clubs to be competitive in European competition. In Scotland in recent years, the conflict has forced questions of league restructuring and the distribution of financial rewards firmly to the top of the agenda, most visibly in the repeated attempts of the Old Firm clubs to seek membership of a more financially lucrative league such as the Premiership or Nationwide Leagues in England or even through the creation of a new league such as the Atlantic League; a league consisting of other big clubs in small countries.

Scotland's lack of competitive balance has long been commented on.[4] But evidence exists that suggests that relative certainty of outcome is becoming a more widespread problem, even within countries that are large enough to be expected not to suffer from problems of minimum efficient scale. For example, in a study of leagues in Italy, Germany, Spain and England over a ten year period from 1988, Hoehn and Szymanski (1999) found that the three biggest teams accounted for between 40 and 50 per cent of all European competition places won.[5] The recent history in terms of the concentration of sporting success within the premier leagues in England, Italy, Spain, Germany, France and the Netherlands is set out in Tables 1.4 to 1.9.

In England, only eight clubs from a possible 25 have found themselves in one of the top-five positions in the last five seasons. The last time the FA Premiership was won by a club other than Arsenal or Manchester United was as far back as 1994/95 when Blackburn Rovers, under the ownership of its benefactor, the late Sir Jack Walker, lifted the title. In the last five seasons, only one club (Liverpool in 2001/02) has prevented Arsenal and Manchester United occupying first and second place at the end of the season, with these three clubs together accounting for 87 per

Table 1.4   England: concentrated sporting success

League position	2001/02	2000/01	1999/2000	1998/99	1997/98
1	Arsenal	Manchester United	Manchester United	Manchester United	Arsenal
2	Liverpool	Arsenal	Arsenal	Arsenal	Manchester United
3	Manchester United	Liverpool	Leeds United	Chelsea	Liverpool
4	Newcastle United	Leeds United	Liverpool	Leeds United	Chelsea
5	Leeds United	Ipswich Town	Chelsea	West Ham United	Leeds United

Source: *International Soccer Servers* (http://sunsite.tut.fi/rec/riku/soccer.html)

cent of the top-three finishes over these five seasons. In addition a fourth club, Leeds United, has achieved a top-five finish in four of the last five seasons.

Murphy (1999a) has carried out research into the overall competitiveness of English elite football. Calculating performance (points) differentials between the top and bottom clubs and between the top six and bottom six clubs, he found that there was no discernible tendency for the level of competitiveness to decline over the period since 1945. However, he also noted that these findings did not exclude the probability that the elite status of some clubs was becoming more secure. Thus the recent picture presented in Table 1.4 is not necessarily inconsistent with the wider empirical analysis carried out by Murphy. While the league as a whole may continue to demonstrate competitive balance, defined in terms of points differential, nevertheless there is an increasingly small number of elite clubs from which the actual winner of the competition is likely to be drawn.

In Italy, only 10 clubs from a possible 25 have found themselves in one of the top-five positions in the last five seasons. Of these, Fiorentina has gone into liquidation and now finds itself beginning again in Serie C. In contrast to England, however, this evidence suggests a greater spread of potential winners of the Serie A title than is the case for the Premiership, with a different club winning the title in each of the last four years. Although no club has managed a top-five finish in each of the last five seasons, three clubs (Juventus, Roma and Inter) have achieved top-five finishes in four of the last five seasons.

Like Italy, in Spain only 10 clubs from a possible 25 have found themselves in any of the top-five positions in the last five seasons. However, if the analysis is restricted to the last four years, the number

Table 1.5   Italy: concentrated sporting success

League position	2001/02	2000/01	1999/2000	1998/99	1997/98
1	Juventus	Roma	Lazio	Milan	Juventus
2	Roma	Juventus	Juventus	Lazio	Inter
3	Inter	Lazio	Milan	Fiorentina	Udinese
4	Milan	Parma	Inter	Parma	Roma
5	Chievo	Inter	Parma	Roma	Fiorentina

Source: *International Soccer Servers* (http://sunsite.tut.fi/rec/riku/soccer.html)

Table 1.6 Spain: concentrated sporting success

League position	2001/02	2000/01	1999/2000	1998/99	1997/98
1	Valencia	Real Madrid	Deportivo la Coruña	Barcelona	Barcelona
2	Deportivo la Coruña	Deportivo la Coruña	Barcelona	Real Madrid	Atlético Bilbao
3	Real Madrid	Mallorca	Valencia	Mallorca	Real Sociedad
4	Barcelona	Barcelona	Zaragoza	Valencia	Real Madrid
5	Celta Vigo	Valencia	Real Madrid	Celta Vigo	Atlético Madrid

Source: *International Soccer Servers* (http://sunsite.tut.fi/rec/riku/soccer.html)

falls to only seven clubs from a possible 20. Again, similar to Italy, this evidence suggests a greater spread of potential winners from within the country's elite clubs, with different clubs winning the Primera League title in each of the last four years. Two clubs (Real Madrid and Barcelona), however, have achieved top-five finishes in each of the five seasons under review, between them achieving three first and two second places.

In Germany, only nine clubs from a possible 25 have found themselves in one of the top-five positions in the last five seasons. In the last two

Table 1.7 Germany: concentrated sporting success

League position	2001/02	2000/01	1999/2000	1998/99	1997/98
1	Borussia Dortmund	Bayern Munich	Bayern Munich	Bayern Munich	Kaiserslautern
2	Bayer Leverkusen	Schalke 04	Bayer Leverkusen	Bayer Leverkusen	Bayern Munich
3	Bayern Munich	Borussia Dortmund	Hamburg SV	Hertha Berlin	Bayer Leverkusen
4	Hertha Berlin	Bayer Leverkusen	1860 München	Borussia Dortmund	Stuttgart
5	Schalke 04	Hertha Berlin	Kaiserslautern	Kaiserslautern	Schalke 04

Source: *International Soccer Servers* (http://sunsite.tut.fi/rec/riku/soccer.html)

seasons the same five clubs occupied the top five positions, albeit in different orders. Two clubs, Bayern Munich and Bayer Leverkusen, have achieved top-five finishes in each of the five seasons under review. Between them these two clubs have achieved three first and four second places, accounting for 70 per cent of the top-two finishes over these five seasons.

The lowest concentration of sporting success is found in France. Here 13 clubs from a possible 25 have found themselves in one of the top-five positions in the last five seasons. In addition, no club has had a top-five finish in all five seasons under review, while only two clubs (Lyon and Bordeaux) achieved top-five finishes in four of the five seasons. Furthermore, a different club in each of the last five seasons has won the league. Whether this greater apparent equality among clubs will continue is debatable. Although French clubs voted in 2002 to maintain the principle of solidarity among clubs, they also voted to revise the redistribution of television rights, with 81 per cent of the total funds going to clubs in the first division. Half of this is shared equally among clubs, one third is distributed according to sporting merit with the remainder being distributed according to 'notoriety' criteria, This includes previous league performances, media exposure and the effect that teams have on their opponents' attendances when they are playing away from home (*Soccer Investor*, 2002i). While the average annual budget for clubs in Ligue 1 has been approximately €35m in each of the last three seasons (up to and including 2002/03), the range of budgets therein has risen markedly. In 2002/03 the highest budget (Olympic Lyon, €101m) was

Table 1.8   France: concentrated sporting success

League position	2001/02	2000/01	1999/2000	1998/99	1997/98
1	Lyon	Nantes	Monaco	Bordeaux	Lens
2	Lens	Lyon	PSG	Marseille	Metz
3	Auxerre	Lille	Lyon	Lyon	Monaco
4	PSG	Bordeaux	Bordeaux	Monaco	Marseille
5	Lille	Sedan	Lens	Rennes	Bordeaux

Source: *International Soccer Servers* (http://sunsite.tut.fi/rec/riku/soccer.html)

Table 1.9   Netherlands: concentrated sporting success

League position	2001/02	2000/01	1999/2000	1998/99	1997/98
1	Ajax	PSV Eindhoven	PSV Eindhoven	Feyenoord	Ajax
2	PSV Eindhoven	Feyenoord	Heerenveen	Willem II	PSV Eindhoven
3	Feyenoord	Ajax	Feyenoord	PSV Eindhoven	Vitesse
4	Heerenveen	Roda JC	Vitesse	Vitesse	Feyenoord
5	Vitesse	Utrecht	Ajax	Roda JC	Willem II

Source: *International Soccer Servers* (http://sunsite.tut.fi/rec/riku/soccer.html)

approximately eight times greater than the lowest budget (AJ Ajaccio, €12.2m), compared to a ratio of only 5:1 in season 2001/02 (*Soccer Investor*, 2002b). That said, it is worth pointing out that in season 2000/01, Lille on the third smallest budget of FF120m (€18.3m) finished in third place, while the club with the largest budget, Paris St Germain (FF500m, €76.2m), could only finish in ninth position (*Soccer Investor*, 2001d).

In the Netherlands, only eight clubs from a possible 25 have found themselves in one of the top-five positions in the last five seasons. More pertinent, however, is the fact that three clubs – Ajax, PSV and Feyenoord, together account for 80 per cent of the top-three finishes over these five seasons. The last season in which one of these three clubs did not end the season in one of the top-five positions was 1990/1991, when Feyenoord finished in eighth position, while the last time the league was won by a club other than one of the big three was as far back as 1980/81 when the title was won by AZ '67. Football success in the Netherlands has always been considered heavily concentrated. Nevertheless it is worth noting that this percentage is actually below that reported for the English Premiership.

Who earns wins? Football's television dependency

For armchair fans, all that remains are memories of great occasions and, as our man in the sheepskin carcoat might have put it, quality words from quality commentators. 'How fitting,' said John Motson, when Manchester United won an FA Cup, 'that a man called Buchan should be first to climb the 39 steps.' Will his successors have time to say that before the commercial break?

(*The Scotsman*, Editorial, 15 June 2000, p. 17)

With the exception of France, for each of these countries there is evidence of concentrated sporting success. Factors such as club ownership structures may have exacerbated the situation (see Chapter 3). Arguably, it is the symbiotic relationship developed between television and football that has most undermined competitive league balance and that has become the most fundamental problem facing professional football (Brown, 2000a; Dobson and Goddard, 2001, p. 425). While sport has become crucial to television's business model, concomitantly the money earned from television rights has become a vital income stream for football clubs.

This dependent relationship can be traced to the fundamental reversal in the economics of broadcasting markets; namely that while in the past programme content had to compete for scarce transmission outlets (i.e. television channels), by the early 1990s large numbers of channels were competing for (relatively) scarce content (Cowie and Williams, 1997; Westerbeek and Smith, 2002, p. 145). This has resulted in clubs throughout Europe, and in particular clubs in those countries with large potential television audiences, benefiting from substantially improved television deals. The extent of football's reliance on, and conversely broadcasters' commitment to football, is reflected in the fact that the combined worth of the contracts covering Europe's biggest leagues in 2001/02 was an extraordinary £1.795bn (Campbell, 2002a). Table 1.10 provides an overview of current deals within some European Leagues while Table 1.11 demonstrates the increasing importance of broadcasting income among Europe's top football leagues.

This change in the wider broadcasting market was accompanied by moves by major clubs in many European countries to put in place mechanisms enabling them to capture a greater share of this increased income. The twin effect of these demands for more lucrative television rights deals, and for substantial modifications in the distribution of these rights, resulted in substantial structural change in some countries – for example, the formation of the FA Premiership in England in 1992 – as well as the metamorphosis of the European Cup into the UEFA Champions' League in 1992/93. In other countries like Italy and Spain, collective television deals were either abandoned in favour of clubs

Table 1.10 Television rights fees

	Time period	Broadcasters	Details	Annual rights fee (approx.) €m
England	2001–04 (3 years)	BSkyB ITV	Live Premier League matches plus highlights	673
France	2001–04 (3 years)	Canal Plus, TPS, France Television	First and second divisions and League Cup, mixture of live plus highlights	380
Germany	2000–04 (4 years)*	KirchMedia		372.5
	2002–04 (2 years)	KirchMedia: ProSieben, SAT 1, Premiere World	Highlights on free to air channels, live games on Pay TV	293 pa plus a one-off payment of 50.6
Italy	2001–02	RAI	Highlights (Serie A and B), live coverage of Coppa Italia	88.8
		Stream, Telepiu	Most Pay-TV deals are arranged individually by club‡	e.g. Inter 44, Juventus 49, Parma 25, Torino 8
Scotland	1998–2002 (4 years)	BSkyB BBC	Live SPL matches Highlights	17.7
	2002–04 (2 years)	BBC	Live SPL matches plus highlights	12.6

* The Bundesliga TV rights were renegotiated after KirchMedia was put into administration in April 2002 and defaulted on its original contract. However, when the rights came back up for auction it managed to secure the contract again but with a significant reduction in its rights fees.
‡ Eight smaller clubs negotiate their Pay-TV deals collectively.

Sources: England (Dobson and Goddard, 2001, p. 437); France (*Soccer Analyst*, 2(1), p. 6); Germany (*SportsBusinessTV*, 19 July 2002, p. 5); Italy (*Soccer Investor*, 106, p. 7 and 109, pp. 1–2); Scotland (various press reports)

negotiating their own individual deals or were introduced in parallel with some form of collective deal.[6]

Within domestic leagues, as Tables 1.1 and 1.4 to 1.9 have demonstrated, there is evidence that a small number of super-clubs have emerged with a consequent reduction in competitive balance within those leagues. One explanation is that the distribution of television income is becoming

Table 1.11 Broadcasting income as a percentage of turnover

	2000/01 (%)	1999/2000 (%)	1998/99 (%)	1997/98 (%)	1996/97 (%)
English Premier League	39*	31	29	26	21
Italian Serie A	54*	56	35	37	36
German Bundesliga	45*	31	29	28	25
French LNF Premiere Division	51*	56	42	43	32

* By contrast broadcasting revenues are relatively less important in other European countries. In Denmark they make up only 4 per cent of total revenue, in the Netherlands 12 per cent and in Scotland 23 per cent.

Source: Deloitte & Touche (various years)

Table 1.12 Distribution of television income – the FA Premier League

	2001/02 (£m)	2000/01 (£m)	1996/97 (£m)	1992/93 (£m)
Top earner	25.7	20.4	6.3	2.4
Median earner	17.3	13.4	4.2	1.6
Lowest earner	10.8	8.4	2.8	1.1
Parachute payment	4.0	3.1	1.0	0.8
Earnings gap*	138%	142%	125%	118%

* Earnings gap = £(top earner – lowest earner)/lowest earner.
Parachute payments are made to relegated clubs for two seasons after their relegation to cushion them from the financial impact of losing their position in the FA Premier League.

Source: FA Premier League Annual Reports (various years)

increasingly skewed towards the top clubs. As mentioned previously, in some countries like Spain, clubs are permitted to arrange their individual television deals.[7] However, even in leagues where the rights have continued to be sold collectively, there is evidence that the distribution of television income is becoming more polarized. For example, Table 1.12 demonstrates the changing distribution of television income within the English FA Premier League. Leaving aside the huge increase in absolute income received by clubs in the last ten years it is important to note that the earnings gap between top and bottom clubs has grown substantially over the last decade.

A further consideration of television's impact on competitive balance is that television income is effectively cost-less, i.e. in contrast with income received from sources like merchandising, margins on broadcasting income are very high. In view of the apparent relationship between investment in players and football success (see, for example, Deloitte & Touche, 2001b; Szymanski and Kuypers, 1999),[8] it is unsurprising that this increased income is often treated as a windfall gain; immediately available to be spent on recruiting and paying for better or more players. Notwithstanding that success in any league is by definition limited, one likely consequence of increased investment in players is thus increasingly concentrated sporting success. While an occasional extraordinary performance by a club like Ipswich Town in England or Chievo in Italy can never be ruled out,[9] nevertheless the picture emerging in these countries is of a handful of super clubs from which inevitably the league champions will emerge. Current systems are designed for continual strengthening of the strongest leagues and clubs; competition is in danger of being replaced by structural self-perpetuation.

The issue of competitive balance within Europe-wide competitions is at least in part dependent on the scale of television deals enjoyed in particular countries. The size of a country's domestic television market-place is generally reflected in the size of its domestic television deal. As a result clubs located in countries with smaller television markets, like the Netherlands, are at a financial disadvantage when competing against a club in say England or Italy. This outcome may be considered unsatisfactory from a sporting perspective, but any debate about its fairness needs to focus on cause rather than effect. Although revenue received from television is an effect arising from the system of distribution, arguably this outcome arises inevitably from the cause, namely the system of market economics that underpins society throughout countries in Western Europe. Issues of financial fairness and sporting equity among competing clubs seem to have far greater legitimacy in the context of competitions organized on a Europe-wide basis such as the Champions' League. Despite the fact that this is a European competition organized within a European market place, in its Champions' League regulations UEFA has adopted discriminatory systems, both sporting and financial, which inevitably favour clubs from major market economies (see the section on 'To those that have ...' later in this chapter).

Up and down – Yo-yos, parachutes and trampolines

Another significant issue in competitive balance is that the gap between clubs in the Premier or top leagues and the lower leagues is shaping to become a chasm. Studying the promotion and relegation of clubs between the two divisions, or inter league mobility, can highlight the consequences of income imbalance between divisions. Dobson and Goddard (2001, p. 428) noted that only nine of the 20 teams promoted to the FA Premier League at the end of its first seven seasons (1993 to 1999 inclusive) avoided relegation in the first season after promotion. On the face of it, things have improved in the two subsequent seasons, with only one club from six (Manchester City) being relegated in its first season after promotion. However, of the other five, Ipswich Town were relegated at the end of their second season, while the ownership structure of Fulham, in the form of its wealthy benefactor Mohamed Al Fayed, and to a lesser extent the return to the top flight of Blackburn Rovers, which still receives generous support from the legacy of its former benefactor, Sir Jack Walker, hardly makes these typical promoted clubs (see also Chapter 3). By contrast, 17 of the 21 teams promoted to Division One of the English League in the seven seasons following the introduction of 'three up, three down' in 1974 avoided immediate relegation (Dobson and Goddard, 2001, p. 428).

This pattern is not restricted to England. However, as the figures in Table 1.13 demonstrate, recent evidence suggests that it is more difficult for a newly promoted club to survive in the English Premiership than is the case in Germany, Italy or Spain.

Football leagues in Europe have always been based on the fundamental principle of sporting competition – playing merit. Irrespective of a club's status or size, if insufficient points are accumulated then a club is relegated. Difficult, as it may now be to believe, it is less than 30 years since one of Europe's super clubs, Manchester United, spent a season (1974/75) outside England's top division. However, there is evidence that rather than having a situation where financial reward simply reflects sporting outcomes, arguably sporting outcomes are becoming increasingly dependent on mechanisms of financial distribution.

For example, in the English Premier League, a system of financial support exists which sees clubs relegated into the Nationwide League receiving a so-called parachute payment (see Table 1.12). This payment cushions relegated clubs from the immediate financial impact of relegation and makes it easier for them to retain their players and is

Table 1.13   Survivability of promotion

	Number of clubs relegated within one season of promotion/Total number of clubs promoted		Number of clubs relegated within one or two seasons of promotion/ Total number of clubs promoted	
	since 1996/97*		since 1996/97[‡]	
England	7/15	47%	9/12	75%
Germany	5/15	33%	6/12	50%
Spain	6/16	38%	8/13	61%

* A club promoted in 1996/97 is included if it was relegated in the following season (1997/98) etc.

[‡] A club promoted in 1996/97 is included if it was relegated in either the following season (1997/98) or the one following that (1998/99) etc.

Source: *International Soccer Servers* (http://sunsite.tut.fi/rec/riku/soccer.html)

thus an implicit recognition of the skewed distribution of television revenues in English football. From a sporting perspective, the receipt of a parachute payment by a relegated club, combined with the experience of having played in the top division, provides it with a significant competitive advantage compared to other clubs in the lower division. Thus it acts to weaken competitive balance in the lower league. As such, the payments contribute to a yo-yo effect and arguably are more akin to a trampoline than a parachute (Murphy, 1999a).

Table 1.14 sets out some comparative financial information for Ipswich Town, a club that has spent time in both the Premiership and Nationwide Leagues in recent seasons.

The implications for a relegated club's income streams are immediately apparent. While the parachute payment is helpful to the club concerned, nevertheless it is markedly less than it would have received had it retained its Premiership status. Its principal difficulty is that while its income streams respond immediately to changes in its operating environment (i.e. which league it is in), its cost base, and in particular, its player wage bill does not, being fixed over the length of players' contracts. (Of course, the situation that a club like Ipswich Town finds itself in has been exacerbated by the collapse of the Nationwide League's deal with ITV Digital, the digital television company set up by Carlton and Granada. Consequently, instead of receiving £315m to be shared over three years, clubs in the Nationwide League will now receive only £95m to be shared over 4 years (Plunkett, 2002).) Notwithstanding this situation, the financial consequences of playing outside the Premiership are clear. Hence, although the relegated club finds itself being financially better off

Table 1.14   Ipswich Town: the cost of relegation

Season	1999/2000	2000/01	2001/02	2002/03
Status:	Nationwide Division 1, promoted (£m)	FA Premiership, 5th position (£m)	FA Premiership, relegated (£m)	Nationwide Division 1, 7th position (£m)
Turnover	10.0	31.3*	37.4	?
Television, radio and share of Premier (or Football) League sponsorships:	1.2	18.5‡	18.5‡	6.5
				made up of:
				5.9 (Parachute payment)
				0.6 (Nationwide League)
TV rights from UEFA Cup games	–	–	1.5	–
Payroll costs	8.5	17.7	24.2	?

* Thirteen month period.
‡ This is divided as follows for 2001/02 (2000/01 in brackets): a basic award of £8.0m (£6.3m), payments of televised games of £5.3m (£4.0m), a merit award of £1.3m (£5.4m) and a share of League sponsorships of £3.8m (£2.8m).

Source: annual reports 2000–2; newspaper reports (2002–3)

than its new competitors in the Nationwide League, it falls further behind the clubs that have retained their Premier League status.[10]

The scale of reward on offer to clubs for top division status, the skewed mechanisms for distribution of these revenue sources and the moves away from inter- and intra-league redistributive principles, all heighten the pressure placed on clubs, encouraging excessively short-termist behaviour and decision making by club directors. Taken together with the evidence of a correlation between investment in players and football success discussed in the previous section, it is unsurprising, therefore, that clubs seek to ensure that they gain or retain top division status by spending heavily on recruiting and purchasing more or better players.

Rosen and Sanderson (2001) liken the escalation of expenditure on player wages by clubs operating within a league to a military arms race among nations. A club has little option but to try to match the spending of its competitors, despite the knowledge that, if all clubs increase spending at the same rate, it will end up no better off at the end than it was at the start. The alternative, abstinence, will result in its losing ground. In football, there is a similar outcome for any league competition, in that one team's ascent up the league must be matched by another's descent (Dobson and Goddard, 2001, p. 429). Thus the consequences of the top-heavy financial reward mechanisms prevalent in leagues like the FA Premiership inevitably put pressure on clubs to spend to survive. Nevertheless, acknowledging this state of affairs and its very considerable pressures surely does not justify apparent mismanagement by so many football club directors.

The difficulty with resolving these problems is that once again we return to the central conflict between solutions that prioritize sporting outcomes and those that prioritize economic or market solutions. In the interests of improving competitive balance within sporting competitions, a case can certainly be made for more even distribution of revenue among different leagues. Policy decisions could be taken that would reduce the skewed distribution mechanisms and might be expected to thus reduce the yo-yo effect. However, all recent trends in the increasingly market-oriented world of football suggest that there is little or no likelihood of such policies being implemented in practice.

Another response would be to reduce or abolish parachute payments. This would be expected to result in a more level playing field within the first division, hence increasing the number of clubs that can aspire to promotion. It would do nothing, however, to increase those clubs' chances of surviving in that top division as their financial resources would be diminished compared to the existing yo-yo clubs, and would be likely to result in more 'one-season wonder' clubs (Murphy, 1999). Further-more, while the likelihood of uncushioned relegation might be expected to introduce financial realism among directors of promoted clubs, paradoxically, it may actually encourage some directors to take greater financial risks in the hope of sustaining a Premiership position. Another possibility is increasing the number of clubs relegated and promoted each season. While this might be expected to level playing standards, unless it was accompanied by radical redistribution of revenues, then any levelling would be likely to be limited to clubs outside the elite or super clubs. As with the abolition of parachute payments, this might be expected to encourage financial realism among directors. But ultimately it would be dependent on decisions taken by individuals.

From the other side of this conflict, one rational economic policy response would be simply to end relegation from top leagues like the FA

Premiership or Serie A. Business risks faced by football clubs are quite unlike those faced by most other businesses. Ultimately, business or financial outcomes are determined by events entirely outside the control, certainly of business managers, and arguably also of football managers. Removing the risk of relegation would enable club directors to plan a sensible and sustainable medium- to long-term financial or business strategy, free from short-term uncontrollable operating risks such as the outcome of one or a few football matches. The more clubs that are promoted and relegated in any one season, then the greater the business risk faced by all clubs. This explains why some consultants in Italian football (where 4 clubs are relegated annually from Serie A) have advocated at least a temporary abandonment of promotion and relegation (interview with Antonio Merchesi, Deloitte & Touche Milan, January 2002). However, even from a financial perspective, though the suggestion may make sense to clubs that find themselves within the elite at the point of cut-off, it is hardly attractive to those left on the other side. More fundamentally, however, while hermetic leagues might be seen by some as the logical extension of the changing financial economy set out above, such a proposal would be entirely at odds, both in substance and in form, with the fundamental principles of sporting competition and rewards for merit. Existing systems of financial redistribution may be far from satisfactory, but in theory they retain the principle of rewarding sporting merit.

Quite probably there may be no practicable policy-based solution that acknowledges both sporting and financial outcomes. Rather, it may be that the focus should be on pragmatic approaches to minimizing the negative aspects of the present circumstances. One possibility lies in improved financial management within clubs. As mentioned previously, the financial consequences of relegation are worsened by the fixed nature of player wages. Concomitant with the introduction of voluntary salary caps, or more accurately voluntary wage restraint,[11] by the G14 clubs[12] as well as the English Nationwide League, one way forward may be the introduction of player contracts where the financial rewards are variable and more explicitly linked to sporting outcomes. In other words, clubs should consider introducing performance-related pay (PRP), something quite common in other areas of business. It might not solve the fundamental problems inherent in the business of football. At a minimum, such pragmatism would concentrate attention on sustainability, if not survival, as clubs' salary bills would be more closely linked to sporting, and by extension, financial performance. While calls for PRP have grown louder during football's 2002 financial troubles,[13] arguably

PRP is not new in football. For example, the success of the less fashionable Scottish club, Dundee United, in the 1980s – which included not only winning the Scottish Premier League title but also reaching the semi final of the European Cup – was based not only on a talented group of young players, but also on a pay structure that relied on relatively low basic wages and high performance related financial incentives[14] (Morrow, 2001b). However, PRP should not be restricted solely to players: where such a system is not already in place, PRP should certainly also be introduced for club directors, many of whom have underachieved substantially in recent years. PRP approaches are consistent with the financial requirements set out in UEFA's proposed club licensing system – which are designed to ensure that clubs live within their means. Under these proposals clubs with outstanding football debts, such as unpaid wages or transfer fees, or which are, or expect to be at the end of the season in a position where their liabilities are in excess of their assets, would be prevented from participating in UEFA club competitions (UEFA, 2002a) (see also sections on 'Players' in Chapter 2 and 'The Annual Report and Accounts' in Chapter 5). It is also worth noting that countries like France already have domestic licensing systems, which encourage good financial management by threatening clubs with relegation if their financial position does not meet agreed standards. There would seem to be a strong case for encouraging domestic governing bodies in other countries like England to adopt similar systems.

To those that have …

If anything the iniquitous financial consequences of football's improved rewards from television and the accompanying changes in the distribution of those rewards are even more vividly illustrated by studying the UEFA Champions' League. Introduced to replace the European Cup in season 1992/93, in practice it bears little resemblance to its predecessor competition. Arguably it is football's closest approximation to a hermetic competition. Participation is dependent on various factors. While domestic league championship success was the requirement for entry to the old European Cup, such sporting success is no longer necessary nor indeed sufficient to gain automatic entry to the league stages of the competition. Instead, entry is based on a country's coefficient as determined by UEFA. Thus, while in season 2002/03 for example, England and Italy had two clubs that automatically qualified for the group stages and a further two clubs that were required take part in the qualifying rounds, the Champions of Belgium (Anderlecht) were required to enter the competition in Qualifying Round 2, while the Champions of Scotland (Celtic) began in Qualifying Round 3. The UEFA coefficients are compiled annually and depend on the performance of clubs representing a particular association in UEFA club competitions in the previous five seasons (UEFA, 2002b, para. 5). The points obtained each season by the participating clubs are added and divided by the number of participating clubs, to produce the coefficient value of that national association (UEFA, 2002b, para. 7).[15] Inevitably it builds a system essentially self-perpetuating.

The UEFA Champions' League has become the most financially lucrative club football competition. Approximately 25 per cent of the total revenues generated by UEFA[16] in respect of the Champions' League are retained by UEFA to cover organizational and administration costs or to allow for solidarity payments to its member associations, made to support the development of football throughout Europe (UEFA, 2002b, para. 24.07 (b)). The remaining 75 per cent is distributed among the 32 participating clubs in the manner set out in Table 1.15.

As Table 1.15 shows, for season 2001/02 approximately 50 per cent of the Champions' League revenues (CHF 383 million) are accrued into a market pool. The allocation of this pool to participant clubs is not, however, based on sporting merit. Instead the market pool is distributed

Table 1.15 UEFA Champions' League revenue distribution 2001/02

Type of payment	Allocated	Amount per club (Swiss Francs, CHF)	Total
Starting fee	Equally	3m	97m
Match fee group stage 1	Equally	3m (0.5m per match)	96m
Performance bonus group stage 1	On merit	0.5m per win, 0.25m per draw	48m
4th place group stage		0.5m	4m
Match fee group stage 2	Equally	3m (0.5m per match)	48m
Performance bonus group stage 2	On merit	0.5m per win, 0.25m per draw	24m
Market pool	See below	See below	383m
Quarter final bonus	On merit	4m per team	32m
Semi final bonus	On merit	5m per team	20m
Final bonus	On merit	Winner – 10m runner up – 6m	16m
Total			768m

Source: www.UEFA.com

Table 1.16   Percentage split of the market pool

Position	4 teams (%)	3 teams (%)	2 teams (%)	1 team (%)
Champions	40	45	55	100
Runners-up	30	35	45	
No. 3	15	20		
No. 4	15			

Source: www.UEFA.com

according to the proportional value of each domestic television market represented by the clubs taking part in the UEFA Champions' League, with this sum then being split among the number of teams (4, 3, 2 or 1) participating from a given association. Half of the sum representing the value of each market is split among clubs, based on their performance in the previous domestic league championship. Hence, the split among the teams from a given association follows the system shown in Table 1.16.

The other half of the sum representing the value of each market is paid in proportion to the number of matches played by each team in the 2001/02 UEFA Champions League. The exact sum received by each club therefore depends on four factors:

1   How many clubs from a market compete in the UEFA Champions' League (for example, two may qualify automatically, and another two via the third qualifying round).
2   The league standing of the club in the previous season's domestic championship.
3   Its performance in the UEFA Champions' League.
4   The performances of other clubs from the same country in the UEFA Champions' League.

The paramount factor in determining what a club receives from the market pool is the television audience size of the country in which it plays. In other words, irrespective of the numerator and the denominator used in the calculation described previously, this fraction is then applied to the respective market value (television value) of a particular country. The consequences of this system of distribution are marked in their sporting inequity. Table 1.17 demonstrates the full consequences of this in respect of the distribution of the 2001/02 Market Pool League table.

Table 1.17   UEFA Champions' League market pool league table 2001/02

		CHF	Stage reached	Group stage 1 points	Group stage 2 points	Domestic league position (no. of clubs from country)	
1	FC Nantes	31.8m	GS2	11	2	1st	(3)
2	AS Roma	29.6m	GS2	9	7	1st	(3)
3	Bayern Munich	29.1m	Quarter final	14	12	1st	(4)
4	Juventus	26.1m	GS2	11	7	2nd	(3)
5	Manchester United	25.4m	Semi final	10	12	1st	(3)
6	Bayer Leverkusen	21.9m	Final	12	10	4th	(4)
7	Real Madrid	21.5m	Winners	13	16	1st	(4)
8	Olympic Lyon	20.1m	GS1	9	–	2nd	(3)
9	Arsenal	19.4m	GS2	9	7	2nd	(3)
10	Schalke 04	17.7m	GS1	6	–	2nd	(4)
11	Deportivo La Coruña	16.8m	Quarter final	10	10	2nd	(4)
12	Liverpool	16.3m	Quarter final	12	7	3rd	(3)
13	Lille	15.1m	GS1	6	–	3rd	(3)
14	Lazio	13.9m	GS1	6	–	3rd	(3)
15	Barcelona	13.4m	Semi final	15	9	4th	(4)
16	Borussia Dortmund	11.6m	GS1	8	–	3rd	(4)
17	Mallorca	7.9m	GS1	9	–	3rd	(4)
18	Celtic	6.8m	GS1	9	–	1st	(1)
19	PSV Eindhoven	6.0m	GS1	7	–	1st	(2)
20	Feyenoord	5.5m	GS1	5	–	2nd	(2)
21	Rosenborg	3.9m	GS1	4	–	1st	(1)
22	Boavista	3.5m	GS2	8	5	1st	(2)
23	Galatasaray	3.5m	GS2	10	5	2nd	(2)
24	FC Porto	3.2m	GS2	10	4	2nd	(2)
25	Panathinaíkos	2.9m	Quarter final	12	8	2nd	(2)
26	Anderlecht	2.8m	GS1	3	–	1st	(1)
27	Fenerbahce	2.7m	GS1	0	–	1st	(2)
28	Olympiakos	2.1m	GS1	5	–	1st	(2)
29	Spartak Moscow	0.8m	GS1	2	–	1st	(2)
30	Locomotiv Moscow	0.8m	GS1	7	–	2nd	(2)
31	Sparta Prague	0.6m	GS2	11	6	1st	(1)
32	Dynamo Kiev	0.3m	GS1	4	–	1st	(1)

Source: www.UEFA.com

This distribution policy is perhaps the clearest example of the market philosophy being applied today in football. Some, such as the G14 group of major clubs, attempt to justify this distribution system as equitable on the grounds that revenues are returned to clubs in the countries from which the television companies and audiences were delivered.[17] But, even from an economic point of view the competition is Europe-wide, its participants are Europe-wide and hence it might be expected that the relevant market would also be a Europe-wide market. More fundamentally, this distribution method effectively disregards reward for sporting merit within the competition itself. While Sparta Prague's market pool reward for reaching an overall points tally of 17 – six points of which were achieved in the second group stage – was CHF 0.6m, Roma was rewarded to the tune of CHF 29.6m for an overall points tally of 16 points, seven of which were achieved in the second stage.

In its Champions' League Regulations, UEFA states that its duty in marketing the commercial rights of the Champions' League 'is to fulfil, within a market economy-oriented environment, its cultural and sporting mandate to protect and foster the interests of football' (UEFA, 2002b, Annexe VII, para. 1.1). It goes on to identity three objectives, the third of which is set out in Exhibit 1.1.

Precisely how the market pool system of distribution fits with UEFA's principles of solidarity within Europe's football family is difficult to comprehend. Sporting merit is largely ignored and financial rewards become dependent on the economic wealth and population base of countries. Clubs from countries with low populations or that are economically poorer are inevitably disadvantaged by the system. Top clubs from these nations are now being hit twice: first, by the lower revenues available from their domestic television deals: second by UEFA's inequitable system of distributing income from its club

Exhibit 1.1   Objectives – UEFA Champions' League

Priority of sport over financial interests

- future oriented financial stability for UEFA, its member associations and clubs, as well as the safeguarding of their independence
- fostering of solidarity within the European footballing community, through the sustained support of financially weaker clubs and national associations

Source: UEFA (2002b), Regulations of the UEFA Champions' League 2002/03, Annexe VII, para. 12

competitions. In these circumstances, success becomes almost a self-fulfilling prophecy, as the reward mechanisms are skewed towards the successful clubs in larger countries, with little or no consideration towards wider issues of sporting competition.[18]

According to Brown (2000a), the distribution systems employed by UEFA now pose long-term questions about the viability of existing structures of European football competition and the sustainability of some clubs. Paradoxically, this is also a view likely to be shared by the G14 group of clubs. Arguably, the changes that have taken place in UEFA's club competitions have arisen from pressure from these clubs; pressure which evidenced itself most publicly in the proposals for a breakaway league to be run outside UEFA's auspices put forward in 1998 by the Italian organization, Media Partners (see later section on 'The economics of change'). One of the issues, which the G14 group is lobbying for, is a Champions' League with an improved filtering process which results in fewer so-called weak teams reaching the group stages (Campbell, 2002b). An inevitable consequence of this is, of course, that there is less chance of any of its members or similar clubs missing out on the financial rewards from the competition simply as a unfortunate consequence of losing football matches!

Changing channels?

Football's relationship with television is a paradox. Television has been responsible for substantially increasing the revenues available in the game as a whole. At the same time it is those very revenues, or rather the manner in which they are shared out, that has most undermined competitive league balance and had led to the emergence of financially dominant leagues and financially dominant super clubs.

Irrespective of the nature of its business, it is unwise for any organization to be over-reliant or dependent on any one source of income. In some areas of economic activity such as auditing, for example, guidance is provided to audit companies to ensure that they do not become financially dependent or potentially compromised by their relationship with one client (Ethics Standards Board, 2002).[19] Football, however, remains a relatively simple business. Most clubs have few substantial sources of income – gate receipts, sponsorship and commercial income and of course, television – and it is not open to all clubs to diversify into other areas of economic activity such as owning and managing hotels (for example, Chelsea, Kilmarnock) or owning other sporting assets (for example, FC København). Furthermore, such diversification has not been universally successful in the past.[20] In view of this it is difficult to see what reasonable steps clubs could have taken to avoid becoming overly reliant on television income, as the value of television rights soared. Equally, however, club directors should have recognized their club's consequent vulnerability and reflected this in its expenditure patterns. While directors could not have been expected to foresee the collapse of companies like KirchMedia or ITV Digital, and certainly cannot be held responsible for the decisions taken by management at those companies with regard to the sums they were prepared to pay for television rights, it does not seem unreasonable to expect them to be cognizant of the changing economics of the broadcasting markets and to reflect this in their own decision making. Yet, evidence suggests that several Nationwide clubs were technically insolvent even before the collapse of the ITV Digital deal. For example, at the end of season 2000/01, 10 out of 24 clubs in Division One had liabilities greater than their assets (Deloitte & Touche, 2002a), figures which are unsurprising given that the average club in that division had a wages to turnover ratio of 101 per cent (Deloitte & Touche, 2002b).

It seems likely that in the absence of new or substantially altered products, football's television rights income may now have peaked (Clarke, 2002). There are several explanations for this: some football specific, others more related to the wider broadcasting and economic environment. First, there has been an economic downturn throughout Europe and beyond, which impinges upon the businesses of broadcasters and media companies most notably through the downturn in advertising revenue. According to investment bank Merrill Lynch, the global advertising market fell by approximately 5 per cent in 2001 compared to the previous year (Clarke, 2002, p. 93). Within the industry itself, there has been a reduction in the number of satellite broadcasters; arising both from mergers and takeovers of companies within the sector (e.g. Sogecable and Via Digital in Spain) and from the collapse of some of the companies (e.g. KirchMedia and ITV Digital). Consequently there will be a reduction in the number of potential bidders for future rights; this reduction in competition seeming certain to reduce the amount broadcasters are prepared to pay for football rights. Many broadcasters, including Sky's Rupert Murdoch, are now on record as stating that the sports rights market has peaked (Mann, 2002).

Another factor has been that to date, Pay-TV or pay-per-view has not been a great financial success for broadcasting companies in most European countries, failing to meet predicted revenues and subscription targets (Clarke, 2002). Even in one of world football's most passionate marketplaces, Italy, Pay-TV has not taken off in the way expected. One consequence is the expected merger of the two main Pay-TV networks, Telepiu and Stream (*Soccer Investor*, 2002a). Many of the Italian clubs that have successfully arranged Pay-TV deals for 2002/03, among them Roma, Lazio and Parma, will receive no more than they received the previous season. Even the deals arranged by Juventus, Inter and Milan show only very modest rises (*Soccer Investor*, 2002a).[21] Further indication of the difficulties faced by Italian football was demonstrated by the delayed start to the 2002/03 Italian League season, a delay caused by the clubs failure to agree a deal for highlights with state broadcaster, RAI, as well as the failure of eight Serie A teams to arrange terms for Pay-TV coverage of their matches (*Soccer Investor*, 2002a).

A further factor is the decline in football's television audience figures, both in terms of domestic competitions (see Table 1.18) and the UEFA Champions' League (see Table 1.19). Several factors may explain this decline. One factor may be the almost saturation coverage of live football now available on television.[22] However, as discussed above, more fundamentally, one rational predicted consequence of competitive imbalance is that audience figures fall in response to what is perceived as a less interesting product. Consequently, it is likely that this decline will be reflected in a lower future rights deals. This is the paradox. Football leagues and clubs seek ever more rewards from broadcasting companies, yet the consequence of those rewards and their manner of distribution is competitive imbalance which thus reduces the attractiveness of the product and leads to lower revenues from rights in the future.

Table 1.18   Domestic League television soccer audiences

	Programme	Type	% change (2000 to 2001)
France	Telefoot	Highlights	−0.3
Germany	Ran-Bundesliga	Highlights	−11.7
Italy	Novantesimo	Highlights	−2.6
Netherlands	Studio Sport	Highlights	−22.0
Spain	Estudi Estadio	Highlights	1.9
Spain	C+ La Liga	Live	11.6
UK	Match of the Day	Highlights	−10.4
UK	Sky Sports	Live	−21.8

Source: Clarke (2002)

Table 1.19   Champions' League (Group Stage 1) television market share*

	2001/02	**1997/98**
United Kingdom:		
Average audience share	31.2%	41.9%
(4 years +)	(7.12m viewers)	(9.56m viewers)
France:		
Average audience share	28.6%	35.6%
(4 years +)	(6.22m viewers)	(7.51m viewers)
Italy:		
Average audience share	22.4%	31.5%
(4 years +)	(5.95m viewers)	(8.7m viewers)

* Market share = those watching Champions' League as a percentage of those homes with television sets turned on.

Source: *SportBusinessTV*, Issue 1, 18 January 2002

Strangely, the difficulties being faced by many clubs as a consequence of the television companies' inability to fulfil their contractual obligations may actually turn out to be advantageous to football. The rapid increases in the scale of television deals, combined with changes in the distribution mechanisms have acted to substantially widen the gap between rich and poor clubs. As was demonstrated in Tables 1.11 and 1.12 the relative importance of television income as a source of income has grown markedly over the last five years, as has the earnings gap between top and bottom clubs in terms of the distribution of that income. If rights income has indeed peaked, then one possible consequence will be a narrowing of the wealth gap, at least in absolute terms, between the richest and poorest clubs in any league.

However, such a benign interpretation is not consistent with recent developments in the business of football. Reduced rights income may be inescapable, but awareness of this new economic reality may in fact reinforce the gap by encouraging bigger leagues and bigger clubs to seek a larger share of a dwindling cake. The market will dictate that a bigger share of reduced rights income will flow to the higher quality leagues with bigger audiences like the FA Premier League, to the detriment of leagues like the Scottish Premier League or the English Nationwide League. Similarly the super clubs within those leagues will act to ensure that they are the main beneficiaries.

Structural change

> It is economics that is driving the tensions which are currently manifesting themselves in European football – club versus country, the initiative behind the restructuring of competitions (both new and potential); the desire for cross-border competitions to close the gap on the big leagues and the ongoing challenge of cost control.
>
> (Deloitte & Touche, 2002a, p. 16)

Clearly European professional football Europe at club level is fundamentally flawed at present. Leagues are increasingly unbalanced; wealth and on-field success are increasingly concentrated among a handful of super clubs in a small number of super countries; audience interest (both direct and indirect) and, by extension, revenue looks set to decline. Such a scenario has consequences not just from a sporting perspective but also from a business perspective.

The economics of change

Within the existing football structure, a particular risk for clubs, particularly the super clubs, is that they are or that they become mature businesses, that is businesses that, owing to their successful growth, have fewer opportunities to develop or expand. In part this outcome is caused by football's regulatory structure and is unrelated to structural change. For example, football authorities place restrictions on the ability of one club owning, or being involved with another club, as a defence against the integrity of sporting competition being compromised. Consequently growth by horizontal integration (taking over a company in the same line of business), which remains a common means of business growth in countries like the UK and is growing in importance in continental European countries, is restricted. Interestingly, vertical integration (where a company expands backwards toward its source of supply or forwards towards its consumers), has also not been common in football. Indeed, the highest profile attempt at a vertical integration, BSkyB's attempted takeover of Manchester United, was prohibited by the UK Monopolies and Mergers Commission (now the Competition Commission) which feared that it would gain undue control or influence within English football (Monopolies and Mergers Commission, 1999. See, for example, Crowther, 2000; Finney, 2000). By contrast, in the United States there is evidence of greater integration of sport franchises into large media and entertainment conglomerates, driven by these companies' desire to own the sporting content (Harvey *et al.*, 2001). As was noted in the previous section, there also exists the possibility of diversifying into unrelated or peripherally related areas of economic activity, as has been successfully achieved by FC København (see Chapter 3).

More fundamentally, in most areas of economic activity, opportunities exist to move into new markets, but for football clubs such decisions cannot simply be taken by a club's directors and/or shareholders. Rather, a football club's ability to develop or expand its business operations is constrained by regulations imposed by governing bodies like the FA or UEFA, which effectively serve to define its market place or to restrain its trade. Such restrictions are interesting. It can be argued that one rational economic response to the current situation would be rationalization of the market place, in other words restructuring of leagues and competitions. At a theoretical level, the economic case for structural change within European football has been considered at length by Hoehn and Szymanski (1999), and *en passant* by others (see, for example, Dobson and Goddard, 2001, pp. 425–8). Hoehn and Szymanski conclude that an economic case does exist for creating a European Superleague, arguing that it should replace existing domestic leagues for its members, rather than being an additional competition to take part in. Furthermore they argue that a hermetic Super League, akin to Major League Baseball or the National Football League would be the market equilibrium, one that would be in the best interests of both the clubs and the consumers (committed or otherwise). This conclusion is entirely rational from an economic perspective. In the context of sport as business, the wealthiest clubs have emerged from the existing football market place, irrespective of views on the merits and equity of that market place. Logically, the expectation of a super league, at least in the short term, would be for a more balanced competition, which might be assumed therefore to be the preference of the consumers.

Notwithstanding the existence of governing-body restraints on trade, there are several examples of clubs investigating issues of structural change. A key dimension has been the willingness to disregard national or geographical boundaries within Europe, with discussions taking place both for cross-border competitions and for clubs from one country participating in competitions organized by another footballing country.

At a policy level, UEFA has shown itself to be demonstrably against structural change within European football.[23] In form this is unsurprising, given that UEFA-stated objectives are 'to promote and further develop the well-being of football in Europe and to foster a spirit of unity and solidarity among the continent's footballing community' (www.uefa.com). However, in practice, many of UEFA's recent decisions can scarcely be considered to live up to such claims and objectives, with the organization having shown itself to be susceptible to pressure or lobbying. This has been most visible with regard to the attempts made in 1988 by an Italian organization, Media Partners, to persuade some of Europe's top clubs of the merits of setting up a Super League outside the control of UEFA. UEFA's response to the initiative was to transform the workings of the UEFA Champions' League to the economic advantage of major clubs in major television markets. This restructuring can be criticized from an equity perspective (see section 'To those that have ...' earlier in this chapter). It can also be interpreted as UEFA attempting to provide at least a limited opportunity for its super clubs to consolidate or grow their businesses. Despite this, it is clear that pressure for change has not gone away as many of the same clubs that were approached about the breakaway league, are now members of the G14 group of clubs, the economic interest group set up to lobby on behalf of its members.[24]

Elsewhere, domestic football associations have also given in to pressure from major clubs and allowed new or super leagues to be set up under their auspices (e.g. the FA Premier League, the Scottish Premier League) for similar financially motivated reasons. In other sports like rugby league and basketball there has also been acquiescence by sports' governing bodies in the creation of new leagues (Caiger and Gardiner, 2000, p. 3). In all of these successful structural changes, perhaps the key factor was market power. Potentially the Media Partners initiative also had the support of Europe's most prominent or powerful clubs, clubs that arguably already transcend national boundaries (Greenfield and Osborn, 2001, p. 187). As UEFA's structures are built entirely around national associations rather than clubs (Greenfield and Osborn, 2001, p. 188), failure to respond could have seen it bypassed and reduced in status. Similarly, the proposals for the FA's acceptance of the Premiership arose from recognition that power rested with its main clubs.[25] One interpretation of UEFA's behaviour, both past and prospective, is that the operation of the free market means that ultimately UEFA has no option but to accept change as '[it] cannot deny the market, [it] cannot deny the economic law' (interview with Peter Foosen, Director of General Affairs, PSV Eindhoven, December 2001). The risk that it runs in trying to deny the market in these circumstances is to watch the major clubs break away and form a league beyond its control.

Clubs outside the major television markets have also been involved in discussion about structural change. One proposal was for a cross-border Atlantic League, involving clubs from the Netherlands, Norway,

Portugal, Scotland and Sweden with this league complementing existing domestic leagues and clubs being promoted and relegated between the two. One of the prime movers has been the Dutch club, PSV Eindhoven (see Chapter 3). According to PSV's Director of General Affairs, Peter Foosen, the Atlantic League is about economics – the survival of bigger clubs in smaller countries – and sporting balance – helping clubs like PSV to bridge the gap with clubs like Manchester United (interview with Peter Foosen, December 2001). What was envisaged was a league running under the auspices of UEFA, alongside the Premier Leagues in countries like England and Italy; a league that would be open and competitive and would thus be a valid (i.e. commercially interesting) product in a market of more than 60m people (interview with Peter Foosen, December 2001).

Several of the clubs involved have used the media as well as public forums such as company general meetings and conferences like Football Expo and SportBusiness[26] to put forward their view on the merits of a cross-border league. No detailed economic analysis on the case for a cross-border league such as the Atlantic League has, however, been published. Many in the press and elsewhere remain sceptical, most notably about whether the product would be sufficiently attractive to broadcasters and audiences (see, for example, Campbell, D., 2000; Glendinning, 2000; Gourley, 2001; Morrow, 2001a). More pertinently, as mentioned previously, UEFA has made it clear that it would not sanction any such cross-border league. Its ability to stand firm on this proposed change is explainable in part by market power, in that arguably within the overall football market, the clubs proposing an Atlantic League simply do not have sufficient power to force UEFA's hand. Moreover, UEFA for the most part communicates not with clubs, but with its member associations. As such it needs to be cognizant of the wishes of its member associations, and is only too aware that a domestic association's power base would be threatened by one or more of its clubs playing outside of its jurisdiction. Nevertheless, it is clear that pressure for change in the shape of some form of cross-border competition has again not gone away. For example, the Chairman of the Scottish Premier League, Lex Gold, raised the possibility of a North Atlantic Cup in a radio interview on 3 August 2002,[27] claiming that such a competition might start as early as season 2002/03,[28] while by the end of the same month press reports were claiming that further secret (*sic*) talks had taken place in Monaco on new cross-border competitions.[29]

Other, more limited, proposals for structural change have also received extensive coverage by the British media, most notably the attempts of Celtic and Rangers to leave the Scottish Premier League to take part in a league organized under the jurisdiction of another country's footballing authorities, namely the English FA Premier League and the English Nationwide League.[30] Leaving aside social and cultural matters for the time being, while the economic benefits for Celtic and Rangers are unarguable (i.e. improved television income arising from participation in a league in a country with a larger television audience and hence more financially lucrative television deal), the benefits to the English clubs expected to welcome their new competitors from the North might best be described, using the language of the Scottish legal system, as *not proven*.

From the point of view of clubs (collectively) in either the FA Premiership or the Nationwide League, the motivation for allowing the Old Firm to play in their league is predicated on the assumption that in financial terms, altering the structure of any football league is not a zero sum game. As far back as 1989, Rosner (1989, cited in Mahony and Howard, 2001) suggested that the sport industry in the United States was a classic case of a product that although dominating its market, was becoming a mature brand with little prospect for expansion. One way to alleviate this type of problem is to alter the product. In the short term, the benefits to the respective league in England would arise from altering the product (the league) by including these new clubs, thus freshening up a mature market place and making it more attractive to customers, in particular broadcasters. Longer term, benefits might arise from an improvement in competitive balance. In view of the level of support and backing, both social and financial, available to these clubs, it might be anticipated that they would be in a position to challenge the existing super clubs in the Premiership; in effect to increase the number of super clubs. As discussed previously, improving the competitive balance may lead to an improved product, one that is more attractive to customers, especially broadcasters.

As a result, a limited restructuring of this sort may actually serve to increase the absolute amount of income available for distribution among the member clubs, by allowing the league to extract more rents from the television companies (or in the current climate, perhaps more accurately, ensuring less of a drop in income), in return for an improved or altered product. More directly the restructuring would have the potential to provide an increase in viewing figures, both from Scotland, but also perhaps more importantly, through the diaspora of Old Firm supporters in England and well beyond.[31]

However, rejecting the idea that a football league is a zero sum game does not mean that there will be no losers from any proposed restructuring, only that there will be more winners than losers.

Furthermore, any evaluation of restructuring initiatives of this type should arguably be concerned not just with the distribution of income, but also with broader issues such as welfare, utility and social goals. However, even in narrow financial or income distribution terms it is clear that some clubs would be economic losers should Celtic and Rangers be accepted into the English league structure; most obviously those clubs whose positions in the league are taken or threatened by the new clubs. An obvious difficulty for Celtic and Rangers is that membership of the new league would be dependent upon the votes of these same clubs. As the former Rangers Chairman and majority owner, David Murray noted, 'the bigger clubs [in the FA Premier League] want us to join but the turkeys aren't going to vote for Christmas' (Waddell, 2001). Other potential financial losers would emerge should Celtic and Rangers ultimately achieve success in the FA Premier League, with any resultant European qualification achieved by Celtic or Rangers inevitably being gained at the expense of one of the present English clubs. Furthermore, the possibility remains that those clubs left behind in Scotland might also lose out financially if the country's two biggest clubs left. Equally, however, given that it is expected that the new SPL would be more equally balanced, then following the logic set out earlier in this chapter, this would encourage spectator and television interest which could translate into increased revenue.

Ultimately, therefore, the economic or financial case for allowing the Old Firm to become members of one of the English leagues comes down to self-interest; not just the self-interest of the two clubs themselves, but also how successful they are in appealing to the self-interest of other clubs. Can they persuade a sufficient number of clubs that they will be winners rather than losers from the new structure?

Policy for change

Any decision on restructuring has implications beyond economics, encompassing social, policy and legal dimensions; both at a micro (club) level and at a macro (nation state) level. Furthermore, given the structure of football and the importance of European competitions and the European marketplace, it is an issue that cannot be fully considered at a nation state level. Rather, the trans-national nature of football in Europe, combined with the fact that it is the most popular and high profile sport, makes regulatory interest from the European Commission inevitable.

Sport, as an economic activity in the sense of Article 2 of the Treaty establishing the European Community (The EC Treaty, 1997) must comply with Community law (Europa, 2001). EU trade law centres on the quest for market integration and this conditions the application of the law of free movement and competition law to sport (Weatherill, 2000). Furthermore, the institutional and constitutional characteristics of the EU system, relating in particular to the watchdog role allocated to the European Commission and the capacity of the individual to pursue violations before the national courts, contributes to shaping a distinctive system. The European Court's finding in the *Bosman* case that the transfer system operated in violation of the EC treaty by infringing worker mobility, provides a high profile illustration of the vigorous potential of EU law in driving change in the practices of sporting organizations (see, for example, Morris *et al.*, 1996). Subsequently, the European Commission has intervened on issues including the employment rights of players in terms of the new football transfer system (Morris *et al.*, 2003) and the application of competition law in areas like the sale and marketing of television rights (see, for example, Caiger and Gardiner, 2000; Ratliff, 2002).

Since the *Bosman* case, the member states of the EU have incrementally developed sports policy guidelines to assist in understanding the relationship between sport and the EU and it is clear that these guidelines have taken a broader approach to sport than was acknowledged by the European Court in *Bosman*. Although there is no specific mention of sport in the EU treaties, following the Declaration on Sport in the 1997 Amsterdam Treaty, the European Union has, on several occasions, emphasized the importance of sport's social function. The European Commission presented its first overall vision of sport at the Helsinki European Council in 1999 (European Commission, 1999). Its approach of seeking 'to preserve the traditional values of sport, while at the same time assimilating a changing economic and social environment' (European Commission, 1999, p. 7) was subsequently endorsed by member states at the Nice European Council in December 2000, who made a declaration on the specificity of sport, presented as a Presidency Conclusion (Nice European Council, 2000, Annex IV, para. 1).

In seeking to take account of sport's special status, the approach being adopted by the European Commission relies on the exception procedure set out in Article 81(3) of the EC Treaty (1997) as a way of allowing sporting authorities supervised autonomy (Foster, 2000). By extension this support of UEFA can be interpreted as support for preserving existing football competition structures. One interpretation is that the European Commission is keen to use sport, and in particular football's special nature, as a mechanism to bring together member states rather than exclude some states, while recognizing their differing cultures and traditions. However, as Brown (2000a, p. 142) notes arguably one interpretation of this movement towards a European Super League is to see it as example of an integration of member states into a single competition and market – a 'Europeanization' of football.

Two major challenges for sport emerge from the Helsinki Report. First, it recommends that sports organizations and federations must define their missions and statutes in order to identify those special characteristics of sport worthy of protection, in other words sport's special status must be more fully defined (European Commission, 1999, para 4.2.3). Second, where sporting organizations have a commercial dimension, sports rules must be 'founded on the principles of transparency and common access to the market, effective and proven redistribution and clarification of contracts, while prominence is given to the "specific nature of sport"' (European Commission, 1999, para 4.2.3).

This second challenge is of particular interest in the context of the current structure of top-level football in Europe, which has seen increasingly concentrated sporting success and wealth and the development of elite super clubs. UEFA's recent record in terms of financial distribution and financial solidarity is poor. By encouraging a league format in its flagship competition, the UEFA Champions' League, it has reduced unpredictability – the adversary of rich clubs. Furthermore, as discussed previously, it is difficult to describe the competition as operating on the basis of one European market place, given the basis on which first, places in the competition are allocated and second, financial rewards for taking part are distributed.

It is clear from the Helsinki Report (European Commission, 1999, para. 2) that the possibility of a breakaway is considered as being economically motivated and at odds with the principles of financial solidarity. Yet, arguably current EU policy is helping to sustain structures that are also economically motivated, being designed around the financial objectives of a small number of elite clubs. In return for its special status, one option open to the European Commission is to demand that UEFA increase its solidarity efforts: both vertical solidarity in the form of redistributing more money towards amateur sport and horizontal solidarity in the form of supporting the poorer football nations (Foster, 2000, p. 60). Disappointingly there is little evidence that issues of financial solidarity, redistribution and social significance have been prioritized by UEFA.

Current policy seems to be based on an assumption that the social function of sport must be best served by the status quo. Hence, much of the EU's competition policy seems to revolve around protecting UEFA's position, in other words, trying to head off the possibility of a league being set up outside the auspices of UEFA. At the very least, pressure should be placed on UEFA to demonstrate its role in preserving football's special status. More fundamentally, however, the assumption that football is best served within the current structure needs to be debated more fully and openly. Competition policy is concerned with consumers. Consumers can not be best served by the failure to examine the case for explicit restructuring. Certainly restructuring may be beneficial both from a social and a sporting perspective and preferable to many consumers to the current structure, which is predicated on the financial demands of a select few major clubs.

Change and the law

The structure and regulation of sport is also influenced by the juridification of European football, that is the intervention of law and lawyers into sport, a process inextricably linked to financial matters (Parrish, 2002). To date, the most prominent intervention arose out of the case brought by the Belgian player Jean-Marc Bosman discussed briefly in the previous section (see for example, Morris *et al.*, 1996). Prior to *Bosman*, players were one of the least powerful stakeholders in football. Football's financial modernization had not been reflected in changes in the status and rights of its players (Parrish, 2002). Although Bosman's case was the assertion of private rights under the law, concerned about the freedom of movement of workers under Article 39 (formerly 48) of the EC Treaty, it demonstrated that major change could be initiated other than through exercising economic power. This may be of particular significance to clubs outside the elite of European super clubs. Certainly there are parallels between Bosman's situation and that in which clubs like Celtic or PSV Eindhoven find themselves, in that any legal challenge would also concern freedom of movement. As Peter Foosen of PSV noted; 'The basic position is that there is one labour market, there is [practically] one European currency ... but there is no single European market for football clubs ... there is no freedom of movement for clubs' (interview, December 2001).

In contemporary European football, clubs already transcend national boundaries in terms of who plays for them and where they play, and also increasingly in terms of where they derive their income.[32] Arguably clubs participating in leagues beyond their national border is simply a logical consequence of globalization. One legal challenge open to clubs concerns whether UEFA is restricting the right of a company to establish itself or provide services in another EU member state (Foster, 2002). Interestingly, the Europa newsletter (which summarizes activities of the European Union) describes the freedom to establish a sports club in another Member State as another important aspect of freedom of movement (Europa, 2001). It goes on to note that ' this right was recently invoked, on the basis of Article 43 of the EC Treaty, by a number of football clubs wishing to establish their registered office in a Member State other than the one of origin, while continuing to play in the leagues of which they were members' (Europa, 2001). In terms of recent history, what this means is that, for example, Wimbledon's proposal to relocate to Dublin as well as the Belgian club Excelsior Mouscron's proposal to play the home leg of a UEFA Cup tie in France would now be within the spirit of Article 43 of the EC Treaty (Mortimer and Pearl, 2000).

However, in neither of these cases were clubs seeking to take part in competitions organized other than under the jurisdiction of the association of which they were members. More fundamental structural change may indeed see clubs seeking to operate outside the jurisdiction of the home association. In this respect, the *Centros* case heard by the European Court of Justice in 1999 may be of relevance. This case centred on Articles 43 and 48 of the EC Treaty (the right of establishment), dealing with the freedom of movement of companies. The European Court of Justice (Case 212/97 *Centros* judgement) ruled that a Danish-owned UK-registered company was not required to set up a branch in Denmark in order to do business in that country (Mortimer and Pearl, 2000). If this decision has general applicability, then it appears that there is nothing to stop European football clubs legitimately planning their corporate location in a Member State other than that in which their fan base has traditionally been located (Mortimer and Pearl, 2000, p. 233). In other words a legal challenge by clubs seeking to participate in cross-border competitions or in competitions outside their own country would seem to have some authority in case law.[33] UEFA's stance could also be challenged on the grounds that it is abusing its dominant position in European football by acting to protect national leagues while preventing other leagues setting up without its permission (Foster, 2002).

However, a legal approach to regulation, suffers from two key problems. First, it is a crude form of regulation, which will only provide a yes/no answer from a court in response to a stated question. Second, it depends on the willingness of a particular club to take on the football authorities with the resultant risk such a challenge brings, both in a footballing sense and in a financial sense. As was discussed in the previous section, UEFA is demonstrably against structural change. Furthermore, its position would appear to be supported by the European Competition Commission which has made it clear that its concern is only with economic matters, not with the organization and promotion of particular sports (Caiger and Gardiner, 2001). A more specific issue arises concerning the possibility of, for example, Celtic and Rangers, taking part in competitions organized under the auspices of the English FA. But as it is the UK that is the EU member state, then there is no basis for arguing that the clubs are being restricted from operating or establishing within another member state, and hence any case would be an internal UK case (Nicolson, 2002).

Agenda for change – social welfare, consultation and research

The question of how best to structure football leagues within European football requires consideration of economic and sporting issues as well as wider issues of social and cultural significance, with many constituencies having legitimate concerns. At a theoretical level, arguably any formal analysis of structures should be concerned with societal welfare and the search for pareto-optimal conditions that maximize the utility of those involved. Pareto-optimality is an evaluative principle according to which the community becomes better off if one individual becomes better off and none worse off (Albert and Hahnel, 1990). In the case of league restructuring what is required is consideration of the benefits and losses arising from league restructuring, taking into account the preferences of all those affected including shareholders, supporters, employees, governing bodies and the community. In practical situations, the presence of losers (people who incur decreases in utility) usually precludes Pareto-optimal solutions. An acceptable lesser standard can be the notion of Pareto improvements wherein a change is potentially good as long as the improvement in welfare of those who gain from a change is more than sufficient to compensate for those who lose (Culyer, 1975, cited in Tower, 1993).

In practice no obvious mechanism exists to determine the preferences of the various stakeholders to allow them to be included in the decision analysis. Consequently, one risk is that wider societal or welfare considerations are simply ignored with change being dictated on the basis of economic power. The likely result of this is that big clubs from large population centres participate in their own lucrative financial competitions, which may result in wider considerations such as incentivizing sporting merit or the use of sport to promote social or community cohesion being disregarded. Another risk is that policy is forced to react to external influences such as legal cases.

Equally, a different risk is that decisions are instead made on the basis of assertions about the social and societal importance and significance of football. As Brown (2000a) notes while the European Commission has committed itself to the idea of upholding sport's social benefits, there is a need for research and understanding on precisely what these benefits are (particularly in the context of spectator sports) and of how they are manifested, distributed and changing. Football's existing structures may well be worth preserving, but such a conclusion should be based on evidence as to whether the asserted social outcomes are actually being achieved. Furthermore, it should also consider whether other structures may not also achieve the same or similar outcomes.

As was suggested in the introduction to this chapter the European football environment is undergoing a period of change; economic, legal, regulatory, social and cultural. Arguably, what is required at this juncture is an open and wide debate and a policy response based on research into how football should be structured in the future, taking into account the preferences of as many of football's constituencies as possible. While consultation with some football stakeholders like UEFA is achievable, determining stakeholder preferences for groups of supporters or community interests will not be straightforward. These groups are fundamental to football's social significance and ways of including them must be found if an outcome that is both socially and economically acceptable is to be achieved.

2 Football Clubs: Businesses or Social Institutions?

The financial transformation of football in the last decade or so has been extraordinary, manifesting itself in so many aspects of football – player wages, ownership structures, distribution of income, stadium developments, ticket prices and so on. However, as is discussed in different contexts throughout this book, how football, or more accurately, football's constituencies or stakeholders, should respond to this ongoing economic transformation remains a contested area. As a business, it could be argued that football's direction and decision making should now be a function of market economics, with an unfettered market approach being adopted to issues like league structure, distribution of revenues and so on, with the emphasis on business objectives like shareholder value, profit and market share. In practice, it has been argued that the way in which English football responded to the stadium safety requirements of the Taylor Report (Home Office, 1990) demonstrated precisely this unfettered application of free market principles (King, 1997).

Yet a more politically informed approach can be adopted which results in football being conceptualized as economic in basis, but social in nature (Nash, 2000). This approach encourages recognition of the social aspects that delineate football from purely economic activity; that is to identify how its economic basis affects its community – those affected by its actions – or, to use the language of business, its stakeholders. It can be argued that the stakeholder concept has greater relevance for football clubs than for more conventional businesses because of the particular features of certain football club stakeholders, specifically their demands for accountability (Morrow, 2000).

The aim of this chapter is to consider whether and how the financial transformation of football, reflected in business performance and behaviour, has affected its social aspects, in particular the relationship between a club and its stakeholders. Consideration is required in particular of its players, its supporters and its wider community, encompassing people and groups who can be affected either directly or indirectly by the existence and operation of a football club within a particular space, usually geographical, but also potentially religious or social (Morrow, 2000).

Players

Nowhere are the changes that have affected top level football over the last decade or so more visible than in the status of players. Legal intervention, most notably the landmark ruling in the Court of Justice of the European Communities in the Bosman case (CJEC, 1995), followed up in March 2001 by changes to the transfer system agreed between FIFA, UEFA and the European Commission after six months of fractious negotiations (see, for example, Morris *et al.*, 2003) has resulted in players having greater freedom of movement and bargaining power than ever before. Coupled with the substantial increases in revenue being enjoyed by major leagues in Europe – revenue increases largely fuelled by television rights – this has resulted in elite players finding themselves in a position to capture substantially improved economic rewards. For example, the average wage for a player in the FA Premiership has increased by 260 per cent since 1995/96, taking the average earnings to over £500,000 per annum (Deloitte & Touche, 2002a, pp. 32–3).

Economists characterize situations in which a few individuals in selected professions earn very high salaries, while even more talented workers in other areas do not earn as much as being evidence of scarcity rents (Lucifora and Simmons, 2003). The social and economic acceptability of the levels of reward are increasingly the subject of extensive public debate in the media. A high profile illustration of this debate in the UK was demonstrated in the often emotive media reporting that accompanied the decision taken in November 2002 by the Professional Footballers' Association (PFA) to ballot its players about the possibility of taking strike action over the PFA's share of the Premiership television deal, a ballot supported by 99 per cent of the country's 2,500 players.[34]

Similar concerns have been expressed in other countries like the United States in respect of the compensation of professional athletes. Hill Zimmer and Zimmer (2001), sought to go beyond the rhetoric and emotion and provide empirical analysis of athletes' earnings in the United States in a broader context than had appeared in the literature hitherto. They identified two critical flaws in previous studies: first, that sports people's earnings should not be discussed in isolation, but rather within the context of an appropriate and well-defined socio-economic reference grouping such as entertainers, and second, that it is important not just to focus on the rewards available to top sportspeople, but also to acknowledge the lower tail of the earnings distribution across the entire profession. Comparing athletes with other professional entertainers, their analysis suggested that athletes are in fact relatively lowly paid.

From an economic or market perspective the entertainer analogy is appealing. In the same way that any comparison between the salary received by a surgeon and the financial rewards earned by an actor like, say, George Clooney for playing the part of a doctor in the medical drama *ER* would be spurious, it might be considered misleading to compare a Premiership footballer's salary to that of say an unskilled labourer or even to the average salary of that club's supporters. The key factor rests in the 'personal scale of operations' effect in sports compared to say medicine or teaching (Mayer, 1960). While no one disputes that a doctor provides services of much higher value than an actor playing the role of a doctor, the difference in earnings is explained by the size of the audience or user group: finite for the doctor, very large for the actor (Dobson and Goddard, 2001, p. 214). The issue is one of technology (Rosen and Sanderson, 2001).[35] Hence, in simple terms, a top footballer's salary arises from the operation of a market for superstars.[36]

If this argument is accepted, then it gives credence to the view that football, at the elite end, has become simply another dimension of the entertainment business. This is clearly problematical for many involved with football – including supporters, policy makers, players' associations and football authorities – who argue that it has social aspects that delineate it from economic activity. Indeed it is an area that highlights the inconsistencies apparent in contemporary football. Nowhere is this more apparent than in the pronouncements of the PFA in England. For example, while advocating market forces combined with incentivized player contracts as the best way of tackling football's financial problems, rather than more interventionist measures such as salary caps (see, for example, *Sunday Herald*, 2002), at the same time the PFA finds itself arguing that interventionist safeguards are required to protect players' (financial) interests and the integrity of the league when clubs are faced by financial difficulties (Conn, 2002a) (see also below). More fundamentally, if the acceptability of market forces to determine player wages and the number of players is accepted, proponents of market-based solutions might legitimately question why the logic of the market forces should not also be applied to issues such as how many teams there should be in a particular city or country?

The issue of the long tail of below average paid players also raises interesting issues. It is clear that the huge financial rewards often discussed in the media are earned by a relatively small number of players, with the distribution of earnings of football players being heavily skewed. Recent empirical research by Lucifora and Simmons (2003) on Italian professional players found that a relatively small number of players earn a disproportionate share of revenues, findings consistent with Rosen's (1981) theory of superstars. In addition, evidence provided by the PFAs in both England and Scotland suggests that there is less job security for players, with increasing numbers of players being released each summer at the end of their contracts (see, for example, Buckland, 1999; Campbell, A., 2000; Campbell, D., 2001; Martin, 2002). The situation became worse in the summer of 2002 for English Nationwide League clubs with the collapse of the ITV Digital deal, although it should be noted that many of these clubs, as well as clubs in leagues that were not directly affected, were in serious financial difficulties before then anyway. But where previously clubs would often have attempted to deal with these financial problems by selling players on the transfer market, recent changes in the football transfer system and the introduction of twice yearly transfer windows during which players can be bought and sold (Morris *et al.*, 2003), has diminished the value of the transfer market as a financial safety net.

Conventional businesses in this kind of situation would normally enter into administration[37] with the objective of negotiating a settlement with creditors, and reducing costs primarily through redundancies. Taking the example of the English Football League, where several clubs have followed the administration route, the freedom available to restructure these clubs has been severely restricted by the Football League's Insolvency Policy. Its objective is to protect the integrity of the league system and to preserve competition, ensuring that clubs could not take on highly paid players in the hope of gaining on-field success, but without having to pay for it (Conn, 2002a). Clubs that fail to comply with it risk losing their league membership. The rules go beyond what the law requires for other companies by introducing a 'super creditors' rule, effectively requiring clubs to honour all sums (including future sums) due to players or former players under the terms of their contracts.[38] In other words, the usual insolvency principle of *pari passu* (i.e. like creditor receiving like treatment) is disregarded in favour of payment of all football creditors.

Proponents argue that football creditor status has maintained financial probity in a market which may be tempted to excess (Hore, 2002). However, in view of the fact that wages and salaries represent the largest expense at most clubs, in strictly financial terms, restructuring becomes more difficult if these amounts are untouchable, and some insolvency experts have called for the policy to be abandoned, at least temporarily (Manning, 2002).

At a more fundamental level, it is becoming increasingly difficult to justify preserving the sanctity of player contracts on social grounds. Players at many bigger clubs are the social elite; the financial rewards they can gain from playing football far outweigh rewards available to most supporters and others in the wider community. Preservation of this policy begins to look little more than the rich looking after themselves at the expense of other stakeholders. On a number of occasions, the journalist David Conn has used his football business column in the *Independent* newspaper (see also Chapter 5) to highlight the unacceptability of the situation. As he notes, the policy 'leads to the appalling spectacle at insolvent clubs of millionaire footballers being paid in full while lowly paid secretaries or kit washers are laid off and a depressing range of local businesses left unpaid' (Conn, 2002a). Another example of the social unacceptability of the consequence of this policy is his revelation that every English club that has gone into administration has done so owing money to the St John Ambulance, a charity of volunteers who look after the sick and injured at football matches, and which receives about £200 per game from English clubs (Conn, 2002b).

Supporters

Supporters are, of course, indispensable to any discussion about the social dimension of football – to quote the legendary ex-Celtic manager, Jock Stein, 'football without fans is nothing' . Several writers – academic and popular –have sought to explain or define the role of the supporter in a football club. In recent years, a proliferation of personalized accounts of fandom have appeared, offering some insight into issues like identity, place and gender in the context of their football allegiances. The most notable contribution of this genre has been Nick Hornby's *Fever Pitch*, in which the author articulates for many the emotional feelings associated with being a fan – of in his case Arsenal – and of following football (Hornby, 1992). Similar accounts now exist for most major football clubs (some examples include Bennie, 1995; Nixon, 2000 and Schindler, 1999). Interestingly, however, the very existence of this populist fan culture form of writing may be interpreted as evidence of the changing economic, social and class status of football, carrying with it the risk of middle-class appropriation of a traditional working-class area of popular culture (Boyle and Haynes, 2000, p. 180). Some would argue that definitions of fandom put forward by authors like Hornby are at odds with traditional notions of fandom. For example, in his Socialist Party pamphlet, *Reclaim the Game*, John Reid sums up Nick Hornby's views on pricing and social exclusion in football as 'the yuppies programme for football' (2001, p. 62).

Fandom has also been explored by some academics, although as Malcolm *et al.* (2000) note, spectatorship has been somewhat overlooked in sports research. Some work has been carried out on issues like the social composition of football crowds (for example, see Waddington *et al.*, 1998 for an overview); hooliganism has been extensively dealt with (for an overview see Giulianotti, 1999, pp. 40–9), as have issues related to supporter activism such as involvement with fanzines and supporter organizations (see, for example, Moorhouse, 1994, Taylor, 1992; Haynes, 1995; Brown, 1998). One concern with such focused work is that it is effectively disregards what might be termed ordinary fans (King, 1998). Using one club, Liverpool FC, Williams *et al.* (2001) attempt to deal with this by adopting a wider approach, examining fan cultures and traditions from a number of perspectives with the aim of locating football, both historically and culturally in the life of a particular city.

The intrinsic nature of fandom is addressed by Jones (1998, cited in Malcolm *et al.*, 2000); an in-depth piece of work which considered football fan identification and identity at Luton Town. In this study fandom was characterized by a particularly strong level of commitment, with fan identity being identified by many supporters as a central component of their overall conception of 'self'. For example, approximately one-third of the fans interviewed identified being a fan as the most important aspect of their identity, with a further 40 per cent suggesting that it was at least equal to any other factor like family relationships. Another interesting finding in this study was that to a large extent success or failure had no influence upon fandom, with strongly committed fans justifying their continued strong identification through the use of strategies designed to rationalize bad experiences (e.g. emphasizing things that differentiate their team, such as the quality or entertainment value of their football) (Jones, 1998, cited in Malcolm *et al.*, 2000). This finding is backed up in American studies, which show that die-hard sports fans continue to support their teams irrespective of on-field success (Meier, 1979; Wann and Branscombe, 1990).

Of particular interest in this book are implications for fandom and the wider social significance of football arising from the commercialization of football. King (1997, 1998) argues that the application of free market principles to transform English football in the 1990s, resulted in the transformation of football supporters into consumers of a football product; a transformation that threatens to undermine the emotional attachment or sense of cultural identity felt by supporters. In a similar vein, Duke (2002) suggests that professional football in England has been infiltrated in the late twentieth century by what he terms 'McDonaldization' and 'Disneyization'; concepts which threaten the traditional fan culture and community linkages. Although he suggests that traditional supporters have the ability to adapt and retain much of their traditional fan culture, he also notes the particular danger of young fans being priced out of attending live matches and not being 'socialised into the pleasure (and pain) of live support' (Duke, 2002, p. 21). These views are backed up by evidence, which suggests that some supporters see issues arising out of the commercialization of football, such as ticket pricing, alteration of match times and dates and the power of individual clubs, as being among the biggest problems faced by clubs (SNCCFR, 2000). A major concern raised by supporters giving evidence to the Football Task Force was that the rate of price increases resulted in some supporters being unable to attend games (Brown, 2000b), while Williams and Perkins (1998) found that among those who used to attend football but no longer did, 70 per cent cited the price of tickets as the main reason for non-attendance, this rising to 80 per cent among the unemployed.

However, Malcolm *et al.* (2000) argue that many assertions made about changes in spectator demographics and social composition of football crowds are largely unsubstantiated: while new fans have been attracted to the game, they suggest that the majority of existing fans have been unaffected in terms of the ways in which they support and consume their team. Nevertheless, at a broader level, what is unarguable is that in recent years entirely new ways have emerged to allow supporters to interact with the game. The advent of satellite television and the Internet means that fandom can now exist as a community without propinquity (Bale, 2000). While the implications of things like pay-per-view (PPV) (see also Chapter 1) may still be limited, other developments like the globalization of football and the increasingly delocalized nature of many football clubs also have potential implications for the social nature of fandom. Several top clubs have positioned themselves as global brands, based upon merchandising, marketing and satellite television, designed at least in part for export and worldwide consumption. Questions such as how such globalized fandom, mediated by satellite television and lacking genuine

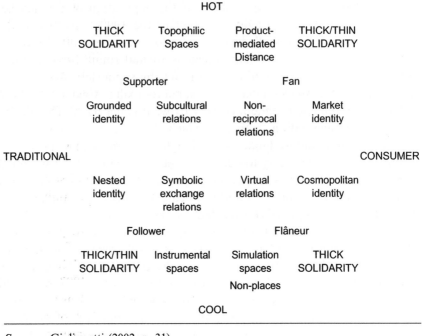

HOT

THICK	Topophilic	Product-	THICK/THIN
SOLIDARITY	Spaces	mediated	SOLIDARITY
		Distance	

Supporter   Fan

Grounded	Subcultural	Non-	Market
identity	relations	reciprocal	identity
		relations	

TRADITIONAL   CONSUMER

Nested	Symbolic	Virtual	Cosmopolitan
identity	exchange	relations	identity
	relations		

Follower   Flâneur

THICK/THIN	Instrumental	Simulation	THICK
SOLIDARITY	spaces	spaces	SOLIDARITY
		Non-places	

COOL

Source: Giulianotti (2002, p. 31)

Figure 2.1 Spectator categories (detailed)

social interaction with the 'home' town or country, affects the nature and identity of fan culture are largely unanswered at present (Nash, 2000).

A theoretical perspective on the nature of fandom is provided by Giulianotti (2002). In the context of what he describes as football's 'fundamental structural transformation', he advances a spectator classification based upon the particular types of identification that spectators have towards specific clubs (see Figure 2.1) (see also Chapter 3).

Notwithstanding the rather inaccessible technical language used in the paper, Giulianotti's theoretical classification is attractive and offers a contemporary insight into the impact of recent changes in football on the contemporary nature of fandom. One strength is that it attempts to recognize the diversity inherent in football supporters, rather than presenting a dichotomous split between old and new or between supporter and consumer, while also allowing for the possibility of overlap and dependency between the different classifications. At one extreme we have the traditional representation of the supporter, where the club is a complex and living symbol of his or her public identity and where the supporter has emotional ties to the club's ground and to its community significance. At the other extreme consumer spectators have a more market-centred relationship centering on consumption of club products. However, beyond this, other categorical differences emerge. For example, in terms of motivation, followers advance various allegiances to clubs as a way of sustaining their involvement in football, while flâneurs seek sensation and excitement, offering only transient support dependent perhaps on success or style. In terms of spatial relationships, for example, flâneurs in fact have no capacity to personally align with a club as a local institution, while arguably the fan's relationship is with stars rather than clubs, consumption of star-focused products serving to affirm and demonstrate fan loyalties (Giulianotti, 2002, p. 41).

The role played by supporters in terms of participation and involvement in their clubs is another area that has been affected by the increasingly business orientation adopted by football clubs (see, for example, Brown, 1998). In the UK, the government in 1997 set up the Football Task Force. In addition to considering issues such as racism and access for disabled people, it addressed others like the lack of supporter involvement in clubs, the conflict created by the emergence of football club plcs and the game's relationship with the wider community. These broad themes of supporter involvement, stakeholder conflict and relatedly corporate governance (see also Chapters 3 and 4) have subsequently been the subject of extensive debate among supporters, politicians, football administrators, academics and the media. One forum in which these issues were debated by many of these groups was a series of conferences held at Birkbeck College in London, from which several publications emerged (Hamil *et al.*, 1999, 2000, 2001b). At a policy level, the terms of reference of the Independent Football Commission, the independent body established in 2001 to scrutinise the performance of the football authorities in England, require it to have particular regard to the issue of supporter and other stakeholder involvement (IFC, 2002).

Supporter trusts

Side before self every time
            (Billy Bremner, former Leeds United and Scotland captain)

Members before profits; what a novel idea.
                        (Nationwide Building Society's campaign
                            to retain its mutual status, 2001)

One of the Football Task Force's recommendations was that collective body supporter trusts and supporter shareholder organizations should be recognized and encouraged by clubs (Football Task Force, 1999). Now only four years on, *Supporters Direct*, a government initiative, funded by public money, has been established to promote supporter involvement in football clubs in both England and Scotland, while supporter trusts have been formed at some 70 clubs (Pendry, 2003). It is perhaps something of a paradox that in the UK it is business influences that have acted as a catalyst for supporters and others, including government, to restate the relationship between football clubs and their communities. Nevertheless it provides an opportunity for fundamental change in the ownership and running of football clubs and one, which it may be argued more fully, reflects the social status and significance of football in the UK.

Supporter trusts are founded on the basis that supporters are the community in which the football club has its being (interview with Brian Lomax, Managing Director, *Supporters Direct*, December 2001). They are founded on democratic, one-member one-vote principles. From a supporters' perspective, Trusts provide a collective structure which enables them to work together to influence behaviour and accountability within their club. Similar to a mutual society or trade union, the sum should be worth more than the individual parts. In simple terms they offer supporters the opportunity to transform the power of their voice from one that can be heard, to one that is listened to (Michie and Ramalingam, 1999). Trusts thus provide supporters (or other members of the community) with a mechanism to activate more fully their stakeholder rights, providing them with an opportunity to influence the direction of their club and to have an input into its positioning as an organization, both in social and business terms. (For discussion of trusts in practice, see the section on Tottenham Hotspur in Chapter 3.)

Notwithstanding the extraordinary success of the supporter trust movement generally to date,[39] major challenges exist for individual trusts. One challenge faced by all trusts is to demonstrate fully their relevance and legitimacy, in other words their rights to representation. Clearly, high membership is one way for a trust to demonstrate its representative rights. Although trusts have been formed at clubs of all structures and financial positions, it is evident that financial difficulty or crisis in clubs can act as a catalyst for the formation of a trust. This means that they often form at a higher level of support and a higher level of membership. For example, the mission statement of the Watford Supporters' Trust set up in September 2002, identified its objective as being to ensure 'the continued existence of Watford FC as a professional football club, at

Vicarage Road Stadium' (www.watfordsupporterstrust.com). The trust with approximately 1,500 members is one of the largest in the country (Fincham, 2003). To date, other trusts formed in less difficult financial circumstances have found it more difficult to recruit large numbers of members.

It would be simplistic, of course, to present this as indicating a lack of legitimacy for trusts, certainly over the short term. While some dimensions of football – for example, managerial tenure, player contracts, demands for success – are self evidently short term, other facets – for example, the loyalty of supporters and geographical immobility of clubs – are equally clearly long-term characteristics (see, for example, Bale, 2000; Malcolm *et al.*, 2000). In clubs where trusts have been established other than as a reaction to immediate financial difficulties or threats, the motivation is to establish a sustainable supporters' trust that can contribute to the long-term success and/or security of the particular club. The coming together of like-minded supporters to form and run trusts arises out of what is termed social capital, a network of personal relationships and social groups that foster co-operative working and community well-being (Jarvie, 2003). Hence, although the voluntary nature of trust membership inevitably results in it taking time to build the organization to a critical size, arguably it is the existence of this social capital that will provide the trust with a strong foundation. Its strength comes from within, and hence external intervention, for example in the form of government funding or other assistance, can only help create a structure in which social capital can flourish; it can not create social capital.

Parallels can be seen in the development of the credit union movement. Credit unions are financial co-operatives, structured on a mutual basis, which operate around what is known as a common bond, something which the members share in common such as being an employee of a particular organization, residence in a particular community or member-ship of an association. One of the strengths of credit unions is the absence of the profit motive, the organization existing only to attain the economic and social goals of its members (Ferguson and McKillop, 1997). Therefore, its strength comes from within. This knowledge explains why governments in the UK and elsewhere, although fully cognizant of the benefits of credit unions in terms of widening access to financial services and reducing financial exclusion, have to tread a careful path between providing sufficient support to encourage the movement to develop without undermining its strength by diminishing its social capital or mutual strength. For example, at the launch of the Scottish Executive's credit union action plan for Scotland '*Unlocking the Potential*' in March 2001, a plan backed by £1.5m of public funding to kick start its implementation, the Minister for Social Justice, Jackie Baillie, was at pains to stress that this funding must not be seen as the government taking control of credit unions, but rather an attempt to create the infrastructure within which credit unions could flourish:

> I say straight away that far from the action plan being an indication that the Executive is trying to take over the movement, we fully recognise the movement's autonomy and that its ethos – community involvement, the role of volunteers, its mutuality – are its strengths, which we wish to support. We wanted to explore how the Executive could best deploy its support and how others, such as the banks, local authorities, the local enterprise companies and the wider voluntary sector, could best contribute to the movement.
>
> (Scottish Parliament Official Report, 2001)

Furthermore, trusts like other voluntary bodies or activities in the UK are faced with a prevalent culture where people are no longer 'joiners of things' (interview with Brian Lomax, December 2001). Certainly there is evidence that supports these claims: for example, the total number of church members in the UK has dropped from 6.6 million in 1990 to 5.9 million in 2000 (UKCH, 2001) while there has been a decrease in union membership in Great Britain since 1991 of 1.3 million, a fall over the ten-year period of 15 per cent (Brook, 2002). Furthermore, in the sports, recreation and culture sector, traditionally volunteers have been active to a much larger extent in countries like Denmark, the Netherlands, Norway and Sweden than has been the case in the UK (Ibsen, 2002) (see also Chapter 3).

Claims for legitimacy or representation in this area are also complicated by the fact that almost anybody can be described as a football supporter. As Brown (1998) notes, fandom contains different constituencies of support, which makes it difficult for any supporters' organization to claim legitimately that it represents the view of a majority of a club's support. But, it is worth noting two things: first, that trusts are not designed to replace or replicate existing supporters' organizations and indeed might be expected to have different areas of concern and interest, and second, that structurally trusts gain their strength through the fundamental principles of democracy and inclusivity: anyone who abides by the rules can become a member; all members are equal. Although individual membership of some trusts remains small, its legitimacy as a collective voice has been strengthened by the support offered to it by supporters' organizations. For example, the Celtic Trust has the backing of the Celtic Supporters' Association, Celtic's largest and oldest supporter grouping, which counts among its membership 170 individual supporters clubs from around the world representing 10,000 members (Carr *et al.*, 2001).

Arguably, however, in the long term it is action by a trust rather than membership statistics that will make the most convincing case for its legitimacy or representative rights. *Ceteris paribus*, how the trust acts in terms of its behaviour, its decision-making and its development of relationships with the directors, other supporters and the wider community will determine whether it receives implicit if not explicit supporter and community support and respect. Trusts provide an opportunity to lead by example, providing a mechanism through which supporters can influence the direction of their club. For example, trusts can take the lead in promoting a social agenda at their clubs, focusing on issues like social inclusion and ticket pricing, racism or charitable giving. In other words they are one mechanism through which it can be demonstrated that a football club has a social dimension, which differentiates it from conventional business organizations.

Communities

The place of sport in the making of communities has been the subject of debate and reflection in political and academic circles (see, for example, Coalter, 2000; Crolley and Hand, 2002; Jarvie and Burnett, 2000, Williams *et al.*, 2001). Within this broad debate, one prominent focus has been on the relationship between football clubs and their communities. Football in the UK, as well as in many other European countries, is regarded as a representational sport with clubs representing geographical locations. The relationship between community, town and local football team is manifestly demonstrated in the social bond that exists between Raith Rovers Football Club and the community of Kirkcaldy, a small Scottish town with a population of just less than 50,000 (Hague and Mercer, 1998). The authors argue that Raith Rovers has played an important role in the development of local identity, culture and a shared memory of living in Kirkcaldy. The link between club and community is evident in one supporter's answer to the question ' Do you support Raith Rovers?' Rather than providing a simple yes/no answer, the authors interpret the supporter's response – 'I'm from the town, I went to school here' – as implying a lifetime of growing up in one place, experiencing childhood, adulthood and numerous memories that have little if anything to do with Raith Rovers or football but can be revived by a simple question about the club (Hague and Mercer, 1998, p. 114).

The communities that identify with clubs need not be restricted to specific geographical areas (Bale, 2000), but may be bound up with wider issues of identity that exist inside and outside the game. Examples include Marseille's particular involvement with the Paris-province divide in France (Crolley and Hand, 2002, p. 6); Barcelona's status as the principal focus of Catalan nationalism (Burns, 1999); Celtic's status as a symbol of identity for Irish immigrants in Scotland (Carr *et al.*, 2001) and Liverpool's cultural significance and its distinctiveness among English clubs (Williams *et al.*, 2001). What is demonstrated in these and other similar examples is how football clubs can provide communities, however defined, with a sense of place or identity; that 'they symbolize a territory, the real or imagined values of which they are expected to convey' (Crolley and Hand, 2002, p. 77).

The relationship between football businesses and community is perhaps less apparent, other than when financial difficulties or adversity acts as a catalyst to encourage communities to demonstrate their commitment to their local clubs.[40] However, arguably the increased business orientation of clubs and its resultant implications for supporters and other communities has also provided an opportunity for positive reappraisal of the relationship (Hamil, 1999b; Morrow, 1999, 2000; Smith, 1997; Williams *et al.*, 2001), challenging clubs and communities alike to renew or strengthen the community or social dimension. In a UK context, the supporter trust model discussed earlier in this chapter is one initiative that seeks to strengthen the community relationship other than at times of last resort (Oughton *et al.*, 2003).

Working for the common good?

That top-level football clubs are now businesses is indisputable. However, the central argument of this book is that there remains much that distinguishes football businesses from more conventional forms of economic activity, most notably their social and community significance. Football clubs as businesses continue to have influence and meaning that extends well beyond the realm of economics or finance. This is not to suggest that football clubs are the only business organizations that have social and community influence. There is a common argument that plcs have substantial economic and social power and that they should seek to exercise their influence for the common good (Dean, 2001). Recent and ongoing developments in areas like Company Law (DTI, 2002; The Company Law Review Steering Group, 2000) (see also following section) and corporate social responsibility (see, for example, European Commission, 2002) suggest that there is an increasing acceptance of this social influence.

The implications for clubs' community or social status arising from increased business orientation of clubs were considered by Morrow and Hamil (2003, forthcoming), and much of the following section draws on this work. Focusing on the 30 top division clubs in England and Scotland in season 1999/2000,[41] this paper had two objectives: first, to consider the extent to which clubs position or present themselves as community or social institutions, and second, to identify the extent to which their subsequent business behaviour or actions are influenced by community or social role considerations.

While the focus is often on how supporters or others in the community perceive clubs in terms of their social or community status, equally significant is the issue of how clubs present themselves. From a financial perspective, such presentation or positioning is noteworthy as it may be used as a way to leverage business advantage. Morrow and Hamil (2003) considered the extent of this presentation in two sources: the corporate annual report and club websites. Evidence of a limited number of clubs making explicit claims about their community or social status was found in corporate annual reports (see Exhibit 2.1), these claims being commonly used to introduce a discussion on community initiatives in practice (see following section). Two clubs that go substantially further in this regard, however, are Sunderland plc and Celtic plc. In the case of Sunderland, its annual report sets out the club's vision and goals in which the club's community and social role is explicitly recognized. In the case of Celtic, disclosure on the Celtic Charity Fund is used to illustrate the club's community and charitable status (see Exhibit 2.2).

One interpretation of this evidence is that a club's ownership structure may have some influence on the likelihood of social or community claims being made in its annual report. In this sample, of the seven clubs identified in Exhibits 2.1 and 2.2, only West Ham United is not a Stock Exchange listed company. The prevalence of Stock Exchange companies is also observed later in the paper in terms of disclosure of CCI (Corporate Community Involvement) activities in the narrative section of the annual report (see Exhibit 2.4). One explanation is that Stock Exchange listed clubs tend to have more diversified ownership structures, with shares being more widely held. Hence the annual report may serve as

Exhibit 2.1   Social involvement (extracts from annual reports)

Chief Executive's Report

Community

The Board continues to place a priority on our relationship with the local community and we maintain proactive lines of communication with local residents and minority groups.

(Leicester City plc, Annual Report 2000)

Review of activities

Manchester United is committed to working on programmes which are able to make a real impact on the community, both locally and internationally

(Manchester United plc, Annual Report 2000)

Chairman's Statement

Working for our community

[we are] pleased to report the continued strength of all of our community initiatives ... [also] implementing strategies that we believe will lead us to be universally recognised for our community activities.

(Newcastle United plc, Annual Report 2000)

Chairman's Statement

Football update

The Academy is an important part of our long term plan to groom players who understand the culture of the Club and appreciate the importance of Southampton Football Club to its local community.

(Southampton Leisure Holdings plc, Annual Report 2000)

Chairman's Statement

Social Responsibility

The success of any community depends, ultimately, upon its ability to include all its people and we continue to work hard through our Community Development Scheme to assist, in our small way, those who have yet to benefit from the economic progress of our region.

(West Ham United, Annual Report 2000)

---

means of communicating with dispersed shareholders. In addition, listed companies exist in a more public space in which there is greater scrutiny and interest in issues like corporate accountability and social responsibility from a range of interested stakeholders (see Chapter 5). Consequently the annual report can be seen by directors as a mechanism to communicate with, and to demonstrate accountability to, these wider stakeholder groups.

Exhibit 2.2 Social involvement (extracts from annual reports)

Our vision

In pursuit of excellence we aim to:

- improve the performance, welfare provision and all-round development of our academy players;
- ensure football is affordable and accessible to all;
- satisfy both our supporters and our shareholders;
- play an active and valuable role in the local community and the region;
- be a club for ALL

(Sunderland plc, Annual Report 2000)

Celtic Charity Fund

In 2000, 112 years after the Club's formation Celtic is involved in more community and charitable work and also, through Celtic Charity Fund, donating more money to charity than at any time during its history.

Celtic Football Club is committed to supporting the community and is proud today that it strives to honour the charitable objectives of the Club's founder Brother Walfrid.

(Celtic plc, Annual Report 2000)

Another source of information, one which emphatically illustrates the changing nature of communities and the resultant changes in the relationship between football and its stakeholders, is the world-wide-web. The company website offers enormous potential for most sports organizations, both from a financial perspective, for example, in terms of facilitating sales of tickets and merchandise, and from a social or community perspective, for example, in terms of engendering fan loyalty and reaching disaffected fans (Mahony and Howard, 2001). Significantly, this tool also provides clubs with a convenient mechanism through which to communicate with their stakeholders; providing an opportunity to present themselves to their communities or stakeholders. The majority of clubs provide examples of their community initiatives in practice using their web pages (see Table 2.2). A few clubs also use this source as a way of explicitly underlining their community or social status[42] (see Exhibit 2.3). The explanation for this is perhaps simply that clubs, irrespective of their ownership structure and legal status, recognize that it is this source which is most relevant and accessible to their communities, both the direct community of supporters and wider notions of community.

Exhibit 2.3   Social involvement (extracts from official club websites)

---

the Club plays a strong role in the local community which supports it and takes seriously its role at the heart of the local community.

Middlesbrough FC Customer Charter, paragraph 5.1
(http://www.mfc.co.uk/, 13 January 2002)

SWFC recognises the role it can play in acting as a focal point for the local community.

Sheffield Wednesday FC Fans' Charter
(http://www.swfc.co.uk/, 13 January 2002)

Our aim is simple, to give something back to our community ...

Everton FC, Football in the Community page
(http://www.evertonfc.com/, 13 January 2002)

the community is at the heart of this club ...

Sunderland AFC, Community home page
(http://www.safc.com/, 13 January 2002)

Corporate Community Involvement

A particular facet of community or social involvement appropriate to corporations is Corporate Community Involvement (CCI), both in terms of direct financial contributions to community/social/charitable projects and through other involvement less easily measured in financial terms. The debate around CCI is closely intertwined with that on corporate governance and more specifically with that on whether companies should be legally obliged to take account of stakeholders other than shareholders. As has been discussed previously, the stakeholder concept has great relevance for football clubs due to the particular features of certain football club stakeholders, specifically their demands for accountability (Morrow, 2000). In this regard, the UK Government's *White Paper on Modernising Company Law* is potentially significant. While reiterating that the goal for directors should be the success of the company in the collective best interests of the shareholders, in deciding what is in the best interests of the company, directors should recognize 'the need to foster the company's business relationships, including those with [its] customers ... [and] ... the need to consider the company's impact on the community and the working environment' (DTI, 2002, para. 3.3).

CCI, via charitable giving for example, can be publicized as a way for businesses to deliver on their side of a social contract with the rest of society. Traditionally the main motive was pure philanthropy (Campbell *et al.*, 1999; Cowton, 1987; Shaw and Post, 1993). However, since the early 1980s, in the wider corporate environment, more organizations have sought strategically to align their CCI activities with the search for competitive advantage as part of the enactment of a stakeholder management strategy (Freeman, 1984). CCI might be deemed to be a rational response in football clubs either on social or instrumental grounds. For those clubs making claims of social or community status, one interpretation is that CCI enables them to action those words. More pragmatically, CCI may be a rational response by management, reflecting the increasing business orientation of their clubs. In other words, CCI at football clubs offers a potential avenue for clubs to meet financial objectives while also meeting social objectives. CCI thus might be expected to reflect a rational management response to pressure from other stakeholder groups, such as community groups, that may exert influence over the business (Hamil, 1999a). There is evidence of this happening in practice through the role being played by supporters' trusts in encouraging clubs to take the interests of the local community into account when taking decisions (Holt, 2003). One example is the working group set up jointly by the Leyton Orient Fans' Trust and the club to tackle the problem of lack of local support for the club. As Holt notes (2003, p. 12), 'playing a positive and genuine role within the community can provide endless benefits for all, both in terms of generating goodwill and the consequent financial rewards.'

Perhaps, the most prominent extant examples of CCI activity among football clubs are the Football in the Community (FIC) schemes and the *Football Aid* initiative. The FIC schemes have been common in many professional football clubs since the early 1990s and were conceived in 1975 as a mechanism to assist in tackling football hooliganism (Watson, 2000). Over one million people per year are currently involved in Football in the Community projects (Reade, 2000). Highly developed schemes can be found at several individual clubs, which have leveraged finance from government initiatives to address problems of social exclusion. One such example is at Leeds United, which has programmes operating in the vicinity of the team's Elland Road ground (Smith, 2000). However, some concern has been expressed that FIC schemes at some Premier League clubs have become increasingly commercial in orientation (Perkins, 2000). Furthermore, the Football Task Force reported that as clubs have adopted plc status there has been a decline in Premier League clubs' involvement in some CCI activities (Football Task Force, 1999).

Football Aid is a relatively recent initiative, which has been developed by the charity, Field of Dreams, to raise funds for voluntary and charitable organizations. Its fund raising is based around holding auctions at different clubs, through which supporters bid for the right to play for their club in a match organized at their club's stadium, encouraged by their club's manager and captain. The 2003 event is being supported by 19 FA Premier League clubs, ten Nationwide League clubs and ten Scottish Premier League clubs. The aims of *Football Aid* include '[supporting] the community investment work of partner clubs and leagues' and '[awarding] grants to their chosen charities' (www.footballaid.com). At one level therefore, the initiative is using the clubs as a way of leveraging funds from supporters. However, at another level it is concerned with enabling 'the football industry to gain due recognition for its community investment and charitable giving programmes' (Paterson, 2002). At this second level, *Football Aid* is explicitly concerned with CCI. As its founder and Chairman states in the organization's promotional literature, 'through association with *Football Aid*, our partners can realise commercial advantage and contribute to community gain' (Paterson, 2002).

Another example of CCI is cash donations to charitable or social activities. Despite fiscal encouragement, recent figures suggest that the contribution of British business to good causes is very modest. At the beginning of the 1990s, leading companies were contributing 0.42 per cent of their pre-tax profits to the community, much of it in cash. A decade on, despite most companies now including the cost of all aspects of their community programme, the £499m contributed in 2000/01 is exactly the same percentage of pre-tax profits as the £225m contributed in 1990/91 (Benjamin, 2002). As is demonstrated in Table 2.1, in terms of direct giving, figures disclosed in the annual reports of football clubs are not out of line with the rest of the UK corporate sector.[43] This table traces the sums donated to charity over a four-year period by the same 30 clubs who made up the top divisions in England and Scotland in 1997/98. For example, in season 2000/01 the average donation per English Premiership club was £20,511, which equates to 0.045 per cent of turnover; £2,801 per Scottish Premier League, which equates to 0.02 per cent of turnover. Arguably, the lack of giving can actually be justified in the context of the lack of reported profits among these clubs. For example, in the 2000/01 season, 83 per cent of the 30 clubs in the sample reported pre-tax losses (Deloitte & Touche, 2002a; PricewaterhouseCoopers, 2002). However, in view of the unprecedented income that flowed into top clubs during the

Table 2.1 Charitable donations

	2000/01	1999/2000	1998/99	1997/98
English Premiership [20 clubs]	£	£	£	£
Total contribution	410,228	367,297	169,131	50,824
Maximum donation	164,000	141,400	67,000	17,740
Minimum donation	762	235	365	200
Number of clubs disclosing donation	12 clubs	13 clubs	11 clubs	9 clubs
Nil donation/disclosure	8 clubs	7 clubs	9 clubs	11 clubs
Scottish Premier [10 clubs]				
Total contribution	28,012	30,229	309,364*	27,277
Maximum donation	13,445	17,150	287,511*	13,385
Minimum donation	554	1,080	2,941	1,531
Number of clubs disclosing donation	4 clubs	4 clubs	4 clubs	4 clubs
Nil donation/disclosure	6 clubs	6 clubs	6 clubs	6 clubs

* The donation of £287,511 is an exceptional donation arising out of a dispute between the players and Chief Executive at Celtic over bonus payments. The compromise reached involved the sum under dispute being donated to the Yorkhill Children's Hospital in Glasgow. The total contribution excluding this sum was £21,853.

period under consideration, such a justification might be considered disingenuous.

Beyond cash donations, several clubs do engage with and provide support to charitable and other CCI activities and provide varied disclosure and communication of this community involvement both in their annual reports and on their websites. For example, Sunderland has set up all its community work as a stand-alone charity, SAFCommunity, while clubs like Arsenal, Aston Villa and Celtic have established or are linked with charitable trusts to which they provide support in terms of lending their name or profile or through the involvement of players. Clubs like Leicester City, Leeds United and Middlesbrough have nominated charities (either at club or player level or both) which are supported throughout the year, while other clubs like Manchester United and Sheffield Wednesday set out a commitment to supporting and working with charities. In addition, the majority of clubs referred to their involvement with *Football Aid*, the annual national charity event discussed earlier in this section, in which football supporters bid for the opportunity to play at their favourite club.

The People's Game?

In terms of narrative disclosure and elaboration in the annual reports, there is a very clear divide. A small limited number of clubs (seven) devote a proportion of their 1999/2000 annual reports to their CCI activities, while the other 23 clubs make no comment at all on CCI activities. As with presentational comments made by clubs, clubs disclosing most about their CCI activities are the Stock Exchange listed clubs (with the important exception of West Ham United). Exhibit 2.4 summarizes the CCI disclosure in the 1999/2000 annual reports in terms of content (both substantive and quantitative) and location.

The majority of clubs provide more detailed CCI information on their websites. Table 2.2 provides a simple disclosure index for information found on club websites in January 2002.

Table 2.2 Club website disclosure index (January 2002)

Disclosure	Clubs	Example
Extensive	7/30	Sunderland
	Aston Villa, Leicester City, Sheffield Wednesday, Sunderland, West Ham United, Wimbledon, Celtic	SAFCommunity and SAFC Foundation. Information on: Shining Through (good citizenship) Education programmes and student information Racism Health Social inclusion
Moderate	10/30	Heart of Midlothian
	Arsenal, Bradford City, Chelsea, Everton, Leeds United, Middlesbrough, Newcastle United, Southampton, Dundee, Heart of Midlothian	Community section has information on initiatives like Soccer Centres, Coaching disabled players, Holiday courses in addition to Football academy community links
Limited	11/30	Liverpool
	Coventry City, Derby County, Liverpool, Manchester United, Tottenham Hotspur, Aberdeen, Dundee United, Hibernian, Motherwell, Rangers, St Johnstone	Discussion in Public Relations section on club's attitude to charitable activities, hospital visits etc.
Nil	2/30	–
	Watford, Kilmarnock	

Source: adapted from Morrow and Hamil (2003)

Exhibit 2.4 CCI narrative disclosure (1999/2000 annual reports)

	CCI issues disclosed/discussed	Location/length
Leeds United	• Football in the community programme • Educational projects such as 'Playing for Success' and 'Learning through Football'	Review of operations 1 page $\frac{1}{2}$ page narrative 1 photograph
Leicester City	• Community Department • 'Contribution to the Community' award • Compliance with Premier League Club Charter	Chairman's report 1 paragraph
Manchester United	• Football in the Community scheme • MU museum/Study Support Centre • UNICEF partnership	Review of Operations 2 pages $\frac{1}{8}$ page narrative, the remainder photographs
Newcastle United	• Football in the Community programme • Showcase video to MPs • Development of a state of the art learning centre	Chairman's Report 2 paragraphs
Sunderland	• Social exclusion pricing policies • Regeneration issues • Environmental/bio-diversity issues • SAFCommunity • SAFCommunity foundation • Champion of initiatives which involve the community	Chairman's Statement 10 paragraphs $1\frac{1}{4}$ page narrative
West Ham United	• Statement on social responsibility • Football in the Community scheme • Initiatives (12) such as Learning Through Football and Holiday Football Centres	Chairman's Statement $2\frac{1}{4}$ pages narrative
Celtic	• Celtic Charity Fund • Aims and areas of support • Past initiatives supported such as Loaves and Fishes, the Glasgow Simon Community • Historical context	Final page in report 1 page narrative

Source: annual reports, Morrow and Hamil (2003)

One interpretation is that CCI is an instrumental response by the directors of increasingly business-oriented clubs to pressures and demands from other stakeholders who may exert influence over the business, and is designed to assist clubs to meet financial objectives while also meeting social objectives. Thus at one level CCI initiatives can be seen as meeting a social objective like strengthening links with supporters (and the wider community). At a second level they can also lead to improved business performance, perhaps, say, in the form of higher spending by supporters. This interpretation is consistent with the philosophy put forward by *Football Aid* (Paterson, 2002), which has been very successful in encouraging clubs to involve themselves with its charitable initiative.

One expectation of increased awareness of the dual social and business benefits of CCI is that clubs would seek better communication of their activities in this area. The above survey is based on the annual reports for the year 1999/2000. Since then there is evidence that more clubs are using publications like their annual report to outline their community involvement. For example, Everton devotes a page of its 2001/02 annual report to community initiatives; Arsenal devotes four pages of its 2000/01 annual report to community initiatives; while Rangers noted in its 2001 annual report both that it was launching a charity foundation for the club and that in addition to direct donations made by the club it helped charities raise a further £250,000.[44]

Communities in transition

As was discussed in Chapter 1, issues that affect football at an industry or league level such as league reconstruction or competition rules, are often presented solely in economic terms. Yet, it is evident that these issues also have social and community implications. This risk of economic or financial considerations dominating the debate is perhaps of even greater concern with regard to such matters as club mergers or relocations. While in football, as in other areas of corporate activity, such initiatives have their foundations in business considerations like the desire to produce more competitive organizations or organizations that are more finan-cially lucrative to the owners, their fundamental importance from a social or community perspective can not be understated.

Mergers of football clubs in Europe in recent times are rare: FC København was formed in 1992 from a fusion of the elite activities of two of the oldest Danish football clubs, Københavns Boldklub and

Boldklubben 1903 (FCK is considered in some detail in Chapter 3); the Italian club, Sampdoria was formed in 1946 out of the merger of two famous Italian soccer clubs, the Andrea Doria, founded in 1900, and the Sampierdarenese Sezione Calcio, founded in 1911; Inverness Caledonian Thistle was formed in 1994 out a merger of two local clubs, Inverness Thistle, founded in 1888 and Caledonian FC, founded in 1886; Rushden and Diamonds was formed in 1992, when local entrepreneur Max Griggs encouraged the merger of Rushden Town (founded in 1889) and Irthlingborough Diamonds (founded in 1947).

There is a long history of local relationships between professional sporting organisations and particular towns, cities and areas. Relocation of European football clubs is relatively rare. This sits in marked contrast with the United States of America, where it is common for professional sports franchises to move to new population centres or to relocate to attract greater financial support from the state or municipality. While the economic effects of sport franchise relocation on cities and municipalities has frequently been considered, little research has considered the social and psychological effects and consequences of relocation on fans. One exception is Mitrano's study on the relocation of the Hartford Whalers ice hockey team (1999). In March 1997, unable to satisfactorily resolve negotiations with city and state officials, the owners of the Hartford Whalers announced the team would not play again in Hartford and would instead relocate to Raleigh, North Carolina. Using 'virtual participant observations' of Hartford Whaler fans who participated in discussion on the Internet, followed up by interviews, Mitrano examines the meanings fans attach to franchise relocation decisions and of how they cope with the loss of civic institutions such as a sports franchise, thus providing a good insight into the nature of fandom and the emotion invested in being a supporter of a sports organization. The depth of feeling is demonstrated by the fact that not one fan observed or interviewed as part of Mitrano's study related losing the team to losing a material object, such as one's car keys or purse. Instead metaphors like death and divorce were used to explain the significance of their loss, suggesting a high degree of emotional attachment and personal involvement in the team. What is apparent is that the sports organization (Hartford Whalers) was viewed as a social institution; 'a bedrock of the community, for which their collective relocation is actually mourned and grieved over, much like human death and divorce' (Mitrano, 1999, p. 137).

In the UK, though the number of relocations has been quite small, there has been a marked increase since the Taylor Report, with about a dozen clubs including Derby County, Southampton and Sunderland moving to new sites (Bale, 2002). Where relocations have taken place, these have tended to be over relatively short distances (Bale, 2000). Bale notes that 'there is a feeling ... that the dislocation of a club from the place bearing its name is anathema to fans and something which clubs have tended to avoid, reflecting a sense of sentiment, place pride or topophilia' (2000, p. 96). Indeed, this topophilic sense often extends beyond the town or city to the stadium itself. Supporters at several clubs have mounted campaigns, the aim of which has been to see their club retain its existing stadium rather than develop a new stadium elsewhere.[45] In some countries the stadium has even wider significance. In Brazil in the 1970s the military regime adopted a policy of stadium building, the result of which was that by 1978, Brazil had 27 stadiums each with a capacity of more than 45,000 and five that held more than 100,000. Having a football landmark became a symbol of a town's self-respect. Bellos (2002) provides one remarkable example of stadium development in the country, the town of Brejinho, which in 1993 built a stadium with a capacity of 10,000, despite having a population of only 3,000 and a further 4,000 living in the surrounding area. Despite the unremitting poverty in the town, Bellos observes that no one questions the political priorities that saw the stadium being built or its cost.

The case of Wimbledon

The ongoing controversy surrounding the relocation of Nationwide League club, Wimbledon to Milton Keynes, brings into sharp focus issues concerned with sentiment, place pride and topophilia as well as highlighting again the potential conflict between business objectives and social or community objectives.

Early in 2001, Wimbledon's owners announced that they intended to move the club to the Buckinghamshire new town, Milton Keynes. The roots of this announcement are found some ten years previously, in the decision taken in 1991 by the club's previous owner, Sam Hammam, to move the club from its home in Plough Lane to ground share with its fellow London club, Crystal Palace. Ostensibly this decision was taken because Plough Lane could not satisfy the requirements of the Taylor Report, but it has been argued that it was motivated by financial considerations, namely the profit to be gained from selling the old ground to a supermarket (White, 2003). Attempts to find a new home for the club did not progress well, and Hammam floated the idea of relocating to Dublin, the only capital city in Europe which does not boast its own full-time professional football club. In a precursor of what was to come, although such relocation could be presented as rational in financial terms, it infuriated the club's supporters who saw themselves being distanced from their club. Although such cross border moves are prohibited by the rules of FIFA, UEFA and the national associations it was reported that Wimbledon and Clydebank (which was also considering a relocation to Dublin) (see also section on 'Change and the Law' in Chapter 1) considered asking the European Commission to test these rules against EU Competition Law (Parrish, 2000, p. 30). However, prior to any such consideration, Hammam sold 80 per cent of his shareholding to a Norwegian company, AKER RGI, controlled by the businessmen Bjorn Rune Gjelsten and Kjell Inge Rokke in 1997, for approximately £25 million (*Lords Hansard*, 2002).[46]

The Norwegians appointed Charles Koppel to look after the club, and in April 2000, Hammam sold his remaining interest to a company in which Koppel was a shareholder (*Lords Hansard*, 2002). Koppel had never been to a football match before he became involved with Wimbledon and gave the impression of being completely unaware of the relationship that exists between a football club and its supporters (White, 2003). What Koppel was interested in was an 'enabling development' ; a business or leisure opportunity of which a new football stadium could be part (White, 2003). Having apparently found difficulty in finding a suitable site in the borough of Merton,[47] he was approached about the possibility of bringing Wimbledon to Milton Keynes, a town with a rapidly growing population, many of them under the age of 19 and the fastest growing local economy in the south east.

The supporters mounted the most sophisticated fans' campaign in history, arguing that their club was being stolen from them and that this move undermined the historical relationship between club and community on which British football is based. One of the many ironies of this case is that Wimbledon had previously established a good reputation in terms of its community presence and relationships. For example, its disclosure of CCI activities on its website was classified as extensive in Table 2.2, while fan surveys carried out in previous years by the Sir Norman Chester Centre for Football Research had identified the success of Wimbledon FC in utilizing its community scheme to attract supporters (SNCCFR, 1997). Despite this, in May 2002, an independent Commission set up by the Football Association approved a request made by the directors of Wimbledon that it should be allowed to relocate to Milton Keynes, thus overturning an earlier decision by the Football League. The directors' argument was predicated on financial issues: that the club was in a unique situation, potentially homeless and haemorrhaging money at an unsustainable rate. The financial or business reasoning, as well as the interrelationship of these issues with planning considerations, has been questioned by some commentators (see, for example, White, 2003). Of greater significance even is the apparent failure to consider the implications of the decision on the club's existing communities, both its supporters and its geographic locale. Supporters, led by the Wimbledon Independent Supporters' Association (WISA) expressed their outrage at the move; ultimately taking the decision to establish their own team, AFC Wimbledon. It is currently playing in the Seagrave Haulage Combined Counties League in front of larger crowds than Wimbledon, which continued to play at Selhurst Park until the end of season 2002/03. From season 2004/05 the club will play its home games in Milton Keynes, initially at the National Hockey Stadium until its new 28,000 seater stadium at Denbigh North is completed. But it is clear that wider supporter dissatisfaction will follow the club to Milton Keynes, as evidenced by Tottenham Hotspur's decision to cancel a pre-season friendly at the National Hockey Stadium, following feedback from its supporters and from the Tottenham Hotspur Supporters' Trust (Ferris, 2003). (For more detail on the relocation from the supporters' perspective, see the website of the Wimbledon Independent Supporters' Association at www.wisa.org.uk. See also Bell *et al.*, 2003.)

Modernization?

It is emphatically clear in the Wimbledon example that little or no consideration was given to the club's existing communities or to the unique characteristics of fandom. To many this will be unsurprising. Utilising case studies of previous club relocations, Vamplew *et al.* (1998) concluded that generally clubs gave limited consideration to the interests of supporters when such moves were being discussed. However, it is also worth noting that discussions about the proposed relocation and ground sharing by the Edinburgh clubs, Heart of Midlothian and Hibernian, announced in June 2003, are to include a consultation process with fans, run by an independent company (Stephen, 2003). Beyond the specifics of the Wimbledon case, however, it is interesting to consider whether it tells us anything about wider policy issues such as relocation or franchising.

In a debate in the House of Lords, the Wimbledon supporting Labour peer, Richard Faulkener noted that the 'owners [of football clubs] should see themselves primarily as guardians of a public asset, as temporary custodians of an entity in which others, such as supporters and the local community, have a genuine stake' (*Lords Hansard*, 2002). Such a view would be shared by many and is consistent with the arguments put forward in this book. But, leaving aside the specific example of Wimbledon, expression of this view must surely not be interpreted as suggesting that all existing football clubs have an inalienable right to continue in existence in their current location. It seems reasonable to suggest that there is an onus on both club and community to ensure that a living relationship exists between club and community, rather than continuing to exist simply as a consequence of history. Clubs must work to make their business sustainable and to develop their community presence. Equally, there is an onus on communities and supporters to support their club. If clubs cannot attract sufficient numbers in one place, or, put another way, if communities are insufficiently enthused to support their team, is there anything inherently wrong with considering moving and looking to draw on social capital elsewhere or looking to build up a new and vibrant community relationship elsewhere?

Some might argue that what is being described in the previous paragraph is franchising.[48] In the United States of America, an active market exists in professional sports organizations or as they are commonly referred to, franchises. Quirk and Fort (1997, p. 49) describe sports franchises as assets that generate a cash flow, positive or negative for an owner, through the team playing its games and through the possibility of a capital gain or loss arising through changes in the price of the franchise. In essence therefore, what is described as franchising is in fact the relocation of a professional sports organization, irrespective of any change in the ownership of the organization itself. The organization is itself a moveable commodity. Relocations are predicated on economic issues and are invariably accompanied by a bidding process among cities and/or the provision of financial incentives. Interestingly, even the Green Bay Packers, often held up as an example of community ownership of professional sports organizations (Michie, 1999) is a publicly held company which has threatened to leave Green Bay if the city did not accede to its demands for stadium improvements (Leeds and von Allmen, 2002, p. 154).

The social aspects of relocation and the consequences for stakeholders first emerged when Tom O'Malley relocated the NFL team, the Brooklyn Dodgers to Los Angeles. Although the Dodgers were already the most successful and profitable team in the NFL, O'Malley recognized the possibilities that would accompany being a monopoly provider in Los Angeles (Leeds and von Allmen, 2002, p. 153). Arguably, it was also the first relocation to generate interest in wider social issues connected with sports organizations, with the residents of Brooklyn having a cultural identification with the Dodgers, rather than the New York Giants, favoured by the more sophisticated and wealthier residents of Manhattan (Leeds and von Allmen, 2002, p. 153).

In the context of football, the term franchising is highly emotive, as witnessed in the debate surrounding Wimbledon's move to Milton Keynes.[49] But it is worth reflecting that issues of so-called franchising and the allegation that money drives football are not new. For example, as far back as 1913 Arsenal FC changed its ground from Plumstead to Highbury, despite some opposition from fans, in order to attract bigger crowds (Vamplew, 1988, p. 5). What was being described then, as now, was the relocation of a club; a decision often motivated by financial considerations. Relocation need not result in any change in the ownership of a club or more accurately company, nor in its legal or football status. But what inevitably does change is its social status or positioning within particular communities.

Of course those communities themselves change over time, reflecting different economic, social and policy decisions. Certainly the demographics of the UK have changed markedly since the end of the nineteenth century when the majority of professional football clubs were formed. Given this, it is difficult to see what is socially unacceptable in principle about enabling clubs to reflect this changing demographic reality and where appropriate to seek out new communities. Yet in debates about relocation or establishing football clubs, little apparent consideration is given to prospective stakeholders of new or relocated clubs – new supporters, businesses in the new town, other community groupings. Instead the analysis or comment is directed almost exclusively towards the implications of the relocation decision for the stakeholders or communities left behind. In some senses this is unsurprising as these communities are already in existence and are identifiable: stakeholders from past and present activities inevitably are in a better position to make their case known. Furthermore, they have something to lose. However, such an approach unavoidably reflects an incumbency bias (Hellwig, 2000).

Denying new communities the opportunity to play host to football clubs seems little more than institutionalized ageism. The case of Inverness Caledonian Thistle (ICT) is perhaps pertinent here. ICT is located in the new city of Inverness, one of the fastest growing areas in the UK. It emerged from a merger of Inverness Thistle and Caledonian FC, a merger which was protracted and at times acrimonious (see, Bannerman, 1997, for an overview). To this day there remain supporters of the previous clubs who will not attend the new club. However, there are also people living in Inverness, particularly youngsters, who now have the opportunity to watch top level football. Is it socially acceptable to deny a future generation of stakeholders an interest in a top division team on the grounds of history? Perhaps what is required in these cases is to attempt to identify a pareto-optimal or at least pareto-satisfing outcome,[50] similar to what was put forward in Chapter 1 in respect of league reconstruction.[51] In other words, to consider the benefits and losses arising from the putative relocation or merger, taking into account the preferences of all those affected including supporters, shareholders, employees, governing bodies and the community, and as far as is practically possible focusing on future stakeholders as well as existing stakeholders. A challenging task certainly, but arguably an improvement from the automatic defence of history and an attempt to keep football relevant in contemporary society.

3   Organizational Forms: Ownership and Governance

Objectives of football clubs

Football clubs are ostensibly uncomplicated organizations: they exist to facilitate participation in organized football. Beyond this plain statement, however, there is a rather more complex and contested debate about the objectives and purpose of football clubs. For example, what is meant by participation? Is taking part in football sufficient or does that participation require to be successful? If so, how do we define success? League championships? Domestic cup competitions? European competitions? Does a football club have a responsibility beyond its own members or supporters, perhaps to other clubs or to their local communities. At a broader level what do we mean by a 'club'?

Like many words in English, the word club has acquired an array of meanings such that it has lost any precision as a label. Daly's Club Law defines a club as 'essentially an association of individuals in a way that involves to some degree the factors of free choice, permanence, corporate identity and the pursuit as a common aim of some joint interest other than the acquisition of a gain, such as those provided by membership of a trade union' (Martin, 1979). In the UK, most top level football clubs have long been incorporated as companies (see section on 'The structure of football in the UK'). In other countries, football is still organized at least in name through clubs, some of which are high profile organizations like Bayern München and Barcelona, which have in the region of 100,000 members. However, in these countries traditionally structured clubs now compete against clubs that are structured or owned by publicly listed companies (see, for example, Wilkesman and Blutner, 2002). How do differences in organizational structures affect the objectives of football 'clubs'? What differences become apparent when the club is a registered company with shareholders?[52]

The debate about these and similar questions has become more prominent in recent years partly as a consequence of the substantial increases in income and financial rewards available within football since the early 1990s.[53] One consequence of football's revenue boom has been to highlight the numerous different interests and motivations among and within football's stakeholders – shareholders, members, supporters, community and so on. While stakeholders in football clubs have probably never had a unitary objective, the objectives of stakeholders in contemporary clubs are arguably more diverse than ever before (Stewart, 1986). The apparent conflict in the objectives of supporters and investors that has come to prominence principally from the decision of some clubs to become Stock Exchange listed companies has perhaps been the most emotive. Bose (1999, p. xxiv) sums up the debate as follows:

'plc' ... [these] three initials are now used almost as a swear word and [are] seen as the fount of all evil, the ultimate triumph of money men over football.

This particular conflict centres on the ownership structure of football clubs. Any discussion of ownership structure is multi-faceted. At one level it is about different organizational forms. At another it is concerned with issues such as the distribution of votes and/or capital and the identity of the owners of those votes and/or capital. It also impinges directly upon issues of corporate governance – how an organization is controlled and managed – and accountability. More fundamentally, however, it is the ownership (and control) framework and resultant corporate governance, which provides the structure through which the objectives of the company are set and through which the means of attaining those objectives and monitoring performance are determined (OECD, 1999, p. 11).

Organizational form

Football has been described as a *lingua franca* (Radnedge, 1998, p. 12). Yet football is also often taken as the manifestation of a particular society, with national teams seen as representing different facets of national identity in their differing styles of play (Crolley and Hand, 2002, p. 9). In a similar vein traditionally there have been significant administrative and business differences between football clubs in the UK, continental Europe and Latin America.

These business differences are not restricted exclusively to football clubs; the nature, structure, funding and governance of general business organizations have varied among countries. Prominent among them was the role played by stock exchanges in different countries. While these typically played a major role in funding corporate activity in the UK and the US where firms prefer to go public, firms in most other European countries commonly maintained private ownership, often relying heavily on sources like bank funding (Solnik, 1996, p. 168). In recent years, however, this factor has begun to be eroded with stock exchanges playing a more significant role in many European countries.

To an extent this erosion of business structures is an inevitable consequence of the process of globalization. In the last decade or so, an increasing number of countries have adopted market-based approaches to economic policy. Financial markets in many countries throughout the world have also gone through processes of deregulation, the outcome being more integrated and internationalised markets and an increase in international investing (Solnik, 1996, p. v). Nevertheless national features remain, particularly in respect of the ownership and control of companies in different countries. For example, companies in several continental European countries continue to have highly concentrated ownership structures, with control being concentrated not only because of the presence of large investors or core investor groups but also because of the absence of significant holdings by others (Becht and Mayer, 2001, p. 36). By contrast in the UK, ownership is more diversified and there are few large shareholders. Not only does the scale of corporate control differ appreciably across countries – so too do the parties who exert it. For instance, while financial institutions are the dominant class of share-holders in the UK, in Italy there remains a dominant role for families, while in the Netherlands the largest blocks of shares are held by administrative offices[54] (Becht and Mayer, 2001, p. 26). Another key difference is the way in which ownership structure can be used to prevent control being contested (Becht and Mayer, 2001, p. 12).

Related to ownership and control is corporate governance. In different countries corporate governance has historically been determined by variations in social, political and legal traditions and reflects the differences in ownership and control structure (Demirag *et al.*, 2000). Of particular significance is the fact that corporate governance is affected by relationships among the participants in the governance system. In other words controlling shareholders (which could be individuals, family holdings, bloc alliances, or other corporations acting through a holding company or cross shareholdings) can significantly influence corporate behaviour (OECD, 1999, p. 13).

Globalizing forces are also in evidence in areas like corporate governance systems (Demirag *et al.*, 2000), as well as in related areas like financial reporting.[55] One effect of market-based approaches to economic policy is a focusing of attention on the importance of private corporations for the welfare of individuals (OECD, 1999, p. 7). At one level this is concerned with helping to ensure that companies use their capital efficiently and hence maintain investor confidence (OECD, 1999, p. 7). At another level, however, it is about accountability: ensuring that companies take into account the interests of a wide range of groups who have an interest in the organization like shareholders, employees, customers and the community and that company boards are accountable to the company and the shareholders (OECD, 1999, p. 7). Interest in corporate governance is highlighted by the number of reports that have been published in European countries dealing with the issue in the last decade or so.[56] Perhaps of most significance in the context of globalization has been the publication of the OECD's *Principles of Corporate Governance*. While recognizing that the multiplicity of legal systems, institutional frameworks and traditions means that there is a range of valid models of corporate governance throughout the world, nevertheless the principles build on common elements in various countries. These underlie good corporate governance and are formulated to embrace the different models that exist (OECD, 1999).

Within football it has been argued that globalization and the international circulation of sports capital have eroded many of the traditional or cultural peculiarities between football organizations in different countries (Giulianotti, 1999, p. 86). Certainly, corporate structures, owned or controlled on market principles, are more prevalent among football clubs (Giulianotti, 2002). This is most visibly evidenced by the fact that listed football clubs are now to be found in Denmark, England, Germany, Italy, the Netherlands, Portugal, Scotland and Turkey. However, very different business structures still remain within European clubs and caution needs to be exercised in judging the extent to which globalization might be eroding distinctive organizational forms.

The remainder of this chapter aims to provide a contemporary insight into these structures in a small number of clubs based in various European countries: to identify aspects of the ownership, control and governance structures in these clubs, both in the context of the particular country's system of corporate financing and governance and also that country's football culture and context. Similar to the approach adopted by the OECD set out above, the analysis does not seek to prescribe a common approach or to identify a single appropriate model of football club ownership and governance. Instead focusing on clubs in countries with distinct legal, financial and institutional frameworks, its objective is to identify common themes that emerge concerning the ownership and governance of these clubs and to provide guidance on elements that underlie successful clubs and good football club governance. To an extent this approach is also in keeping with that reflected in the *UEFA Club Licensing System* document (UEFA, 2002a), which allows individual associations flexibility in developing their own licensing systems based upon the UEFA master document. Although not explicitly stated in that document, this approach is presumably based on recognition of the differing legal, financial, cultural and social frameworks within which each association's member clubs operate and which would render a common approach meaningless.

Interviews were carried at different dates in 2001 and 2002 with club directors and/or management at each club and also, where possible, with supporter representatives. These interviews are referred to throughout the remainder of this chapter.

The United Kingdom

Home to a population of 59.6m at July 2001, the United Kingdom (UK) is a leading trading power and financial centre. Its per capita GDP of $24,500 in 2000 is comparable to other OECD countries like France ($24,400) and Italy ($25,100) (OECD, 2002). The largest proportion of GDP is accounted for by services, particularly banking, insurance and business services, while industry continues to decline in importance (CIA, 2001). While a prominent member of the EU, to date the UK has not yet elected to adopt the single European currency, the euro. Constitutionally, the Westminster Parliament governs the UK, but regional parliaments and assemblies with varying degrees of power are to be found in Scotland, Wales and Northern Ireland.

The UK deploys an essentially capitalistic economy with the majority of major business organizations structured as limited liability companies.[57] The limited liability company arose as a response to demand for risk capital during the industrial expansion of the late nineteenth and twentieth centuries (Rutterford, 1993). The important point about a limited liability company is that it does not require its members to contribute more than a certain amount of capital, no matter what financial difficulties the company may get into. In other words the risk of members being called upon to contribute unlimited amounts of capital is removed and they are less likely, therefore, to find themselves being forced into bankruptcy (Dyson, 1992, p. 115).

In view of this need for risk capital is it is unsurprising that there is a long history in the UK of corporate activity being funded through the London Stock Exchange and that its development precedes that of exchanges in other European countries. Today, the UK is home to one of the world's largest stock markets, the London Stock Exchange. At September 2002, some 2,849 companies were listed on the London Stock Exchange. Among these were 1,738 UK companies listed on the main market and 425 foreign companies, while domestic market capitalization was £1,105bn (€1,750bn) (www.londonstockexchange.com). It is also important to note that the London Stock Exchange has retained a relatively greater importance as a source of finance than stock exchanges in countries with greater economic activity than the UK like Germany and France.

The structure of football in the UK

Football in the UK, however, is not organized at a national level. Instead separate leagues exist in England (in which some Welsh clubs also participate), Scotland and Northern Ireland. In each country, a separate governing body also exists (e.g. the Scottish Football Association), while each country has its own international side. Separate administrative bodies like the FA Premier League within each country govern individual football leagues.

Although it has been Stock Exchange listings that have highlighted the conflict between supporters and investors in some UK football clubs, in fact, its roots lie much deeper in the limited liability corporate structure, which has been prevalent among UK football clubs since about the late nineteenth century (Szymanski and Kuypers, 1999, pp. 5–6; Vamplew, 1988, p. 4). Although motivated initially by a desire to protect the founders and officers of the club from personal liability in the event of the club developing unpayable debts, particularly as wages rose, it effectively resulted in a division being created between those who owned and ran the clubs and those who supported them.

Recognition of the potential conflict that might arise in limited liability football companies between sporting and financial objectives prompted the Football Association (FA) in England to introduce Rule 34. This restricted the payment of dividends to owners – initially to five per cent but increased in 1981 to fifteen per cent of the nominal value of the shares – and prevented the payment of directors (Conn, 1997, p. 39; Hamil *et al.*, 2001a, p. 4). However, the listing of Tottenham Hotspur on the London Stock Exchange in 1983 effectively ended any meaningful attempt by the football authorities in England to distinguish between a football club and a football company. In order to make itself an attractive financial investment proposition, Rule 34 was circumvented through the setting up of new holding company (Tottenham Hotspur plc) of which the football club became a subsidiary. Key to this was that the holding company was not subject to the FA rules and hence the financial restrictions set out in Rule 34 did not apply. The FA's feebleness as a regulator was epitomized by its failure to make any attempt to enforce Rule 34 and subsequently a number of clubs adopted similar corporate structures prior to flotation. Rule 34 was finally abandoned altogether by the FA in 1998 (Brown, 2000b).

In the UK, football was in fact one of the last major industries to adopt the limited liability or joint stock model. However, by 1888, the *Athletic News* was recommending that football clubs with an annual turnover of £1,000 should convert from private associations to limited companies (Birley, 1995, p. 39). Normally the limited liability model results in a separation of ownership and control of the company. In football, however, the two often continued to overlap, with many British clubs being owned by small groups of businessmen and a few hundred small shareholders, most of them fans. A study in 1982 found that in half of the 92 English Football League clubs, more than 40 per cent of voting shares were held by directors (FIR, 1982). More recently, Table 3.1 provides a classification of the top division English and Scottish football companies by ownership type in 1997. What it demonstrates is that most clubs continued to either have concentrated ownership (where one or a few individuals or institutions own a large percentage of shares in a company) or concentrated control (where notwithstanding a more diversified ownership structure, one or a small group of dominant shareholders remain in a position to exert effective control).

As of October 2002, there are 20 UK clubs listed on either the London Stock Exchange Official List (main market) or on the Alternative Investment Market (AIM), the market for smaller, young and fast-growing companies that are not ready or which do not wish to join the Official List. In view of the historical importance of stock markets as a means of funding UK corporate activity, it is perhaps unsurprising that

Table 3.1 Classification of football companies by ownership type, 1997

Concentrated ownership		Diversified ownership – concentrated control		Diversified ownership
Dominant owner	**Family/ director control**	**Dominant owner**	**Family/ director control**	
Blackburn Rovers	Arsenal	Aston Villa	Leicester City	Caspian (Leeds United)
Derby County	West Ham United	Newcastle United	Nottingham Forest	Manchester United
Everton	Dundee United*	Sheffield Wednesday	Aberdeen	Sheffield United
Liverpool	Motherwell*	Sunderland	Heart of Midlothian	Southampton Leisure (Southampton)
Wimbledon		Tottenham Hotspur	Burnden Leisure (Bolton Wanderers)	West Bromwich Albion
Dunfermline Athletic		Celtic	Charlton Athletic	
Hibernian		Birmingham City	Silver Shield (Swansea City)	
Kilmarnock		Loftus Road (Queen's Park Rangers)		
Raith Rovers		Preston North End		
Rangers				
Middlesbrough				

* This classification reflects the very small number of shares in issue at each of these clubs: 13,004 in the case of Dundee United; 266,996 in the case of Motherwell.

Note: Lack of publicly available information on the nature of the substantial shareholdings in Chelsea Village (Chelsea) and Coventry City Football Club (Holdings) Ltd makes classification of these companies impracticable. In general terms, it should also be borne in mind that any classification of this nature is, of course, subjective.

Source: Morrow (1999, p. 83)

there are more listed football clubs in the UK than anywhere else. However, what is perhaps surprising is that most of those listed clubs, including Manchester United, arguably the world's most prominent listed sporting company, did not list until the mid 1990s.

Tottenham Hotspur

Tottenham Hotspur Football Club was formed in 1882, its unique name originating from a small cricket club, The Hotspur Cricket Club, which played on a field in the Tottenham area of London and whose members were looking to find a winter pastime to keep the club together when the cricket season was over (Goodwin, 1988, p. 9). The need for an injection of new funds and the wish to restrict the personal liability of the members resulted in a meeting of the club's members on 2 March 1898 agreeing to transfer the club's assets and liabilities to a limited liability company – The Tottenham Hotspur Football and Athletic Company Limited. A share issue in which 8,000 shares of £1 each were offered to the public accompanied this. Interestingly, while the share issue that accompanied the company's listing on the London Stock Exchange in 1983 was a great success, being oversubscribed by four times, this initial share issue did not go well, with only 1,558 shares being taken up in the first year (Goodwin, 1988, p. 14).

Ownership and structure

Tottenham Hotspur has long been of significance to those with an interest in the financial aspects of football. In addition to being the first European football club to list on a stock market, it was also one of the first major clubs to try to diversify its business away from core football activities; ill-fated ventures into sportswear, women's fashion and ticketing took the company almost to the edge of bankruptcy in 1990. It has led the way in financial reporting in football clubs too, being the first British club to recognize the services provided by its players as assets on its Balance Sheet back in 1989 (Morrow, 1999).

Its more recent history is still of interest. In February 2001, the entertainment and leisure group, ENIC (English National Investment Company), which has holdings in a number of European clubs, acquired a *de facto* controlling stake in Tottenham Hotspur plc. ENIC's initial holding of 27.4m ordinary shares (29.9 per cent) of the ordinary share capital in Tottenham Hotspur plc was purchased from former Chairman, businessman Sir Alan Sugar. Prior to ENIC's involvement, the ownership structure at Tottenham could be classified as one of diversified ownership, concentrated control (see Table 3.1). In other words, notwithstanding its Stock Exchange listing, Tottenham continued to be under the effective control of one individual, Sir Alan Sugar. This structure is not at all uncommon among listed clubs, with similar dominant individuals remaining in control at clubs like Aston Villa (Doug Ellis), Lazio (Sergio Cragnotti) and Roma (Francesco Sensi) (see also Italy section).

The ownership structure of Tottenham Hotspur plc in September 2002 is set out in Table 3.2.

ENIC has ownership interests in several football clubs. Over a number of years it has built up a portfolio of shareholdings in European clubs, with stakes in AEK Athens, Basle, Rangers, Slavia Prague and Vicenza. ENIC's original plan was a pyramid of clubs. At the top would be a major club (a position for which apparently Tottenham was identified) which ENIC had influence over. Below, there would be clubs, often in underdeveloped (footballing) countries like Greece or the Czech Republic, which had potential to grow. Originally, the rationale was that such clubs would share in and benefit from the commercial ideas and expertise of Tottenham. Tottenham in turn would utilize, on an arms length basis, players from these clubs. In Chief Executive, Daniel Levy's terms 'it was the inter-relationship between various clubs which we thought would bring mutual benefits to both' (interview, August 2001). However, this synergistic initiative was effectively blocked by UEFA when it prohibited multi-club ownership. It ruled that two clubs controlled by the same organization or individual could not take part

Table 3.2 Ownership of Tottenham Hotspur plc

Shareholder	Percentage holding	Number of shares
ENIC	29.80	30,406,649
Amshold Group Limited*	13.13	13,396,026
Hodram	8.67	8,850,000
H. Shore[‡]	0.99	1,000,000

* The Amshold Group Limited is wholly owned by Sir Alan Sugar, former Chairman of Tottenham Hotspur plc.

[‡] H. Shore is a potential beneficiary of a discretionary trust that holds 1,000,000 shares in Tottenham Hotspur plc.

Source: Tottenham Hotspur plc Annual Report 2002, information at 3 September 2002[58]

in the same UEFA competition on the grounds that it damaged the integrity of the tournament and introduced the possibility of matches being fixed. This decision was then upheld by the European Court of Arbitration for Sport in 1999. ENIC subsequently challenged the rules arguing that they infringed EU competition regulations. However, in a ruling in 2002, the European Commission accepted that a firm or individual should not be permitted to control more than one club thus calling into question ENIC's investment strategy (Cohen and Guerrera, 2002).

Given Tottenham's long history as a Stock Exchange listed company, it is interesting that one of ENIC's other clubs, AEK Athens, is currently prohibited under Greek regulations from becoming a public company. According to Daniel Levy, two of the most important advantages of public listed company status are first, facilitating access to capital and second, improving transparency and governance (interview August 2001). Consequently, in ENIC's view, Greek clubs and Greek football are held back through being denied these advantages.

The business of Tottenham Hotspur

[Y]ou have a duty to protect the assets of the club for its fans today and its future fans, future generations, not just its shareholders.

(interview with Daniel Levy, August 2001)

Notwithstanding its status as a Stock Exchange listed company, according to its controlling shareholder, the objectives of Tottenham Hotspur are broader than those commonly associated with UK market listed companies – maximization of profits or maximization of shareholder value. Instead, what are espoused are objectives that envisage a symbiotic relationship between what happens on and off the field:

This is initially a football club and a business second ... it is the success on the pitch which drives the revenue streams ... My opinion is that you have to have ... football success first, but, in order to make sure it is properly managed you have to have the appropriate business structure in place to ensure that you can take advantage of the fact that you have got football success.

(interview with Daniel Levy, August 2001).

Levy's use of the phrase 'business structure', as distinct from ownership structure, is of interest. Despite his enthusiasm for football clubs to be allowed to become publicly listed companies, it is clear that ownership structure *per se* is not considered the key factor in achieving the corporate objectives. Rather what is important is how the company is run, not who owns it. In other words, does the company have the structures in place to allow it to benefit from football success?

The phrase 'business structure' may conjure up images for some of conflict between football-minded supporters and business-minded directors. However, at Tottenham there is evidence of a willingness to define the football business in a broader or more inclusive way that recognizes the social significance or social role of the club. At one level this may be motivated simply by business priorities. In other words, the directors recognize that the factors that make the club a valuable social asset are often the same factors that will make it a successful business, and hence their behaviour aims to cultivate that social relationship to the benefit of the company's financial position. While concerns have been expressed about the free-market transformation of football club supporters into customers or consumers (see, for example, King, 1997; Morrow, 1999), often this has been expressed as a discrete choice. Giulianotti (2002), however, provides a more thorough analysis of the supporter identification, identifying four ideal types – supporters, followers, fans and flâneurs. A simplified version of Giulianotti's classification is set out in Figure 3.1 (the more detailed version is found in Figure 2.1).

The 'traditional'/'consumer' split focuses on an individual's investment in a specific club: 'traditional' spectators have a longer, more localized and popular cultural identification with a club: 'consumer' spectators have a more market-centred relationship centering upon consumption of club products. The 'hot'/'cool' split focuses on the extent to which a club is central to an individual's self-formation. For example, 'hot' loyalty

	HOT	
	Supporter	**Fan**
Traditional		Consumer
	Follower	**Flâneur**
	COOL	

Source: adapted from Giulianotti (2002, p. 31)

Figure 3.1   Spectator categories (simplified)

indicating intense kinds of solidarity and identification with the club (Giulianotti, 2002, pp. 30–1). However, while the nature of a spectator's social relationship with a club differs markedly within these four categories, arguably there is less variation in the economic relationship, or at least in the outcome of that economic relationship. While some spectators are clearly more market-centred than others – a fact reflected in their willingness to consume products associated with a club ranging from merchandise to shares – all categories require an economic relationship with their club to enable their spectating.

One aspect of Tottenham's business structure involves a more explicit recognition of the importance of the club's supporters and of its community and of the need to build a genuine relationship with them. As Daniel Levy noted 'football clubs have taken their fan base for granted too much' (interview, August 2001). At Tottenham the directors are attempting to build this relationship in a number of ways. Key to this building process is improved communication, of promoting dialogue. At one level this is personal communication – things like the Chief Executive reading and responding to all non-abusive mail that he receives; or inviting two season ticket holders at random to the directors' box for every home game. At a structural level it involves things like developing the club's website and improving communication with the press. It also involves improved corporate communications and reporting to share-holders: 'a fuller statement in terms of the activities of the business … how things are going, rather than just a couple of sentences' (interview with Daniel Levy, August 2001).

Arguably the most substantive change, however, is the recognition afforded to the Tottenham Hotspur Supporters' Trust (THST). The Trust is a mutually structured membership organization, developed with the help of *Supporters Direct*, the government-funded initiative designed to encourage supporters to take a stake in their club (see also Chapter 2). The THST website sets out its informal mission statement as being:

- To help THFC [Tottenham Hotspur Football Club] achieve constant and sustained success.
- To unite and represent all Spurs' fans and to exercise their collective power.
- To improve communication and understanding between the Club and its supporters.

(Tottenham Hotspur Supporters' Trust at
http://www.tottenhamtrust.com)

The willingness to work with the Trust was formally expressed by the club's Vice-Chairman, David Buchler, shortly after the appointment of Glenn Hoddle as manager, when he talked in terms of '[embracing] the supporters' trust ...' of having 'a communication route with its supporters' and of '[working] together in a real team work effort, to build the future of the club that we all seek' (Wynne, 2001). Daniel Levy described its practical support of the Trust – in terms of allowing the Trust to use facilities at the stadium, allowing it to advertise in the programme, allowing it to put details on the website – as being about promoting dialogue and communication (interview, August 2001).

It is clear from the above that both the directors and the THST are ostensibly committed to communication and dialogue as a way of achieving their ultimate aim, making Tottenham Hotspur as successful as possible. Congruence in terms of the ultimate aim, however, does not mean that the two sides necessarily share the same motivation for seeking to achieve that aim, a point noted by Joff Wild of the THST:

> in roundabout ways the goals of Daniel Levy are the same as the goals of the Spurs supporters. Levy wants to be in the Champions' League because that is how he justifies the purchase of Tottenham to ENIC shareholders and [the supporters] want to be in the Champions' League because that's where we want to be.
>
> (interview, December 2001)

As discussed previously, at the end of the day the directors want to develop the relationship with the supporters because an improved relationship will be beneficial for business in the long run. However, while the supporters want an improved relationship because the club is something they love, that they are part of, equally, they recognize that the club needs them in order to be financially successful:

> ENIC have not come into Tottenham, and Levy is not there as a Spurs supporter. He's not there because he loves Spurs, he's there because he is chairman of ENIC and he believes that he can make money out of Tottenham ... what we need to do ... is demonstrate to [Levy] that he cannot maximize his investment in Spurs as chairman of ENIC unless he has a constructive dialogue with the supporters, because the supporters can actually show him the way, in many ways, to maximize his returns.
>
> (interview with Joff Wild, December 2001)

Governance and accountability in practice

It is something of a paradox that it is those football clubs that have adopted the most business-like structures that offer the greatest opportunity to adopt inclusive approaches to governance. Key to this are Stock Exchange listing requirements, that companies adopt certain standards of transparency in terms of business behaviour and reporting and governance. Arguably these demands for transparency and govern-ance force a discipline on boards of directors that might not be present if a club were a private company, particularly where it is controlled by one individual (interview with Daniel Levy, August 2001). The benefits of transparency arising from public listing are also recognized by some supporters. For example, THST's Joff Wild, was of the opinion that 'taking clubs public ... is not necessarily the disaster for supporters that people portray it as ... it institutionalises the relationship between the supporters and the club ... There is a far greater degree of scrutiny in a plc than in a privately owned football club' (interview, December 2001).

What the Trust is seeking from its relationship with the directors in the long term is both accountability and influence – having the ability to ensure that the board of directors explain their decision-making processes and about giving the supporters an opportunity to change the way things are run through persuasion (interview with Joff Wild, December 2001). However, Trust members need to be aware that the successful development of the relationship requires them to be realistic in their aims and rational in their behaviour. In practice this relationship operates through formal meetings between the Trust and directors, and informally through the Trust having a point of contact within the club whom it can contact for information. Communication, however, works both ways. For example, the club approached the Trust to ask it to survey its fans to get their views on the workings of the ticket office.

The extent to which there is genuine communication, accountability and influence will only become clear over a period of time. However, Tottenham Hotspur plc is a market-listed company and its directors will be judged by the rules of that market. To that end, while the directors may encourage communication and inclusivity, ultimately decision making rests with them, a point noted by Daniel Levy: 'we listen to [the Trust's view] but at the end of the day, we have a duty to protect the financial assets of the club and that may be in conflict with what the fans want' (interview August 2001).

Unpalatable as that observation may be to some supporters, potentially of greater concern is where market logic extends beyond individual decision making and individual clubs. In arguing against regulation of the football industry, Daniel Levy suggests that ultimately it is market forces that act as a discipline on clubs (interview August 2001). In other words, the market will reward those clubs that look after their fans and community because this translates into customers and increased income, which makes it easier to compete on the field. Where a club fails to act in this way then the outcome is either that the owner sells up, disenchanted at being unable to bring success or unable to sustain the operation financially, or at the most extreme the club goes out of business. Financial or economic issues thus determine the outcome.

Both in a football and in a wider economic context, concerns exist about the desirability, and indeed feasibility, of allowing the market to operate in this way. A particular concern is whether the market mechanism is appropriate for industries where there is a lack of competition or supplier choice (Letza and Smallman, 2001). In theory the economic choices of both product substitution and non-purchase exist for football customers. In practice, however, no such social choices exist for most football supporters. Hence, arguably, in substance if not in economic form, the football market is one in which the behaviour of a key participant (supporters) renders the choices redundant. While a supporter is always a customer, most supporters are never just customers. Particular difficulties exist for supporters if they are faced with an owner who they believe is not acting in the best interests of their club. While economic logic might advocate staying away from the club and allowing the market to resolve the issue, such rational behaviour may often be rejected as an option by supporters, motivated by non-financial considerations like identity and belonging.

Arguably, the prospects of genuine communication, accountability and influence are dependent not only on market-based economic considerations, but also on social considerations. An inclusive approach to business is one that focuses less exclusively on shareholders and gives consideration to all stakeholder relationships (RSA, 1995). The theoretical case for supporters' trusts being intimately involved in communication is strong as they are by definition democratic and have the potential to be representative of the club's supporters and its community. However, the Trust needs to be able to demonstrate its legitimacy in practice, both to the directors, but also to other supporters and members of the community (see section on 'Supporter Trusts' in Chapter 2).

As discussed in Chapter 2, notwithstanding the long-term nature of the *Supporters Direct* initiative, and the fact that trusts are community initiatives being developed by supporters in their own time, it is apparent that very few of these trusts yet have a substantial number of members. For example, in the summer of 2001, the Tottenham Hotspur Supporters Trust, which was one of the biggest supporters trusts at that time, had approximately 600 members. By way of comparison, the average home attendance at FA Premier League matches in season 2001/02 was 35,001 (2000/01: 35,421). From the directors' viewpoint, any perceived lack of weight has the potential to become more of an issue should the relationship between club and trust deteriorate. On the other hand, too close a relationship with the club leaves the trust open to accusations of being captured or being seen to be captured by the club management; then being challenged by other supporters who perhaps do not share the trust's view on particular issues (see Chapter 2).

Netherlands

Home to a population of 16.0m at July 2001, the Netherlands is an advanced economy, which combines high per capita income (2000: $27,800 (OECD, 2002)) with relatively even income distribution. It is one of the most open and outward looking economies in the world, a fact explained both by its geographical position as a hub of Europe's transportation system and the small size of its domestic market (EIU, 2001). The economy is dominated by the services sector, which accounted for over 70 per cent of GDP in 2000 (EIU, 2001).

The country's economic model is similar to the social market model found in Germany, with extensive social welfare provisions, an important role for workers' councils at corporate level and trade unions at national level (EIU, 2001). Interestingly, however, its financial system is more akin to the Anglo-American rather than the Germanic model, with corporate finance being provided primarily through share issues, with banks acting as intermediaries rather than as long-term investors (EIU, 2001). It was a founder member of the EU and it was among the first 11 EU countries establishing the euro currency zone on 1 January 1999.

There are various legal forms of business entity in the Netherlands including associations, foundations and cooperatives. However, the largest legal entities are limited companies. These are either public limited companies – *Naamloze Vennootschap* (NV), of which there are approximately 2,000 – or private limited companies – *Besloten Vennootschap* (BV), of which there are approximately 150,000. A BV is usually smaller than a NV, and is less open in its behaviour. For example, the statutes of a BV must limit the transferability of shares. NV status is usually a prerequisite for listing on the Amsterdam Stock Exchange (de Jong *et al.*, 2001). All companies which employ at least 100 employees must have a works council – *ondernemingsraad* – to allow representation of, and consultation with, employees. Among other things the council has a right to relevant information and to advise on major decisions such as transfers of ownership and relocation.

For large companies a variation exists in the form of a 'structure NV' (*structuurregeling*) for which special rules apply. (A large company is defined as employing at least 100 employees in the Netherlands, having equity capital of at least €13m, and being legally required to have a works council (SER, 2001).) The structure regime includes the requirement to set up a supervisory board (*raad van commissarissen*). This board consists of at least three members and new members can be co-opted by the board itself. It takes on many of the powers otherwise held by the shareholders such as the evaluation of managerial decisions, and consequently, de Jong *et al.* (2001) argue that, in practice, ordinary shareholders end up with little influence or say over the supervisory or management board.

As mentioned previously, the Dutch financial system follows the Anglo-American model, with share issues being a primary source of finance. In September 2001, the Amsterdam Stock Exchange merged with the exchanges in Brussels and Paris to form the Euronext Exchange, which aims to be the first fully integrated, cross-border, European market for equities, bonds, derivatives and commodities. Securities are listed on either the Official Market or the Euro.NM Amsterdam market. Approximately 225 Dutch companies, 140 foreign companies and 220 investment institutions are listed on Euronext's Amsterdam Official Market. The market capitalization of the Dutch companies only, amounted to €671 billion on 31 September 2000 (www.euronext.nl). The economic significance of the stock market is also evident in earlier periods. Historically, the Amsterdam Stock Exchange was heavily concentrated. Prior to its merger, fifteen companies, among them Philips, accounted for about 75 per cent of total market capitalization of the exchange (de Jong *et al.*, 2001).

The structure of Dutch football

The structure and operations of Dutch clubs are regulated by the KNVB (Royal Netherlands Football Association). Traditionally, only clubs legally structured as associations (*vereniging*)[59] or as foundations (*stichting*)[60] could be members of the KNVB, and thus could be granted a licence to take part in its competitions. However, since January 2002, the statutes of the KNVB have been changed to allow limited companies (BVs) and public companies (NVs) to become members of the KNVB (correspondence with KNVB, April 2002), the argument being that more business-like corporate structures would allow clubs, for example, to raise capital while still maintaining their licences.

For a number of years, three clubs have dominated Dutch football: Ajax, Feyenoord and PSV Eindhoven (see Chapter 1). These clubs have also had a strong presence in European football, between them winning 11 European trophies since 1970: six for Ajax, three for Feyenoord, and two for PSV.[61] Their significance is also reflected in the fact that both Ajax and PSV were founder members of the G14 group of clubs (see also Chapter 1).

The dominance of clubs from the Netherlands' two main cities, Amsterdam and Rotterdam, is perhaps unsurprising. Part of the rivalry, which exists between these two clubs, relates to a contest between these two cities for the right to represent the Netherlands. However, as Giulianotti (1999, p. 11) notes, the contest to represent the nation is based on more than geography, with the conflict also being contested on ethno-class lines – the club of the commercial, Jewish, middle-class bohemia versus the club representing the industrial, working-class superport. Such representational contests are also evident in other European countries like Greece, Portugal, Scotland and Turkey.[62] The presence, therefore, of what was in effect a works teams, albeit a multinational works, from a small town in the South East of the country, might at first sight seem a little odd.

Philips Sport Vereniging (PSV)

As a donor, sponsor, investor and credit bank, Philips has pumped hundreds of millions of guilders into the club over the past forty years. In the meantime PSV has reached the point where it will manage even without Philips. In Eindhoven there is a club of international standing: a club with its own heart and soul which is able to charm other lovers as well as Philips. Yet they are faithful to each other. That is also love.

Oosterwijk (2002, p. 150)

The Philips Company, Eindhoven's major employer, gave its name to the club – Philips Sport Vereniging – formed in Eindhoven in 1913. PSV effectively started life as a factory team – a football club for the Philips workers. Since then there has been a close but evolving relationship between Philips and PSV. At its formation, however, in order for PSV to be granted a licence by the KNVB allowing it to participate in its competitions, the club was required to adopt the legal structure of an association, a membership organization, with those members electing the board. While some are exclusively football associations, others encompass several sports. The association at PSV, *Eindhovense Voetbal Vereniging PSV* (EVV), continues to exist today within the new organizational structure.

As football became more professional, a second legal entity was set up – *Stichting PSV Voetbal* or PSV foundation.[63] In the mid 1980s, the club's current president, Harry van Raaij, wrote a policy proposal, the essence of which was to put in place a more business-like structure between PSV and Philips (Oosterwijk, 2002, p. 131). This was the first of several such attempts to formalize the relationship, and the essence of it was that in return for a fixed amount of sponsorship money, PSV would provide services such as shirt sponsorship, stadium advertising, hospitality and promotional matches (Oosterwijk, 2002, p. 131). Part of the new strategy, involved a restructuring of the relationship between the association (EVV) and the foundation. Under the new structure, the foundation was assigned a crucial role, taking over ownership of all the assets including the transfer rights of the players and collecting the sponsorship money from Philips. The players were then hired out to the association (EVV) which paid their salaries, and the association retained the licence from the KNVB to play as PSV (interview with Harry van Raaij, December 2001). The significance of this was that control was effectively passed from the association, or more pertinently its members, to the foundation, a corporate body with no members. Effectively, therefore, it removed the delaying effect of club democracy (Oosterwijk, 2002, p. 131).

The significance of the Philips company in PSV was clearly evident in the board of the foundation, which at that time was made up of two members: one was the president of the association (EVV), the other was the President of Philips. According to the current PSV President, Mr Harry van Raaij, himself an employee of Philips since 1954 and ultimately its Director of Corporate Accounting, the structure at that time was such that while PSV was the football club (the association), the (financial) power rested indirectly with Phillips through the foundation (interview, December 2001). In simple terms, Philips acted as a financial safety net for PSV – if PSV had a loss at the end of the season, Philips covered it; if PSV needed a loan Philips provided it (interview with Fons Spooren, Director of Operations PSV, December 2001).

As the opening quotation in this section illustrates, until recently PSV remained financially dependent on the Philips company (see Oosterwijk, 2002, for a detailed discussion of the development of the relationship between PSV and Philips). Lately, however, the relationship between PSV and Philips has been transformed, on a mutually agreed basis, from one of dependency into a purely business or commercial relationship. At present Philips acts as the company's main sponsor, but like any sponsorship agreement this is subject to renewal and renegotiation. To an extent the transformation arose from a recognition that time had moved on, both in terms of Philips and in terms of the football industry. While Philips still has interests in football, clearly football is not Philips' business.[64] On PSV's part, the perception is that new professional managers brought in at PSV could see the benefits in running the club on a more professional and independent manner. PSV now seeks to run itself as a sustainable operation, with appropriate operating and governance structures in place. This is the driving force behind its structures. One consequence of the transformation of the relationship into a purely commercial one is that Philips were willing to enter into a lucrative arms-length 5-year sponsorship contract with the new PSV.

Ownership and structure

As part of the development of PSV's relationship with Philips, a limited liability company, PSV NV (*Naamloze Vennootschap*) was set up. The activities and assets and liabilities of the Association and the Foundation were transferred on 30 June 1999 to PSV NV through the issue of shares to these legal bodies (PSV Annual Report, 2000/01, p. 21). As part of this restructuring, the Foundation received preference shares in PSV NV

Table 3.3 PSV share capital at 30 June 2001

Issued/placed paid up share capital	
9,989 ordinary shares, nominal value €10	99,890
10 preference shares, nominal value €10	100
1 golden share, nominal value €10	10
	€100,000

Source: PSV (2001), Annual Report 2000/01, p. 37

(*prioriteitsaandelen*) with the Association receiving a golden share (*bijzonder aandeel*). PSV's share capital is shown in Table 3.3.

The special rights of the preference shares and golden share as detailed in the 2000/01 annual report are:

- *Golden share*: The share capital [includes] one golden share at the nominal value of €10. This share belongs to the Eindhoven Football Association PSV. The right of approval has been linked to this special share concerning a number of decisions by PSV plc.

  The approval of the Eindhoven Football Association PSV is required for: the changing of the name or a trade name of PSV or changing the description of aims and goals of PSV NV; changing the PSV logo or the PSV club colours; changing the PSV football location; changing the location; the structure or the design of the youth training coordinated by PSV, the independent application for a licence for professional football from the KNVB.
- *Preference shares*: To the holder of preference shares, now called the PSV Football Foundation, among others the following preferential rights have been awarded:

  deciding the number of directors and commissioners; binding nomination for appointment of management and commissioners; suspension and/or dismissal of directors and commissioners; giving consent before the decision for legal mergers, legal splitting of the company, change of statutes and dissolution.

As a result, the current structure is that the Foundation is effectively the legal owner of PSV NV, while moral ownership is retained by the Association (and its members). Further change to the ownership structure, in terms of PSV NV becoming a Stock Exchange listed company has been ruled out at least for the time being. Different reasons emerge for this; some relate to the nature of stock markets, others to the nature of PSV and Dutch football clubs more generally.

The importance of running the organization on a sound and proper financial basis was something that was stressed by the PSV directors (interviews, December 2001). A key objective for the organization is financial sustainability – matching normal or recurring expenditure with recurring income. Acting as a primary market, stock markets exist to provide an accessible form of long-term funds to companies (Morrow, 1999, p. 63). At this stage, quite simply the directors of PSV do not consider it appropriate to go public, as they have not identified a requirement for long-term funds. While some clubs have chosen to invest share-issue proceeds in short-term assets, most noticeably players, the PSV directors' focus on financial sustainability and appropriate matching of funds and assets, leads to, for them, a perfectly rational economic decision. In the words of the president, Harry van Raaij: '[When I am asked] why are you not going [to the stock exchange], I say I don't know how to write the paragraph on how we will use the proceeds' (interview, December 2001).

A second reason is the historical ownership structures prevalent among Dutch clubs, namely associations and foundations. Among other things these structures have restricted clubs' ability to raise funds other than through retained profits, with the result being that even if it was deemed to be a desired route, most Dutch clubs are simply not ready for market listing in structural or financial terms. While PSV has taken steps to adopt a more business-like ownership structure from which it could consider moving toward flotation, evidence suggests that, instead, the focus is on continuing to develop the club's management and governance structure through, for example, the creation of a new supervisory board rather than on issues of ownership *per se*. The purpose is to demonstrate PSV's credibility as a stand-alone football business, separate from Philips. Thereafter, other structural changes may be opportune but these are more likely to involve strengthening relationships with the club's existing (business) partners or stakeholders, perhaps by the private placing of shares.

A third reason for its caution is the experience of other clubs that have sought listing, both in the Netherlands (Ajax) and also elsewhere, particularly the UK. In addition to broad issues such as marked negative price movements on the secondary market, concern was also expressed about the excessive publicity that Ajax has encountered owing to its position as the country's only listed club. Any rumour about the club, however small, is likely to be reported and highlighted (interview with Harry van Raaij, December 2001).

Governance

In terms of governance structures, PSV has adopted the system of governance and management outlined previously for a structure NV (*structuurregeling*), namely a supervisory board or board of commissioners (*raad van commissarissen*) and a management board (*raad van Bestuur*).

The supervisory board has 5 members. Its independent Chairman, Mr J. D. Timmer is a former president of Philips and he is joined by a current

Philips director (Mr A. P. M. van der Peol), a representative from one of PSV's sponsors, the President Director of Daimler Chrysler Netherlands, a representative from a local Eindhoven-based company, the President Director of the VDL Group and the Vice Chairman of the association (EVV) (full details can be found on the PSV website at www.psv.nl; see also Figure 3.2). Furthermore, the Chairman of the Supervisory Board now also has a role as one of the three board members of the foundation (along with Harry van Raaij and the President of Philips).

The role of the Supervisory Board is to give approval and guidance to the directors, both on an operational level (e.g. any investment greater than 5,000 guilders [approximately €2,270] has to be approved by the supervisory board) and at a strategic level, on issues that will have a long-term impact on the business (interview with Harry van Raaij, December 2001). According to Mr van Raaij, a key requirement of the board must

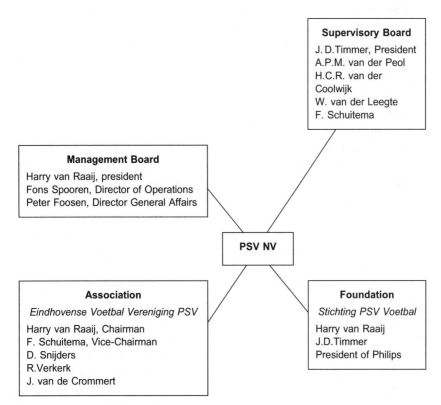

Source: www.psv.nl, interviews

Figure 3.2 Organization structure at PSV Eindhoven

be its unity or unitary nature. The Management Board consists of van Raaij, plus two other full time directors, Mr Fons Spooren and Mr Peter Foosen. It is responsible for the day-to-day running of the club and is accountable to the Supervisory Board for financial results.

It is clear from Figure 3.2 that PSV is in a position to draw on very well qualified, well-connected and experienced individuals for its boards, from both its Philips connection and from the wider business community. However, in view of the nature of many football clubs and their broad range of stakeholder groups, the structure presented is arguably somewhat exclusive or closed. Returning to the notion of what was described for PSV as a 'unitary supervisory board', one can easily see why such a unitary board may well be desirable from the management board's perspective, as it might be presumed to reduce the risk of discord within the organization's decision making. But it is debatable whether such a unitary board truly reflects the nature of many football clubs and their stakeholder groupings. As mentioned previously, stakeholders in football clubs do not, and probably never have, operated with a unitary objective (Stewart, 1986). The association's members are represented on the supervisory board together with business representatives. Objectives and preferences potentially differ among these groups. Presently there is no formal mechanism for them to be reflected within the governance structure at PSV.

The failure to encourage broader stakeholder representation is surprising and perhaps uncharacteristic. Dutch corporate governance already actively involves stakeholders such as employees, both through formally established works' councils and also by allowing employees to elect representative members of the supervisory board. Taken with the prevalence of the two-tier board structure, in which supervision and management are split, then a formal structure already exists in a club like PSV for encouraging and developing wider stakeholder involvement and having a more inclusive supervisory board.

Notwithstanding these comments it also important to recognize that companies can involve their supporters in a variety of ways. At PSV, regular meetings are held with supporters and the directors visit the official meetings of supporters' groups to provide explanation and participate in discussion. However, attendance is usually low, with only somewhere in the region of five per cent of members attending. One explanation may be cultural. For example, Harry van Raaij, suggests that English supporters are more willing than Dutch supporters to participate in the sense of making a financial effort to support their clubs (interview, December 2001).

Operational issues

Any study of PSV quickly reveals an organization that is run on a business-like and professional manner. To a large extent this can be traced to the development of the relationship with Philips from one of dependency to one of partnership. Nothing illustrates this more visibly than the fact that when the directors were negotiating a new sponsorship deal in 2000, first, they were prepared to negotiate with other companies, and second, that although ultimately they stayed with Philips, PSV were successful in securing a new five year deal that was substantially better than the deal that had been agreed during the dependent phases (interview with Fons Spooren, December 2001).

More generally, a distinguishing factor between football clubs in the Netherlands and other European countries is the dependence on sponsorship and other corporate income (see Table 3.4). At a club like PSV, media revenue constitutes only 8 per cent of the club's total turnover. In total, broadcast income for the Dutch Eredivisie constitutes only 12 per cent of total income, compared to 39 per cent in England, 54 per cent in Italy, 51 per cent in Spain and 45 per cent in Germany (Deloitte & Touche, 2002a, p. 9). Consequently, a club like PSV is more reliant on sponsorship and other corporate match day contributions.[65]

According to its President, PSV's objective is 'to play a role in European football ... [to be] one of the 40 or 50 big clubs in Europe'. This ambition is not new. In the late 1980s, with the support of Philips, it sought to position itself as a European player, rather than a provincial Dutch club. High-profile signings such as Ruud Gullit, the top Dutch

Table 3.4   Turnover PSV

	2000/2001 €000s	1999/2000 €000s
Gate receipts	17,775	11,067
Sponsorship	15,208	10,705
Merchandising	447	388
Media	4,172	2,035
Corporate matchday income	8,247	7,450
Other income	4,299	2,389
	50,148	34,034

Source: PSV Annual Report, 2000/01, p. 30

player of his generation, and subsequently the Brazilian internationals, Romario and Ronaldo, saw it branded as a multi-national club, charged with destroying competition within the Dutch league (Oosterwijk, 2002, p. 139).

In the current climate, however, this ambition is very much expressed in terms of financial stability and sustainability. PSV's position within one of Europe's smaller domestic marketplaces, of course, makes this objective increasingly difficult. Its principal problem, shared with clubs in leagues in countries like Scotland, Denmark and Portugal, is that although its income is largely dependent on the domestic Dutch market, its cost base in terms of player transfer fees and salaries is dependent on a single European market (interview with Harry van Raaij, December 2001). PSV is one of a number of clubs that have been intensively lobbying for new league structures to be developed within Europe, arguing that these are essential from both a sporting and a financial point of view (see section on 'Structural change' in Chapter 1). As Harry van Raaij explains, the relationship between PSV and Philips makes the connection between sport and finance quite explicit:

> Philips does not sponsor us out of charity or considerations of subsidy. They are interested in their projected image and the management of business connections. Of what use is their projected image to Philips in the Netherlands? Of no use at all! Philips needs to be able to invite business contacts from Milan or Madrid. PSV must represent added value for the company. If it is unable to deliver it, it is no longer of interest (quoted in Oosterwijk, 2002, p. 143)

PSV's directors recognize that the club will struggle to increase revenue any further from sources like sponsorship and from its stadium, which unusually among continental European clubs it owns. (The Philips Stadium is debt-financed and passed to PSV as part of the redefinition of the relationship between the club and Philips). Its focus, therefore, is on looking to generate revenue from other sources such as the development of real-estate projects beyond its stadium, improving its use of player image rights and the development of interactive media.[66] This last area would seem to offer a great opportunity for a club like PSV given that approximately 42.5 per cent of the population of the Netherlands; some 6.8 million people were estimated to have Internet access in the year 2000 (CIA, 2001).[67] PSV is also developing an initiative provisionally titled *PSV plaza*. Essentially this is a form of Customer Relationship Marketing (CRM) where PSV is aiming to create an environment, both a physical space and a virtual space, which will allow it to maximize the financial benefits to be accrued from its supporters by linking the club into other businesses (interview with Fons Spooren, December 2001).

This type of initiative is unlikely to be appreciated by all of the club's supporters. Indeed, one director did comment that some supporters already believe that the club is all about money. However, this aspiration to leverage value from its supporters needs to be placed in context, in that it forms part of a two-tier approach to supporter relations. Dutch clubs derive far less income directly from supporters in the form of gate receipts than clubs in countries like England (Deloitte & Touche, 2002a, pp. 9–11). Average season ticket prices at PSV are approximately €200, compared to approximately €600–700 in the UK. The club's pricing policy for match attendance is about affordability; prices are set at a level that aims to ensure that everyone who enjoys football can come and visit the club. There is also a recognition that the club needs to do more to leverage value from these same supporters, but not at the risk of alienating supporters or pricing them out of the live football market.

Denmark

Home to some 5.3m people, until recent political upheaval, Denmark might best have been described as a thoroughly modern market economy located within a traditional social democratic society. This description is seen in features such as a highly educated population, extensive government welfare measures, comfortable living standards, modern small-scale and corporate industry, high-tech agriculture and a high dependence on foreign trade. Its economic success is reflected in a GDP per capita figure based on current purchasing power parities of $29,100 in 2000 against an EU average of $24,400 (OECD, 2002). Like its Nordic neighbours, Denmark also has had a high level of state expenditure compared to total economic activity, a fact reflected most visibly in the importance of the public sector in terms of total employment, which is considerably higher than the OECD average (EIU, 2001).

Private sector economic activity in Denmark is dominated by small and medium-sized enterprises, with firms having less than 50 employees accounting for about one-half of total employment (EIU, 2001). The prevalence of small and medium-sized enterprises in the Danish business environment is also apparent in the ownership concentration of the Copenhagen Stock Exchange. At the end of 2002, 201 companies were listed on the exchange, with a combined market capitalization at that date of DKK 564 billion (€76bn). The Copenhagen Stock Exchange is heavily concentrated. At its 2002 year end, 50 per cent of market capitalization was accounted for by six Danish companies, which had shares worth more than DKK 25 billion each, with many of the remaining companies being relatively small in international terms.

Politically, the Social Democratic Party has dominated the country since the post-World War II period. The November 2001 election, however, resulted in a coalition government that included not only the Liberal Party and the Conservative Party, but also the far-right Danish People's Party. This move to the right is somewhat at odds with the foundations of the democratic system in Denmark, which is based on broader community and social values.[68] These foundations are created in people's involvement and commitment to local community; where by working together with others in an atmosphere of respect and tolerance they can help maintain a foundation for democracy (DGI, 2002).

The corporate governance debate was slow to take off in Denmark. It was only in 2001 that the Danish Ministry of Business mandated the Nørby Committee to consider whether there was a need for a set of recommendations for good corporate governance in Denmark. The resultant Nørby Report was in fact the first set of recommendations regarding corporate governance adjusted specifically to Danish circumstances (Nørby Committee, 2001). As the report's authors note this is all the more surprising given that Denmark has been active in the globalization of both capital markets and companies that has taken place in recent decades (2001, p. 1).

The structure of Danish football

These democratic foundations are very apparent in the provision of sport (including football) in Denmark, which both historically and today continue to be arranged through associations. The forming of associations as a way of sharing a common interest is one of the most fundamental characteristics of the Danish people and is even embodied in the Danish constitution which dates to 1849 (DGI, 2002). There is a saying in Denmark that whenever three people get together to share a common interest, they immediately form an association! This is a very common feature. Many Danes belong to more than one association and it estimated that about two million Danes – about 40 per cent of the country's population – actively engage in association sport (Jacobsen, 2001). However, as Ibsen (2001) observes associations are an international phenomenon that are found in almost all democratic countries.

Denmark has three national sports associations – the Danish Sports Confederation and Olympic Committee (DIF), Danish Gymnastics and Sports Associations (DIG) and the Danish Federation of Company Sports (DFIF).

Associations are founded on the principles of democracy, openness and communication. The informal objectives of one of the national associations (the Danish Gymnastics and Sports Association) attempts to summarize the role and place of associations in Danish society:

> Through practising sports in an association, members learn how to value other people and how to see themselves as parts of a fellowship, whether this is the association itself or society in general … the association is the hub or focal point, and as a centre of activities in the local community, it therefore acquires an indispensable social and democratic value (DGI, 2002).

Others, however, argue that most associations focus on the well-being of the association itself, rather than wider societal well-being. Consequently they are oriented inwardly towards the club and their own members, rather than being oriented towards a local community, with social responsibility being limited to the club fellowship (Ibsen, 2001). Nevertheless, within this associational context and the wider social democratic structure of the country, it is perhaps surprising to find that after the UK, Denmark is home to the largest concentration of listed football clubs anywhere in the world, with six listed Danish clubs (see Table 3.5).

Table 3.5   Listed Danish clubs

| | **Price** | **12 month** | | **Market capitalization** | |
| | | **high** | **low** | | |
	(DKK)	(DKK)	(DKK)	(DKKm)	(€m)
Aab Aalborg	53	68	45	42.49	5.72
AGF Kontrakfodbold	16	74	16	3.63	0.49
Akademisk Boldklub	11	28.5	8.5	13.88	1.87
Brøndbyernes IF FO	57	75	53	165.30	22.27
Parken Sport & Entertainment	220	275	175	406.74	54.82
SIF Fodbold	23	63	20	6.06	0.82

Source: *Soccer Investor Weekly*, Issue 111, 3 September 2002, p. 15
(Exchange rate €1 = 7.42 DKK)

Table 3.6   Financial statements (extracts) – Brøndby

	2000/01 (DKKm)	1999/00 (DKKm)	1998/99 (DKKm)	1997/98 (DKKm)	1996/97 (DKKm)
Turnover	90.814	85.440	112.379	92.844	87.299
Operating profit	(16.438)	0.437	28.069	13.759	23.271
Total assets	444.463	461.195	298.380	258.082	162.011

Source: Copenhagen Stock Exchange at www.xcse.dk, accessed 30 May 2002

Of these six clubs, four have very small market capitalizations and the primary motivation for floating on the stock market in each of these cases evidently was the requirement to raise capital.[69] The other two clubs, Brøndby and FC København (FCK), which is part of Parken Sport and Entertainment (Parken), however, are of more interest in a wider context given that they are the two most prominent Danish football clubs.

Located in a working class suburb of Copenhagen, Brøndbyernes IF FO, or Brøndby, for short, has been the most successful Danish club in the last 15 years. Since 1985 it has won the Superliga on nine occasions, most recently in season 2001/02, and has been a regular participant in the various UEFA competitions, including reaching the semi-finals of the 1991 UEFA Cup. Less well known is the fact that Brøndby was the second club in the world, after Tottenham Hotspur, to become a Stock Exchange listed football club, when it listed on the Copenhagen Stock Exchange in 1987. The original club, Brøndbyernes I.F. Fodbold, which through a combination of holdings of A and B class shares, has 50 per cent of the voting rights, controls the company[70] (see also section on Italy later in this chapter). Brøndby owns the GildhoCentret, but remains primarily a football club. The club also has a very strong fan culture and its official fan club has more than 10,000 members (www.brondby-if.dk).

Some key financial figures for Brøndby are noted in Table 3.6.

FC København (FCK)

FCK has a more recent history. Founded in 1992, it arose from a merger or fusion of the first team activities of two of the oldest Danish football clubs, Københavns Boldklub (KB), founded in 1876 and the oldest football club outside the UK, and Boldklubben 1903 (B1903). Rather than being a merger, it is perhaps more accurate to describe FCK as arising from an umbrella agreement. The two original clubs became parent clubs in FCK. In return for the majority of shares in FCK, the original clubs gave up their right to take part in organized football beyond a given level.

The term 'merger' (or even more palatable versions such as 'fusion') tend to evoke immediate hostility in the football world (see also section on 'Communities in transition' in Chapter 2). However, one thing, immediately apparent in this case is that reaction to the formation of FCK was far from hostile. The most likely reason for this is the associational structure of sports clubs discussed previously, which meant that the fusion could only take place if the members of the two existing clubs, KB and B1903, voted in favour of it. In short the decision rested with the key stakeholders in these two clubs. In fact, it was accepted almost unanimously by the members of both clubs (interview with Anders Larsen, FCK Fan Club, 26 October 2001).[71] One important indication of this acceptance is that the official FCK fan club was founded prior to the formation of the amalgamated club (interview with Dan Hammer, Commercial Director and Anders Larsen, FCK Fan Club, October 2001). Both of the original clubs, however, continue to exist and serve their members. For example, KB has tennis and cricket clubs, as well as a thriving football section. Over the last 10 years, the stakes held by the original parent clubs have diminished, resulting in KB and B1903 being among the most wealthy sports clubs in Denmark. Both parent clubs still each have holdings of between 4 and 5 per cent in the new parent company Parken Sport and Entertainment (see Table 3.7).

While FCK's own history may be short, it has not, however, been without incident. On the field of play it has won the Superliga three times, in 1993, 2001 and 2003, as well as winning the Danish Cup twice. Off the field, things have been more dramatic. The company came close to bankruptcy in 1997; its second major financial crisis in five years. At that time, a group of investors, including current Chairman, Flemming Østergaard, took stakes in the club. Unsurprisingly shares in FCK were then very modestly priced. About eight months later, the directors had an IPO (public issue of shares) and FCK became listed on the Copenhagen Stock Exchange. Many of the investors who bought into FCK prior to the IPO have made substantial paper gains on their investment. As a result, like the situation that arose in the UK after numerous clubs floated (see, for example, Conn, 1997), the motives of those investors have been questioned.

Two factors need to be borne in mind here. First, once FCK had become a Stock Exchange listed company, the rules of the market must be expected to apply. When considering any security an investor is always concerned with the return expected on the investment and the risk of the investment, that is, how likely it is that the return expected will be achieved. When Østergaard and others bought into FCK in 1997, to invest in a company perilously close to bankruptcy was clearly a high-risk investment. At its most simple, the observation of FCK's current Commercial Director, Dan Hammer, that from a personal point of view he 'would not have put one Krone in the club at the time' (interview with Dan Hammer, October 2001) is apposite. Irrespective of one's views on whether football clubs should be public companies or not, to deny investors a potential return based on the risk they have taken in buying shares simply renders the market mechanism impotent.

Second, many of the investors who bought into FCK in 1997, including Østergaard as well as the major current shareholder, Lønmodtagernes Dyrtidsfond (the employees capital pension fund), have demonstrated long-term commitment to FCK in terms of their shareholdings (FCK annual reports, various years). Perhaps the best UK parallel is with Celtic, which was rescued in 1994 by the Canadian-based businessman Fergus McCann, a matter of minutes before it was to be put into liquidation. Many would argue that McCann's estimated return of approximately £40m on his five year investment in Celtic, while undoubtedly substantial, was a fair return for the risk that he took in 1994, a risk that others were unwilling or unable to accept at that stage (Morrow, 2000).

Ownership and structure

Along with Manchester United, the parent company of FCK, Parken Sport and Entertainment (Parken) has perhaps the most conventional corporate structure of any listed football club: a low degree of ownership concentration and a high percentage of shares owned by professional or financial investors. The remainder of the shares are highly dispersed, with about a further 6,454 shareholders having very modest individual holdings. The current ownership profile is set out in Table 3.7.

To date, no dividends have been paid on Parken shares. Nevertheless, the share price has performed well since 1997, and has been almost the sole consistent performer among European football club stocks in recent years. Investors such as LD and Danske Bank have, apparently, invested in Parken using the same criteria that they would use to make any other kind of investment; in other words, they have confidence in how the management of Parken will run that business. That confidence to date has been justified as turnover and profits have grown (see Tables 3.8 and 3.9), a fact reflected in the stable share price (see Figure 3.3). An

Table 3.7 Ownership of Parken Sport and Entertainment

Shareholder	Percentage holding	Number of shares
LD (Lønmodtagernes Dyrtidsfond)	18.10	334,633
Danske Bank	9.95	183,956
PSE 2123 A/s	9.12	168,611
Michael Kjaer	4.90	90,591
KBs Fodbold Fund	4.70	86,894
B 1903	4.30	79,498
Flemming Østergaard Management A/S	4.20	77,650
Others	44.83	826,967
Total	100.00	1,848,800

Source: Copenhagen Stock Exchange at www.xcse.dk, accessed 22 March 2002

Table 3.8 Profit and loss account (extracts) – Parken

	2001/02 (DKKm)	2000/01 (DKKm)	1999/00 (DKKm)	1998/99 (DKKm)	1997/98 (DKKm)	1996/97 (DKKm)
Turnover	275.589*	180.119*	152.875*	159.933*	50.902	34.228
Operating profit	74.414	20.239	20.974	22.689	2.682	0.920
Retained profit for the year	48.500	16.017	15.012	20.064	5.642	0.100

* This includes DKK 74.7m (2000/01, 63.3m; 1999/00, 61.5m; 1998/99, 65.0m) of revenues from Sports Café, Bowling Centre and Conference Centre and DKK 24.6m (2000/01, 38.4m; 1999/00, 25.4m; 1998/99, 23.3m) of Stadium Rental Income.

Source: annual reports

Table 3.9 Balance Sheet (extracts) – Parken

	2001/02 (DKKm)	2000/01 (DKKm)	1999/00 (DKKm)	1998/99 (DKKm)	1997/98 (DKKm)	1996/97 (DKKm)
Total assets	841.261	359.076	252.055	350.966	109.697	19.722
Shareholders' equity	483.926	300.742	197.125	183.143	100.400	12.412
Amounts invested in:						
Parken Stadium	567.000	111.316	4.180	142.297	–	–
Transfer fees	54.900	35.483	22.855	21.812	16.679	12.441

Source: annual reports

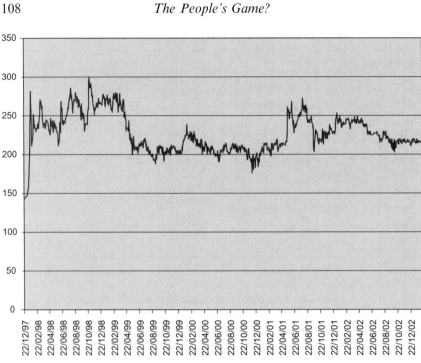

Source: www.xcse.dk, accessed 14 February 2003

Figure 3.3   Movements in Parken share price

important factor is that the company's decision to list on the Copenhagen
Stock Exchange, along with subsequent decisions to raise capital, have
been motivated entirely by rational economic consideration, i.e. on each
occasion its share issues have been motivated by its need to raise funds to
finance specific projects. For example, its offer for sale in 1998 raised
funds to purchase the Parken Stadium, while its 2001 share issue enabled
it to invest in a unique sliding roof for the Parken stadium, thus
transforming a football stadium into a modern, heated indoor arena.

Since 1997, the company has been transformed into a leisure and
entertainment company. Its sporting activities are centred on its
professional team, FCK, which plays in the *Danish SAS Ligaen*, but
also encompasses a Handball team with a turnover of approximately
£1m. In addition, the company also runs the Parken National Stadium,
with associated sportscafé, bowling and conference centres, and runs an
outdoor travelling Rock Tour Show. Its purchase of its home arena, the
Parken National Stadium in July 1998, was arguably the defining
moment for the organization. Its importance to the organization was
demonstrated in 1999 when the company changed its name from FCK to

Parken Sport and Entertainment, reflecting the fact that a substantial proportion of the group's revenues are now derived from activities not directly associated with FCK (see Table 3.8). The football club, however, remains known as FCK.

From a business perspective it is unarguable that this is a very well run company. Notwithstanding the peculiarities of this company – particularly its diversified asset base and consequently income streams – the basic principles that underlie Parken's operations have relevance for other clubs, both in terms of running the business and the governance thereof. The (management) objectives of FCK, which will be used as a basis for analysing FCK in the following sections, are:

- Optimum organizational performance;
- Success on the pitch;
  - Objective: to qualify for Europe each year;
  - Objective: streamlined player development;
- Seamless cooperation with parent clubs;
- Developing a strong fan culture;
- Raising the number of spectators significantly;
- Well-structured care of commercial partners;
- Going public; and
- From 'just football' to an entertainment experience.

Source: interview with Dan Hammer, October 2002

The business of FCK

One thing that distinguishes FCK from several other clubs is its explicit prioritization of financial or economic objectives. Of the objectives set out in the previous list, almost all ostensibly have a financial focus. These specific objectives are underpinned more generally by the fundamental belief of the directors who have been involved with the club since 1997, that things required to be done in the correct order – i.e. the first priority was the company's economic or financial position (described as 'optimum organizational performance'). Only when the financials were in order was it considered appropriate to think about on-field success. Key to this approach was the desire not to end up like so many other clubs, both in Denmark and beyond: unprofitable. While recognizing that football is about feelings and emotion, the fundamental philosophy underpinning how the club operates is that decisions must always be made according to common sense business principles like 'not spending more than you are earning' and 'monitoring your costs'.

Notwithstanding this philosophy, however, there is also recognition that to run a successful football club, sooner or later you do need to have football success. FCK's two objectives in this area both have footballing and financial dimensions: first, to qualify for European competitions each year, and second, for the club to streamline player development. An important and explicit financial actualization of this second objective is that the club seeks to be independent of transfers [income] (interview with Dan Hammer, October 2001).

Arguably this ordering of objectives is easier to achieve in a country like Denmark than it would be say in somewhere like Italy. One consequence of the cooperative spirit prevalent in the country and of its social democratic culture is that football club directors are subject to less fan pressure; there is far greater tolerance of decisions.

Fan culture

Many supporters would question whether a club should or indeed even whether it could 'develop a fan culture'. However, irrespective of whether we consider football clubs as social institutions, conventional business or something in between, it is indisputable that these organizations operate within an economic market place. To that end, an objective like developing a fan culture might be deemed to be a rational response by directors on both social and instrumental grounds.

Whatever else they may or may not be, supporters are the core customers of football organizations, and hence it would be negligent of directors not to seek to develop and harness that relationship. Rather than criticize those who explicitly articulate that objective, it might be more valuable to focus on directors whose behaviour and decision making suggest that they arrogantly take the relationship for granted. While the nature of a supporter's relationship with his or her club suggests that it may never be terminated (see Chapter 2), diminution of the relationship weakens both the social base of the club and its business base.

The recent history of FCK and its emergence from its two parent clubs, KB and B1903, means that the logic of trying to develop a fan culture is more apparent at this club, both in terms of its social purpose and role, and in financial terms. Evidence exists that suggests that FCK has been successful both in terms or retaining its original communities and also developing new ones. For example, the club's official fan club, which has a membership of approximately 12,000, is actually older than the club itself. Furthermore, the club has increased its attendances in the six year period since Østergaard took over the club, from less than 9,000 in season 1996/97 through to an average attendance of 20,000 in season 2002/03, more than treble the average of Danish super league teams. Perhaps the most significant thing is that the club did not lose supporters in the two seasons (1998/99, 7th; 1999/2000, 8th) when it was not enjoying any on-field success, with average attendances being maintained at approximately 12,000.

A good example of the social and financial perspective of the role of supporters at FCK arises from the physical positioning of the club's supporters in the stadium. The most colourful, exuberant and noisiest FCK supporters are those who occupy the *Fredgaard tribunen* or *Nedre C* stand. These supporters occupy some of the best positions in the stadium, at a good height and opposite the pitch. The reasoning behind not moving these supporters to allow the premium seats to be sold at higher prices, perhaps to corporate spectators is illuminating. One reason is social or community-based, a reward for supporter loyalty (or in the language of business, customer care). These supporters have always occupied that area of the stadium. The directors are aware of the loyalty shown to the club by these supporters and not moving them is one way of reciprocating that loyalty. A second reason is more instrumental. Those supporters are in the line of the television cameras and are perhaps the most important element of the club (interview with Dan Hammer, October 2001). Given the peculiarities of football as a product, therefore, those supporters become a prime factor in the product itself (King, 1997, p. 236). To show the product at its best, the most colourful, exuberant and noisiest supporters are of most value precisely where they are. In other words, it is not only a question of honouring loyal customers or fans, it is also because they are the prime factor in the product itself (interview with Dan Hammer, 2001).

A wider re-positioning is evident in the objective of moving from 'just football' to 'entertainment experience'.[72] Arguably this is concomitant with the instrumental approach involved in trying to generate a fan culture. Retaining the most colourful supporters in the prime television seats is but one example of the move towards the notion of football as being part of an entertainment experience. This notion is articulated most clearly through the football/television nexus. Clubs and leagues throughout Europe have been eager to sell their product as content to television companies. Even prior to 2002, which saw several television companies like Kirch and ITV Digital get into serious financial difficulties and have to seek to revise their contracts with various football leagues (see Chapter 1), the relationship between football and television was something of a double-edged sword. While improved income to clubs meant that supporters were often treated to better players on the field, there was often great dissatisfaction concerning issues like match scheduling and so on.

However, the movement to entertainment can also be viewed more benignly. For example, FCK's family stand – the *NesaFamilie Tribunen* – unlike that of many other clubs, is more than just a secure area. It is all encompassing family entertainment, almost akin to Copenhagen's famous Tivoli. In addition to the football on the field, within the stadium (behind the stands) there are things like live entertainment with stars from children's television, face painting, penalty shooting competitions, popcorn and so on. The initiative has been hugely successful, bringing in an extra 2,500–4,000 spectators per game. From a business perspective, it is also viewed as a way of locking in the supporters of the future. In other words, in a few years' time, today's children will take their places in the *Fredgaard tribunen* (*Nedre C*), so the initiative is quite clearly an investment for the future (interview with Dan Hammer, October 2001). The initiative is all about entertainment, in particular recognizing that football clubs have to do more in today's world to compete for supporters.

The entertainment dimension is also in evidence in other parts of the stadium. For example, FCK has something called 'Carlsberg Corner'. This is located in the 'fan stand' (*Fredgaard tribunen* or *Nedre C*) and hosts post-match live entertainment, usually including a live band as well as things like a 'man of the match' celebration. Among other things beer is also sold at a discounted price in the Carlsberg Corner.

Key to this discussion on developing fan culture is that before embarking on such an approach, it is vitally important that you know your customers, or more precisely, know how they will react when you make a business out of football. Undoubtedly there is evidence of instrumentality in FCK's approach to its supporters. According to Dan Hammer (interview, October 2001), FCK probably do more for their supporters than almost any other European club, but to a large extent this is motivated by the fact that commercially it makes sense. In FCK's view, the supporters and the wider community will accept change if it makes the underlying business stronger and if they have been involved in considering the implications of any changes.

The relationship between football clubs and their various communities is continually evolving and consequently directors need to get to know their supporters on an ongoing basis. Available evidence suggests that FCK is working hard to know its supporters. Nevertheless examples exist which demonstrate the difficulty of managing the supporter/club relationship in the context of an entertainment business. The first relates to the decision taken by the club's directors in 1999 to change the name of the organization (but not the football club) from FCK to Parken Sport and Entertainment (Parken). Interestingly, while floating the club on the Stock Exchange was not identified as being a major issue to supporters, the decision to change the name to Parken was viewed very negatively and the name continues to be ignored by the supporters (interview with Anders Larsen, October 2001). Other supporters viewed the name change more enthusiastically, with the supporters of Brøndby in particular relishing the opportunity to taunt FCK supporters about commercialization by referring to the club as Parken (interview with Anders Larsen, October 2001).

Arguably the most important dispute between the club and its supporters, however, arose out of Parken's successful bid to host the 2001 Eurovision Song contest. As a result of the contest, FCK was forced to play one of its home Superliga games away from the Parken stadium. Partly due to pressure from the players who were involved in a championship race and who wanted the game to take place on the best available alternative surface, the club chose to move the game to the stadium of its main rivals, Brøndby. This decision was extremely unpopular with the supporters. Many of them boycotted the match while others saw it as conclusive evidence that when it came down to it, Parken was not a football club. To its credit, the club has acknowledged that a mistake was made and that it underestimated the symbolism of the act and that no similar decision would be taken again (interview with Dan Hammer, October 2001).

Governance and communication

The governance system that exists within Parken has two apparent dimensions to it: first, corporate governance in the context of the company, arguably focusing on the efficient use of capital, and second, stakeholder governance or management in the context of the football club focusing in particular on the supporters. Interestingly, although many of the supporters are themselves shareholders,[73] this is not perceived as particularly relevant in terms of governance by company management. Rather the view is expressed that the corporate structure really acts as another layer between management and supporters that has to be managed (interview with Dan Hammer, October 2001). However, there is a strong view that the company does need to take account of the interests of its stakeholders (and in particular its supporters) but that this relationship is best managed at a football club level.

At FCK the supporter stakeholder relationship is essentially managed through the official FCK fan club. While there are regular meetings between the management and the fan club, communication between the club management and the fan club is for the most part informal, and takes place in person as well as by phone and email. Where the club has a decision to take then it will normally contact the fan club to discuss the matter. Similarly, there is an open door for the fan club at FCK (interview with Anders Larsen, October 2001).

What the club aims to develop is a culture of communication, based on the principles of cooperation and trust, principles which of course have their foundation in the Danish sporting associations as well as in wider Danish society. For example, at a strategic level when the club took the decision to list on the Copenhagen Stock Exchange, consultation meetings were arranged between directors and the fan club (interview with Anders Larsen, October 2001). On a more day-to-day basis, the club's Chairman, Flemming Østergaard regularly walks about the stadium prior to matches, talking with supporters. While some supporters may view this as a cynical PR ploy, others view it as exercise in stakeholder management. Undoubtedly the strength of Østergaard's personality is important here. At the Fan Club's 10 year anniversary dinner, not only were Østergaard and other management present, but the Chairman was quite happy to use his speech to remind the supporters that football was now a business! However, this treatment cuts both ways. So impressed was Østergaard at the commitment of a bus load of FCK supporters who made their way overland to attend the club's UEFA Cup match against Serbian side Obelic, that he invited them to corporate hospitality in the next home game.[74] It is difficult to imagine either of these two events happening at most other major European clubs! Nevertheless, despite the existence of these communication channels, it is important to stress that FCK (Parken) is run as a business and that ultimately decisions are taken by management.

Italy

Home to a population of some 57.7m as of July 2001, Italy has a diversified industrial economy. Although its GDP is comparable to other OECD countries like France and the UK,[75] within the country itself the economy remains clearly divided on a north–south basis. While private companies dominate the developed and prosperous industrial north, the south of the country is less developed and primarily agricultural, with unemployment in the south being in the region of 20 per cent. Persistent problems include illegal immigration, organized crime, corruption, high unemployment, and the low incomes and technical standards of southern Italy compared with the more prosperous north (CIA, 2001).

Interestingly, corporate control and governance in Italy has not followed models that have developed elsewhere, such as the Anglo-American model or the banking relationship-based model prevalent in, say, Germany. Study of the corporate governance system in Italy reveals a high concentration of direct ownership in both listed and unlisted companies. While the amount held by financial institutions is limited, a prominent ownership role is played by family groupings and, particularly in listed companies, through holdings by other non-financial or holding companies in pyramidal group structures (Bianchi *et al.*, 2001, p. 154). OECD statistics show that single majority stakes account for about 60 per cent of total stock market capitalization in Italy compared to about 5 per cent in the UK (Price Waterhouse, 1997). These structures enable one or a few individuals to control a wide range of assets and activities with a limited amount of their own capital. This is achieved by concentrating their voting rights in the company at the top of the pyramid, while spreading the voting rights of minority shareholders over a large number of firms, in other words, separating ownership and control. Several well known Italian companies like Fiat (owned by the Agnelli family) and Pirelli, which play a significant part in the economy, continue to be family controlled, with control being maintained despite relatively small shareholdings, through holding companies and cross-shareholdings with industrial and financial partners (EIU, 2001). Both the Agnelli and Pirelli families have football links: as owners of Juventus and minority shareholders in Inter Milan respectively.

Historically the public markets have not played a major role in the Italian economy. However, as can be seen from Table 3.10, the economic importance of the Italian Stock Exchange has been increasing in recent years, partly through the privatization programme, which has acted to reduce the weight of the state in the ownership of listed companies.

Nevertheless it is the smaller and medium-sized family owned companies that remain the strongest part of the Italian economy (EIU, 2001). Bianchi *et al.* (2001) carried out a study in 1992 in which, using a sample of manufacturing firms, they investigated the separation between ownership and control by classifying unlisted companies into various 'control' groupings. The aim of the study was to identify the corporate

Table 3.10   The importance of Borsa Italiana

Year	Listed companies	Capitalization	
		(€m)	(% GDP)
1981*	177	23,562	9.8
1991	272	99,081	13.3
1996	248	202,732	20.6
2001	294	592,319	48.5

* Data for companies listed on the Milan Stock Exchange
Source: Borsa Italiana (www.borsaitaliana.it)

governance models prevalent in Italian unlisted companies at that time. What they found was that the most frequent model was the hierarchical group control, which accounted for 52 per cent of manufacturing firms' total employment and was more frequent among larger firms. The second most important model was the family control model, where links existed among the individuals in control or between them and non-controlling shareholders (Bianchi *et al.*, 2001, p. 179). These types of control are further strengthened by the *salotto buono* – literally the good drawing room – which refers to the role played by an exclusive grouping of industrialists and bankers who confer in secret over major decisions (Edmondson, 2001). Indeed, Becht and Mayer (2001, p. 12) assert that the popular complaint about the *salotto buono* is 'not the way its members exert control, but the fact they shield each other from control challenges'. However, in the last couple of years some evidence has emerged of a move to more open forms of decision making.[76] Nevertheless, the reluctance of many of these companies to go public to finance expansion has held back their growth and left them exposed to foreign predators seeking an entry to the lucrative Italian market place (Pagano *et al.*, 1995 cited in Shleifer and Vishny, 1997).

The structure of Italian football

Nowhere in Europe, arguably, does football matter as much as in Italy. It has been estimated that about 24 million Italians are interested in football with 17 million of them following it regularly on television (Deloitte & Touche/Lega Calcio, 1999, p. 3). Attendance at Serie A and B matches in season 1999/2000 was approximately 12.4m people (Deloitte & Touche, 2001, p. 22). Around 5.8m people read its three daily sports newspapers (see also Chapter 5), while 61 per cent of total television sports viewing figures were in respect of football (Deloitte & Touche, 1999, p. 3). It is even common for football in some shape or form to be discussed in Parliament.[77] Back on the pitch, the power of the Italian game is also reflected in its clubs' success in European competitions.[78]

Unsurprisingly, football clubs are often reflective of the ownership and corporate governance models prevalent in the wider corporate environment. Several Italian clubs continue to be controlled either directly by individuals or families or indirectly via corporate groupings. However, in contrast with companies in the wider economy, often there is little evidence of separation between ownership and control. The importance of this familial style of corporate structure is heightened by the wider Italian passion for football, with in many cases wealthy individuals or families owning the club that they support.

A prominent example of direct family control is Inter Milan, which is owned by the Moratti family (see following section). The foremost examples of the corporate/familial ownership structure are Juventus, which is controlled by the Agnelli family, through its holding company, Istituto Finanziario Industriale (IFI), and AC Milan, whose majority shareholder, Fininvest, is a company owned and controlled by Italian Prime Minister, Silvio Berlusconi. Another interesting example is Parma, which is controlled by the Tanzi family, via the Parmalat Finanziaria company.[79] However, the rationale behind the Tansi family's holding is arguably as much about an instrumental approach to its wider business interests as deep-rooted football passion, with football and other sports being used as a vehicle for promoting the Parmalat company.

In recent years, a few Italian clubs have started to make use of the Stock Exchange to raise funds. However, even in these cases, it has not been common for the controlling family or grouping to relinquish control of the club, or more accurately company. The first Italian club to have some of its shares publicly traded was SS Lazio, which listed on the main market of the Borsa Italiana in 1999. Its owner, Sergio Cragnotti, head of the food processing company Cirio del Monte, bought the club in 1992. His financial investment has enabled the club to attract top class players to Rome, helping it to win several trophies. However, even after the public offer of shares in 1999, an offer which was 10 times oversubscribed, 51 per cent of the club continued to be controlled by Cragnotti and his family through stakes held by Cirio Finanziari (35 per cent) and Cirio Holding (16 per cent) (*Soccer Investor*, 2002h). In addition, the familial structure of the company is strengthened by the fact that Sergio Cragnotti along with several members of his family continues to work for the company.

Shares in its Roman neighbour, AS Roma, were listed on the main market of the Borsa Italiana in 2000, the share issue being oversubscribed by 3.5 times. After the share issue, however, 65.6 per cent of the shares continued to be owned by Roma 2000, a company controlled by club president, Francesco Sensi. The club continues to be run by Sensi, while other members of his family, including Chief Executive, Rosella Sensi are also employed. In other ways, there is evidence that Roma continues to be run as a Sensi family company. For example, it was reported that Francesco Sensi lent the club €62.6m prior to its 2001 accounting year end to fund the bonuses due to the players for winning the 2000 Serie A title and to maintain the financial stability of the club (*Soccer Investor*, 2001c).

Most recently (December 2001), Juventus raised €164m when it offered 37 per cent of its capital on Borsa Italiana. The shares, which are listed on the STAR market, were taken up by both retail investors (59.5 per cent) and institutional investors (40.5 per cent), with the offer being oversubscribed by 1.2 times. The remaining shares, however, continue to be held by Istituto Finanziario Industriale (IFI), the holding company of the Agnelli family, which also owns and control, the automobile maker, Fiat. The shareholder structure of Juventus after its IPO is shown in Figure 3.4.

However, it is worth noting that even prior to the listing Juventus operated on a more business-like structure than other Italian clubs. This is evidenced most clearly in its enduring ability to report profits. For example, Juventus reported profits in 2002 and in each of the previous 5 years (Gerlis, 2002b). Unlike most Italian clubs, Juventus is a model of fiscal rectitude and is run by a well-respected management team (Glendinning, 2002). In this regard, it is also interesting that it sought a listing on the STAR market. This market is specifically aimed at

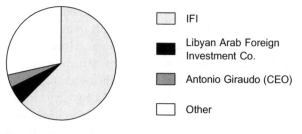

Source: Banca IMI, 2002

Figure 3.4 Juventus shareholder structure

companies with a market capitalization of less then €800m, but which undertake to satisfy higher requirements in terms of transparency, corporate governance and liquidity (www.boursaitaliana.it).

Internazionale Milano

By any measure, FC Internazionale Milano (Inter) is one of world football's big clubs. Founded in 1908 by a breakaway group of disgruntled members of Milan FC (which became AC Milan), Inter now shares the 85,443 seat *Giuseppe Meazza* stadium in the San Siro district of Milan with its main rival, AC Milan. It has won the Serie A title on 13 occasions, although its last title was in 1989, and has won the European Cup twice (1964, 1965) and the UEFA Cup three times (1991, 1994 and 1998) (Cresswell and Evans, 2000, p. 357). It is often the best supported team in Italy. For example, in season 1999/2000, Inter attracted 1.13m supporters to its Serie A home games, the only club to attract more than 1m supporters (Deloitte & Touche, 2001, p. 18).

Inter is owned and controlled by the Moratti family which has a 65 per cent holding. As such it is reflective of the wider economic and social fabric of Italy where most businesses remain family-owned. Inter has one other substantial shareholder, the tyre manufacturer Pirelli which has a holding of 13 per cent, but in substance this is very much a Moratti family company.

Although Inter is family owned and controlled, no family members other than the Chairman and President, Massimo Moratti, are employed full-time at Inter, although several are directors of different companies within the Inter group. Although he is best known for his involvement with Inter, Massimo Moratti, is also a prominent businessman in the oil industry as CEO of the family company of Sardinian refineries, Saras. The Moratti family bought their stake in Inter in 1995 and Massimo Moratti has been President since then. His involvement restores a previous family connection as Massimo's father, Angelo Moratti had been president of the club in the 1950s and 1960s. Moratti Snr invested heavily in the club and was the man responsible for taking the legendary Helenio Herrera to the club (Cresswell and Evans, 2000, p. 359). His reign coincided with one of the club's two most successful on-field periods, the other being in the 1930s when Guiseppe Meazza was the main striker.

Massimo Moratti bought his stake in the club in 1995 for only $25m (€23m) from Ernest Pellegrino, a catering millionaire. Since then, Moratti has invested heavily in the club, purchasing and paying the salaries of stars such as Christian Vieri and until his transfer to Real

Madrid in October 2002, the Brazilian Ronaldo. One advantage of the archetypical Italian family-controlled structure found at Inter is that historically, when resources have been required, then they have been available in-house, from within the family. However, notwithstanding his substantial investment in Inter, Moratti is also sitting on a large paper gain, with the club's current value probably being in the region of €400-500m. Despite this paper gain, to most observers Moratti's involvement with Inter and subsequent decision-making is not about business or profit but is fuelled by his passion and fanaticism for the club; by his desire to see a successful Inter Milan. As Jeff Slack, CEO of Inter-Active, a subsidiary of FC Internazionale Milano SpA which manages the club's business affairs observed 'everyone knows how much money Massimo Moratti has put into this exactly . . . he's worn his heart on his sleeve . . . [it is] totally his passion but nobody would come up and say this is a business' (interview, February 2002). One consequence of this attitude existing in the boardroom, is that conflict is less likely to arise between supporters and directors at a club like Inter, given that Moratti is to all intents and purposes a supporter, distinct from other supporters only in that he is wealthy enough to try to have a positive influence on the outcome of his supporter dreams or aspirations. Such goal congruence could thus be expected to improve the nature of the relationship between supporters and directors. However, as will be considered later in this chapter it can also cause problems.

The finances of Italian football

As shown in Table 3.11, in recent years the financial position of Italian clubs has deteriorated markedly. Collectively Serie A clubs have reported an operating loss in each of the last four seasons. The key factor for this is that while total income has been relatively static between 2000 and 2001, wages and salaries have risen by approximately 32 per cent (*Soccer Investor*, 2002g). Revenues are also now heavily dependent on television, with approximately 55 per cent of the revenues of Serie A clubs in 2001 coming from television rights, the next biggest income source being gate receipts at 16 per cent.

Several factors explain the current financial problems of Italian clubs, some football-specific, others cultural. As the business side of football developed, most clubs were slow, for example, to recognize the potential rewards to be made from marketing their business and the need for some kind of customer relationship marketing. Nowhere is this more pronounced than in respect of merchandising. The slowness of clubs to

Table 3.11   The finances of Italian Serie A clubs

	2001 (€m)	2000 (€m)	1999 (€m)	1998 (€m)
Revenue	1150.5	1058.9	713.5	649.8
Operating profit/(loss)	(710.4)	(406.4)	(335.2)	(222.2)
Profit after player trading and taxation	(133.4)	34.7	(11.2)	(37.6)

Source: *Soccer Investor* (2002g, p. 12)

harness their merchandising opportunities is partly cultural, with for example, many arguing that the market for things like replica football tops was always going to be more limited in a fashion conscious country like Italy than in say England. Perhaps, more serious, however, is the unresolved national problem of the extent of criminality in the economy. Recent research claimed that one-fifth of the country's economy was in the hands of the Mafia with the volume of business amounting to around £100bn (€145bn); equal to 15 per cent of the country's gross domestic product (Lloyd, 2002). Counterfeiting is a huge problem for Italian clubs in terms of their merchandising activities. At least one major club now has an agreement with the main organization of counterfeiting producers under which counterfeiters are allowed to sell semi-official replica shirts, alike in all respects other than they do not have the manufacturer's logo on them, resulting effectively in the creation of a parallel market (interview with Antonio Merchesi, Deloitte & Touche, February 2002).

Another contributory factor is that most Italian clubs do not own their stadium, these often being owned by local authorities. This long tradition of local authority involvement in the financing and administration of football has also been common in other European countries like France where municipalities have had a statutory duty to promote and develop sport (Dobson and Goddard, 2001, p. 102). The consequence of this is that clubs are restricted in their ability to utilize their stadium as a revenue-generating asset, with stadium income being restricted primarily to match-day ticket revenues. However, some clubs are now beginning to address this problem. Part of the rationale behind the Juventus Initial Public Offering (IPO) was to generate funds to acquire and develop its Delle Alpi stadium (*Soccer Investor*, 2001b, p. 12), while the two Milan clubs are working with Milan City Council, owner of the Giuseppe Meazza stadium, on a €4.3m redevelopment, the primary aim of which is to facilitate the generation of revenue for both clubs from hospitality and entertaining. Both clubs, however, have insisted that ticket prices will not rise in order to fund the redevelopment (*Soccer Investor*, 2002f, p. 9).

The financial position of Italian clubs is also influenced by mutuality; the system of allocation of shared resources adopted by the Lega Calcio (Italian League) (Deloitte & Touche, 1999, p. 7). This involves the redistribution of football pools revenues and television income from the richest clubs in Serie A (18 clubs) to the other professional clubs, with some commentators arguing that the levels of redistribution are higher in Italy than in other top European football countries (interview with Antonio Merchesi, February 2002). Irrespective of the accuracy of the claim, it is nevertheless clear that as in most major European football leagues, the majority of television income is now captured by the top (division) clubs.[80] For example, in season 1999/2000 television income was split as shown in Figure 3.5.

Salary levels among top Italian clubs are extremely high. Personnel costs of €660m accounted for 63 per cent of revenues among the Serie A clubs in 2000 (Deloitte & Touche, 2001), while in season 2000/01 approximately 30 per cent of players earned more than €1m (gross) per annum (*Soccer Investor*, 2002d). One factor that puts upward pressure on these salary levels are the social costs of employment in Italy. Italian players wages are currently taxed at the highest rate of 46 per cent, which although lower than the highest Spanish rate of 48 per cent, is greater than the top rate in the UK of 40 per cent (Banca IMI, 2002, p. 8).[81] Equally significant, however, are the rates of other social contributions such as employees National Insurance or Social Security contributions. The consultants, Andersen, have estimated the effective rate of taxes and social security charges in Italy is 45 per cent, a rate comparable to Spain (46 per cent) and substantially better than Germany (50 per cent) or France (57 per cent), but which is significantly higher than in the United

☐ Serie A (individual clubs)

■ Serie B (individual clubs)

▨ Championship (Lega Calcio)

☐ Italian Cup (Lega Calcio and other clubs)

Source: Deloitte & Touche 2001, p. 25

Figure 3.5   The distribution of television and radio rights, season 1999/2000

Kingdom, where the rate is only 39 per cent (*Soccer Investor*, 2001a). The effect of these differential rates is that it costs Italian clubs more than their English competitors for a player to receive a given level of net salary.

Another significant tax factor which acts to reduce profits, is that Italian companies are also required to pay a local tax known as IRAP. It is particularly significant for football clubs as it is currently charged at a rate of 4.25 per cent on the net value of production, i.e. gross profit before among other things players' salaries and capital gains on player trading. For example, in 2001, Juventus IRAP charge was €3.7m. However, it should be noted that the Italian government recently presented a tax reform proposal, which included the possible deductibility of players salaries and capital gains on player trading costs in determining IRAP (Banca IMI, 2002, p. 8).

Ownership structure – a cause of financial strife?

Arguably, however, it is the combination of familial ownership corporate structures and the population's passion for football that are the most significant explanatory factors for the current financial situation of Italian clubs, and in particular the rising employee/player costs.

In an organization like Inter, for example, the ownership structure results in the functions of ownership, control and residual claimant being internalized (Moerland, 1995). This has consequences both for decision making and for accountability. First, ownership structure would be expected to have an impact on the demand for accountability, with the overlap between ownership and control predicted to reduce the need for external monitoring, i.e. the incentive alignment effects of managers also being shareholders are predicted to reduce the corresponding demand for monitoring (Peasnell *et al.*, 2001). In contrast in organizations where ownership is widely dispersed, i.e. where the directors are agents acting on behalf of a disparate group of owners, whether those owners are shareholders or members, then greater reliance is placed on governance mechanisms such as audit (see, for example, Jensen and Meckling, 1976; O'Sullivan, 2000).

Second, in making operating decisions the dominant owner (in Inter's case, Massimo Moratti) is assumed to be maximizing his personal utility (Moerland, 1995). Consequently, one interpretation of decision making and subsequent accountability in organizations with this type of ownership structure is quite simply that an owner is free to use his or her funds as he or she see fit.

However, while such an interpretation is quite rational in the context of maximizing the utility of an individual owner within an individual firm, even leaving aside wider issues of stakeholder responsibility or account-ability, it has broader implications that require to be examined. First of these arises from a definition or understanding of utility. As indicated, Italians are passionate about football. Thus it would be surprising if this cultural environment was not reflected in how a supporter-owner like Massimo Moratti defined his utility. It is quite conceivable that his utility is defined in terms of on-field success; that maximization of utility can be equated, say, to winning the *Scudetto*. Taken together with evidence that suggests that, over the long term, there is an apparent relationship between spending on wages and league performance (Szymanski and Kuypers, 1999, pp. 157–93)[82] and the previously discussed reduction in demand for accountability or external monitoring arising from the ownership structure, then it is perhaps to be expected that financial discipline is not prioritized and that consequently the actions of dominant owners tend to bid up wages and salaries.

Second, as is well documented, football has certain peculiar economic characteristics. This peculiarity centres on the interdependence of the participants, i.e. it has been argued that professional sport organizations are different from other business organizations because the nature of sport means that such organizations must function together to provide a saleable product. Furthermore, it is argued that the essence of a professional sports league is genuine competition, i.e. participants in a league need to have sufficient financial and resource backing to allow them to compete with one another on a relatively fair basis (see Chapter 1). While bidding up wages may be considered logical from an individual company perspective in the context of maximizing an owner's utility (defined as on-field success), in view of these peculiar economic and competition characteristics the drive of one or a few organizations to act in this way does have potential consequences for the league or industry as a whole.

One difficulty is that it encourages other clubs to try to compete with the bidded-up salary levels. Ultimately the risk is that these clubs live beyond their means and that their financial position becomes unsustain-able. The financial position of many Italian clubs in 2002, most notably Fiorentina, provides some evidence that this has already happened in Italy.[83] Alternatively, the utility motivations of clubs with dominant owners may act to distort the operation of the industry, by threatening the sporting equilibrium required for a fair contest. In other words, clubs apart from those that are acting to bid up wages, can not or do not seek to compete in terms of salaries. This results in a near monopoly situation for clubs with dominant owners in terms of attracting the top players. This type of argument is not, of course, new. In England, Jack Walker, the benefactor of Blackburn Rovers, was accused of being responsible for bidding up transfer costs and player salaries in his quest to bring success to Blackburn Rovers (Horrie, 2002a, pp. 114–15),while similar arguments have been advanced in Scotland concerning the role of David Murray at Rangers.

In this context, one interesting issue is whether public listing has altered the behaviour of clubs. Although clubs like Lazio and Roma are subject to increased financial accountability and scrutiny, in terms of financial discipline, the evidence to date suggests that public listing has made little or no difference to their behaviour, with both clubs reporting substantial operating losses in the year ended 30 June 2001, principally as a result of salary related expenditure (see Table 3.12). It has subsequently been reported that both clubs are aiming to reduce substantially their salary costs from season 2002/3 onwards, by 29.1 per cent in the case of Lazio and 11.5 per cent in the case of Roma (*Soccer Investor*, 2002c).

The ownership of both clubs remains under the control of family groupings or individuals, and for the most part new capital that has been raised has come primarily from supporter investors. Once again the fact that the majority shareholder in each club – Cragnotti at Lazio and Sensi at Roma – is also a supporter of the club, is likely to act to reduce the demand for accountability or external monitoring from small supporter-shareholders. Consequently, controlling groupings can continue to run the clubs as they see fit relatively unfettered, with the fragmented small supporter-shareholder base supporting the ownership whims of the large supporter-shareholder because he is seen to be prioritizing on-field success (interview with Antonio Merchesi, February 2002). In this sense one can argue that clubs going to the market have not altered behaviour as it has simply brought in a number of small shareholders who share the

Table 3.12   Financial performance of listed Italian clubs

	AS Roma 2001	SS Lazio 2001
Operating loss	€56.8m	€99.6m
Labour costs/turnover	66.6%	82.9%

Sources: *Soccer Investor* (2001c); Banca IMI (2002)

same objective as the controlling shareholder. Of course, this behaviour is not restricted to either family controlled or Italian clubs. For example, membership organizations like Barcelona and, particularly, Real Madrid have been guilty of fuelling player salary and transfer fee inflation by offering terms and conditions that would not normally be considered prudent or sustainable. Explanations can be found for this behaviour in issues like business culture, legal systems and financial systems and responsibilities. Another important factor is the potent mix of politics and personality at clubs like Real Madrid and Barcelona. For instance, the presidential campaign of current Real Madrid President, Florentino Lopez, included an open-ended financial commitment to acquire, Portuguese star Luis Figo from Barcelona, a commitment that was achieved at a purchase cost of £37m (€54m) and an annual salary of £3.5m (€5.1m) (Harverson, 2000). More recently, a major factor in Joan Laporta's campaign to be elected as President of Barcelona in June 2003 was his promise to negotiate with Manchester United to bring David Beckham to the Camp Nou. But while Laporta successfully won the Presidency, Beckham instead opted to join Barcelona's archrival, Real Madrid. Similar to circumstances at Roma or Lazio, anecdotal evidence suggests that the fragmented membership might be expected to lend its support to those candidates or owners whose promises or behaviour seem most consistent with maximizing their individual utility functions.

Accountability – from financial to public?

Football in Italy is very inwardly focused. Partly this is reflective of the country's footballing culture and history (Cresswell and Evans, 2000, pp. 339–45), partly it arises from the closed family-ownership structure. Football club owners see themselves as being separated; their attitude is one of 'let's do business among ourselves' (interview with Antonio Merchesi, February 2002). This is perhaps unsurprising, however, given the historical prevalence of the *salotto buono* in Italian corporate life. Nevertheless, this combination of ownership and attitude results in a lack of transparency in terms of how clubs are run. Among other things it has implications for the relationship between club owners and other interested groups such as supporters, particularly in terms of things like governance and financial accountability.

However, accountability is not simply about providing some kind of financial account for actions. It entails a relationship in which people are required to explain and take responsibility for their actions: 'the giving and demanding of reasons for conduct' (Roberts and Scapens, 1985,

p. 447). Sinclair describes accountability as having chameleon-like qualities in the sense of being much sought after but nevertheless elusive (1995, p. 219). Rather than attempt to override this chameleon quality she suggests that accountability can be made to mean more by recognizing that the multiple ways in which accountability is experienced can enhance it (Sinclair, 1995, pp. 219–20).

Arguably what operates in Italian football is a form of public accountability – informal but direct accountability to the public, interested community groups and individuals (Thynne and Goldring, 1981) – which can act as a way of aligning managerial and public interest. Those involved – players, managers, directors – are effectively being held publicly to account every time a game takes place. Even beyond the immediate sporting contest, however, media interest in football provides for further public accountability. Italy has three daily sports newspapers as well as some five hours per day of programmes devoted to football comment on television. Everyone connected with football in Italy is under intense public pressure and scrutiny, particularly in terms of newspaper and media coverage. A prominent figure like Inter's Massimo Moratti is in the newspapers every day and is therefore 'accountable every day to the fans' (interview with Jeff Slack, February 2002).

To date, however, there is little evidence to suggest that supporters are seeking increased financial accountability or indeed involvement with their clubs, their financial interest being awakened only to the extent that it impinges upon the team. In contrast with some other European countries, it has been suggested that supporters see themselves as being 'moral owners of the team not the club' (interview with Antonio Merchesi, February 2002).[84] In the context of legal ownership, Italian supporters are remote from their clubs partly because most owners are both extremely wealthy and also are such identifiable supporters themselves. Nevertheless this remoteness should not be taken as indicating subservience. Where supporters are dissatisfied with players, managers or directors, their communication is direct. For example, at the other Milan club (AC Milan) in season 2000/01, during a poor run of play for the team lasting three or four games, a favoured chant among the most loyal supporters in the Curva Nord area of the ground was the unambiguous 'Berlusconi, Berlusconi – get the money out' (interview with Antonio Merchesi, February 2002).

4   Where Business Meets Society: Learning From the Case Studies

The previous chapter was devoted to analysing aspects of the ownership, control and governance structures in a number of European clubs, both in the context of the particular country's system of corporate financing and governance and also that country's football culture and context. In this chapter, themes and differences that emerge from the case studies are identified and analysed. Drawing on the academic literature in these areas, the chapter aims to specify the extent to which these findings can inform our understanding of ownership and governance structures among other football clubs in that country. To what degree are there examples of best practice that may have relevance beyond a particular club or company; beyond a particular country? However, it is important to reiterate that only four clubs in four countries were considered in any detail in Chapter 3 – Tottenham Hotspur (England), FC København (FCK) (Denmark), PSV Eindhoven (PSV) (Netherlands) and Inter Milan (Italy).[85] Consequently, some caution needs to be exercised in interpreting the findings.

Structural rationale

Perhaps the most marked finding is the continuing importance of country-specific cultural factors on ownership structures and models of business behaviour and practice. In Italy, while substantial changes are occurring in the country's wider corporate culture, nevertheless traditional familial ownership structures, as well as pyramidal and cross-holding structures, remain important within companies. These structures remain common within football clubs, even where those clubs have become Stock Exchange listed organizations.

One consequence of the overlap between ownership and control can be a reduction in external monitoring, which can lead to a lack of transparency in these organizations. However, this is not to suggest that there is a lack of accountability within Italian clubs. Rather, enormous public and political interest in football leads to a different kind of accountability, with the political system and the media focusing on and reflecting the stakeholder interests of their constituencies, arguably the supporters and the football public.[86] Consequently, emphasis is placed upon more public forms of scrutiny or accountability as opposed to financial accountability.

By contrast in the UK, the historical importance of the limited liability corporate structure among football clubs, in conjunction with wider economic and financial issues such as the importance of stock markets, had led to shareholder-centric corporate and governance structures. In view of this broad framework, it is perhaps surprising that with the exception of Tottenham Hotspur, it was not until the early 1990s that using the Stock Exchange as a means of raising finance gained popularity with British clubs. The need to raise capital to fund the stadium safety requirements of the 1990 Taylor Report was put forward as the principal motivation, but other reasons included the strengthening of playing squads, development of commercial operations, investment in youth training programmes, improvement of training facilities, widening supporter share ownership, providing improved liquidity to (existing) shareholders, reduction of borrowings and provision of additional working capital (Morrow, 1999, pp. 63-64). Certainly, within a market economy, where a company wishes or requires to raise long term capital to fund investment in long term assets like a football stadium or training facilities, then using the Stock Exchange as the means of achieving this objective is financially rational.[87] However, it has been powerfully argued that the main catalyst behind several UK clubs' public listings was in fact nothing to do with funding stadium redevelopments, but rather was simply about the greed of directors and shareholders and about their desire to personally benefit from football's economic boom through liquidating part or all of their shareholdings (Conn, 1997, pp. 168–80). Consequently, while flotations have been beneficial for some individuals, their benefits for clubs are more debateable.

Furthermore, irrespective of the economic validity of the initial rationale for flotation, once listed thereafter a club is inevitably exposed to unfettered market control.[88] In other words, flotation means that the club is in effect always up for sale (Szymanski and Kuypers, 1999, p. 74). Nowhere is this more apparent than at Manchester United, where rumours continually circulate about potential bids for the company and stake building.[89] In addition, there is also an increased likelihood of stakeholder conflict, most notably between utility motivated supporters and possibly directors, where utility may be football success, and financially motivated investors. While this conflict has been well rehearsed (see, for example, Morrow, 1999), the reporting of the reactions and comments of those involved in the transfer of Rio Ferdinand from Stock Exchange listed Leeds United plc to Stock Exchange listed Manchester United plc provides another clear demonstration of the issues involved (see Exhibit 4.1).

However, arguably, the importance of cultural issues is most pronounced in Denmark. At first sight a club like FCK might be

Exhibit 4.1   Stakeholder conflict

'Man Utd board attacked over new acquisition'

The Financial Times, 23 July 2002, p. 21 (extracts)

After a less-than-triumphant season on the pitch, Manchester United gave its legions of supporters reason to be cheerful when it completed the transfer of Rio Ferdinand from Leeds United in a deal worth up to £33.3m.

But while Manchester United supporters ... celebrated the arrival at Old Trafford of yet another world-class player ... investors were far from happy.

Shares in the Club fell 8.5% to close at 110p as the City expressed doubt over the Manchester United board's decision to break the British transfer record for the second successive year ...

'I can think of no other industry in the world where this sort of money would be spent on a depreciating asset' said one seller of the shares ...

analysts questioned whether the Ferdinand purchase could be justified. ... 'While football clubs must clearly buy players, Manchester United shareholders, who have seen the share price fall over the last couple of years, may have preferred to see less money risked in player trading and more returned through the certainty of dividends.'

'Ridsdale prepared to consider offers'

Morning Star, 18 July 2002, p. 12 (extracts)

[Leeds Chairman, Peter Ridsdale said] 'we are a public company, I am merely an employee and I have a duty to shareholders to maximize the value of our assets'.

The 23-year-old [Ferdinand] is already talking about Leeds in terms of the past, and a senior source at Leeds plc confirmed that Schroders, the investment giants who are the major shareholders in the club's parent company, would not stand in the way of a sale.

---

considered as being the epitome of the contemporary football business – new club, run by successful businessman, Stock Exchange listed, diversified operations etc. However, closer inspection reveals that FCK is reflective of wider Danish culture and society. This is most pronounced in the way in which the country's historical tradition of social democracy continues to impinge upon and inform the club's operations.[90] At its simplest this is evidenced in principles such as cooperation, openness and inclusivity. Nevertheless, it also important to stress that Danish clubs operate in a somewhat less demanding sporting and social space than clubs in say England, Italy or Spain. Hence, supporter expectations and pressure on directors are evidently diminished in contrast to these other countries.

As for the Netherlands, given the distinct history of PSV, it is more difficult to draw conclusions about cultural influences in the wider country.

Concentration – ownership, control and power

In previous work, UK clubs were classified according to certain ownership and control categories (see Table 3.1). Concentrated ownership exists where one or a few individuals or institutions own a large percentage, usually a majority, of shares in the company. Concentrated control exists where effective control can be exercised with a holding of less than 50 per cent, either as a result of cross-shareholdings or due to the fragmented nature of the shareholder base, which in practice makes it difficult for them to act in concert. Using the same categories, Table 4.1 provides a classification for the clubs considered in detail in this study. Examples from the earlier study are also included for comparison.

A particular problem noted in the literature on governance and ownership is the disinclination of small shareholders to exercise their ownership rights actively to influence management activity or strategy (Vives, 2000),[91] a fact usually explained by reference to issues like the difficulty in monitoring and supervising companies, the transaction costs involved in exercising and enforcing voting rights and the fragmentation of ownership (see, for example, Shleifer and Vishny, 1997; Strätling, 2001; Webb *et al.*, 2001). This disinclination is not aided, however, by directors adopting methods, the result of which is to effectively disenfranchise shareholders (Monks and Minow, 2001, p. 95). Consequently, where shareholders are dissatisfied, the only option left open to them is passive monitoring and control, in other words, disinvestment (Vives, 2000).[92]

Table 4.1   Classification of football clubs by ownership type

	European clubs (2001)	UK clubs (examples) (1997)
Concentrated ownership	Inter Milan (Moratti family, 65% shareholding)	Arsenal (director controlled, 87.5% shareholding)
	PSV Eindhoven	Rangers (dominant owner, 61.0% shareholding)
Diversified ownership – concentrated control	Tottenham Hotspur (ENIC, 29.8% shareholding)	Aberdeen (director controlled, 29.5% shareholding)
		Aston Villa (dominant owner, 33.4% shareholding)
Diversified ownership	FC Copenhagen	Manchester United

Yet in those football clubs in which the share capital has been opened up or the ownership broadened, in practice there is little evidence of selling by football club shareholders. Trading in football club shares, even in listed football clubs, which in theory should provide an active secondary market for shares, remains highly illiquid (Morrow, 2000).[93] Thin trading can be caused by a variety of factors, most of which arise simply enough from a lack of buyers or a lack of sellers. On the supply side, concentrated ownership or control effectively reduces the availability of shares to be traded. On the demand side, the nature of investors is key: even in listed clubs there are few substantial holdings by institutions which might be expected to follow an active investment policy. Arguably the most significant issue, however, is the investment rationale of individual investors. Many individual shareholders are supporters of the club. Often there are family connections that have seen shares held for a long time. When clubs first became companies and issued shares, often people bought the shares not to get rich but for reasons more to do with civic pride or the desire to be someone in the local community (see, for example, Birley, 1995, p. 39 with regard to the UK). More recently, as clubs made public issues or floated on the Stock Exchange, it is commonly accepted, if not empirically justified, that supporters' investments have primarily been motivated by emotion rather than financial logic. In one of the few studies to consider this issue,

De Ruyter and Wetzels (2000) found that the social norm of reciprocity – a sense of indebtedness and feeling of obligation to help the club – and the level of personal attachment to the club, were factors that instigated supporters to provide financial support by means of buying football club shares.[94] Irrespective of the precise investment motive, what is unarguable is that once purchased many supporter-shareholders are disinclined to see their shares as marketable assets, and hence are unlikely to exercise the disciplinary right of exit or sale (Morrow, 2000).

Of course, demand and supply side issues are not necessarily independent. One consequence of the nature of the investors outlined above is that it can result in effective control being concentrated in relatively modest shareholdings in some football clubs. The literature on the merits and demerits of a large shareholder intervening in a company is extensive. What concentrated ownership does is converge power in the hands of a dominant owner or family. Different types of ownership and control are suited to different types of activities, with Carlin and Mayer (2000) arguing that concentrated ownership benefits activities that require long-term, committed investors as it can provide both stability and certainty of purpose. They argue further that concentrated owners can display a greater degree of commitment to other stakeholders than can dispersed shareholders, and unlike dispersed shareholders, large block-holders cannot anonymously withdraw from past commitments. Interestingly, Carlin and Mayer (2000) also suggest that activities which require a lot of irreversible investment by other stakeholders, in for example, human capital formation or knowledge about customer markets, benefit from having large rather than diversified share holders.

Relating these arguments to football clubs, several observations can be made. First, that supporters contribute to a club is indisputable. As discussed in Chapter 3 ('The business of Tottenham Hotspur' section), while there are different kinds of spectator, all spectators contribute to a club; that contribution being part financial, part emotional. Giulianotti's 'classic supporter has a long-term personal and emotional investment in the club. [While] this may be supplemented ... by a market-centered investment, such as buying shares in the club ... the rationale for that outlay is still underpinned by a conscious commitment to show thick personal solidarity and offer monetary support toward the club' (2002, p. 33). This definition leaves one in no doubt that for these supporters; support in its different guises involves an irreversible investment in their club (see also Chapter 2). Even from a narrow financial perspective, much of the value of a club is predicated on the investment made by supporters. Second, in terms of time scale, as a grouping, their investment is ongoing as well as irreversible. Hence, logically this investment is long term, albeit those supporters may also seek to place short-term demands on the owners. Third, it seems plausible to suggest that football supporters will prefer a dominant owner to anonymous, dispersed owners. As well as the greater commitment which Carlin and Mayer (2000) argue will emerge, dominant ownership ensures that a football club has a figurehead to be rallied around or vilified as the case may be, and thus sits in marked contrast to the mythical 'men in grey suits'. In other words, there is someone who can be held to account.[95]

Another argument in favour of concentrated ownership in areas of activity like professional football is based on the assumption that dominant owners will act as utility maximizers. Demsetz and Lehn (1985) argue that in certain types of firm (like professional sport and the mass media), a concentrated ownership structure makes sense as it allows owners to ensure that decisions are taken which are consistent with their utility preferences. In other words large shareholders represent their own interest. Thus taking the example of Inter Milan, Massimo Moratti's concentrated ownership allows him to take decisions the aim of which is maximization of his utility, for example, attempting to win the *Scudetto*. However, concentrated ownership can also present problems, in particular it can create private benefit of control problems (Carlin and Mayer, 1998). What this means is that the structure allows the potential expropriation by large investors of other investors and stakeholders in the firm (La Porta *et al.*, 1999; Shleifer and Vishny, 1997). In the literature, this is primarily considered in the context of cash flows. While this is likely to be of relevance to some minority shareholders in some football clubs (as well as to other financial stakeholders such as banks and other lenders), the possibility of expropriation is also relevant in the context of utility. In other words, where a dominant shareholder is running the club with the aim of maximizing his or her utility, then problems will arise where the utility functions of the minority shareholders or other stakeholders do not coincide with that of the dominant shareholder.

Arguably, therefore the supposed structural benefits of concentrated ownership may be dependent on something as intangible and transient as the behaviour and personality of the dominant owner. However, the *de facto* removal of passive monitoring and controlling (disinvestment), taken together with the disinclination of small shareholders to intervene actively in influencing management activity and monitoring, leaves other shareholders (and stakeholders) impotent and exposed to the whims of the dominant controller. At its most extreme, within the confines of Company Law and the protection of minority interests, this may manifest itself as entrenchment by the dominant owner, irrespective of the wishes or utility functions of other shareholders and stakeholders.

In view both of these observations and of the public nature of the football industry, it is unsurprising that concentrated ownership and control is often accompanied by the presence of a dominant personality. Most common in family or otherwise closely controlled private companies of which Italian clubs have historically been the most prominent example, dominant personalities have also been prevalent in other countries, including the UK. Masimo Moratti at Inter Milan is a perfect example. In many ways, Moratti is the personification of Inter: the figure behind whom supporters can rally, the figure who can be vilified by them. However, one suspects that few doubt his commitment to Inter; his family has repeatedly demonstrated in the past that it has the resources to sustain the club, and hence supporters and other stakeholders, have benefited from the largesse of the dominant football owner. However, football's history is littered with examples of clubs where it would be a little more difficult to put such a benign interpretation on the role of a dominant owner.

Interestingly, the importance of personality does not necessarily diminish with changes in the ownership structure such as market listing. Whether ownership is concentrated or diversified, control of a listed club can remain concentrated in the hands of a dominant owner or owners. Within Italy, for example, notwithstanding their market listings, control of Juventus, Lazio and Roma, remains firmly in the hands of the Agnelli family, Sergio Cragnotti and Francesco Sensi respectively. The issue of concentrated control is most pronounced at Lazio and Roma where the dominant owners (and their family) continue to be employed by the company. In this regard, Tottenham Hotspur is interesting. Although ENIC has a minority stake in the company (29.8 per cent), it is evidently the dominant shareholder, with Chief Executive, Daniel Levy, being its public face. At first glance this structure would appear to be in marked contrast to that which existed when Sir Alan Sugar was the dominant individual shareholder. Ostensibly, one might presume that the objectives and motivations of an organization like ENIC would be more business-focused and hence potentially more likely to be in conflict with the supporters than those of someone like Sugar, apparently a supporter-owner.[96] The reality, however, both in words and action is quite different. Sugar's approach to Tottenham was unpopular with some supporters, not, it is argued specifically, because of his financial focus, but rather because at a deeper level, he simply did not understand the things that defined the club, its heritage and style (interview with Joff Wild,

Tottenham Hotspur Supporters' Trust, December 2001). By contrast, despite its business focus, through its willingness to engage in dialogue with the supporters, to date ENIC has succeeded in convincing supporters of its approach and of how it can also be beneficial for the football side. It is also interesting to note that while the supposed fan, Sugar, appointed former Arsenal manager, George Graham as manager, much to the chagrin of the supporters, it was ENIC which brought former Tottenham legend, Glenn Hoddle, back to the club.

While someone like Massimo Moratti is both a dominant personality and a dominant shareholder, arguably effective or *de facto* control need not necessarily be dependent on share ownership or voting control. In other words, irrespective of a club's ownership structure, the strength of personality of a key individual may itself form the basis for a controlling influence. A prominent example of the importance of personality in structure and business behaviour is FCK's Chairman, Flemming Østergaard. Despite a personal holding of less than 5 per cent, Østergaard is clearly the dominant influence at FCK. His background as a stockbroker, combined with his personality and profile has allowed him to forge relationships or alliances with key groups, including financiers and supporters, developing in governance terms, an insider system of control, in which he has managerial autonomy. In addition, this control or dominance has been cemented by success. Financial success and belief in his managerial abilities means he has the backing of shareholders; footballing success allied to the strength of his personality, means he also has the backing of the supporters. Interestingly, however, even in Denmark, there is an Italian influence, with Østergaard being christened *Don Ø* on account of his Italian manners and his friendliness and treatment of the club's supporters (interview with Dan Hammer, November 2001).[97]

Market principles and business ethos

One area in which there is evidence of common ground among three of the clubs (FCK, PSV and Tottenham Hotspur) is in their adherence to market principles as a guide to their behaviour and decision-making. Such a conclusion is perhaps unsurprising given that the countries and societies within which these clubs operate are governed by market principles. Taken with the increases in income available to the elite clubs throughout the 1990s, arguably a new political economy has emerged in football of which this emergence of market principles as a guide within clubs to behaviour and decision-making is but one symptom. Further, as we have seen, two of these clubs, FCK and Tottenham Hotspur are in fact Stock Exchange listed companies.

This is not to suggest, however, that these clubs are being run solely as market-based enterprises, whose primary objective is something like the maximization of profit or the maximization of shareholder value. Rather what emerges is the portrayal of a symbiotic relationship between on and off the field activities: in which football success can only be sustained within an appropriate business structure. Interestingly, even at a club like Inter with its familial ownership structure, as well as at other Italian clubs, the need for the adoption of market principles and for the prioritization of financial discipline seems to have been belatedly accepted (see, for example, Glendinning, 2002).

At a more conceptual level, the very appropriateness of the market mechanism for organizations, which many would consider to be primarily social institutions, remains a contested area (see Chapter 2). Ultimately, a consideration of the case studies reminds us of perhaps the fundamental issue – what and who is a football club for? While three of the case study clubs and many others beyond are now being run in more business-like ways and in accordance with market principles, the nature of the product or industry remains fundamentally different from other areas of business or economic activity, a point accepted by all of the interviewees. In particular, the intense and usually unvarying loyalties of supporters, means that clubs become effectively monopolistic, with resultant implications for issues of governance and accountability. In particular, the possibility emerges of the needs and wishes of other stakeholders being prioritized at the expense of those of the supporters.

Some parallels can be drawn between football supporters and utility customers, where privatized companies have been charged with the provision of essential public goods. For example, in a paper on governance within the UK's privatized water industry, Letza and Smallman (2001) contend that while Yorkshire Water continued to meet its commitment to raising shareholder value during the 1995 summer drought, it failed to meet the needs of its other stakeholders. Of course, the analogy with say the water industry only goes so far. First, while football might be considered a social good, it is clearly not a public good like water or power. Second, as was discussed in Chapter 3, while it can be argued that product substitution or non-purchase is not likely to be an option for football supporters in social terms, for utility customers no economic choice of product substitution or non-purchase may exist. Third, football supporters do have wider choices of non-purchase. In other words, their rights of non-purchase can be exercised in respect of products other than match attendance. Notwithstanding these differences, however, it is clear that the nature of the relationship between a club and its supporters can have monopolistic attributes, with resultant consequences for governance and accountability. But football club businesses do have the opportunity to prioritize the needs of other stakeholders. Indeed there are rational economic and social reasons why they should adopt a more inclusive approach to all their stakeholders. Notwithstanding their adoption of market principles, certainly, the evidence from the case studies indicates that clubs are aware of the need for inclusivity.

Inclusivity

As even the few examples in this chapter demonstrate, football clubs in Europe continue to have distinctive organizational forms. Inevitably this leads to markedly different structures and approaches to corporate governance and to accountability. However, what events in the wider corporate economy like Enron and Worldcom have demonstrated is that corporate governance is not just about structures and controls (ICAS, 2002). Accountability is socially constructed and hence people and their behaviour can be as important as structures.

This is of particular significance in football clubs; organizations that may be considered as both businesses and social institutions. Evidence from at least two of the case study clubs suggests a new willingness on the part of directors to see clubs operating in ways that include and involve groups that have a stake in the club like supporters and the community, and to work to improve those stakeholder relationships.

Motivation for more inclusive approaches to business behaviour and governance differ among clubs, and perhaps, more fundamentally among its stakeholders. For example, astute directors may recognize that improved customer relationships are likely to be good for business, even if they do not accept the notion that their club is a stakeholder organization. Similarly, supporters and community groups can use the directors' business focus to improve communication and dialogue to ensure that directors take better account of and are more accountable to them. However, differing motivations need not diminish the benefits of adopting an inclusive approach to business and of seeking improved accountability – there is surely no requirement that stakeholders must share the same views on the role and purpose of the club.

Interestingly, while it is common to assert that football is in some way different from other areas of economic activity, it is worth observing that no less an organization than the OECD advocates precisely such an inclusive approach:

> Corporations should recognize that the contributions of stakeholders constitute a valuable resource for building competitive and profitable companies. It is, therefore, in the long-term interest of corporations to foster wealth-creating co-operation among stakeholders. The governance framework should recognize that the interests of the corporation are served by recognizing the interests of stakeholders and their contribution to the long-term success of the corporation.
>
> (OECD, 1999, p. 35)

Judging the extent to which clubs are operating inclusively is both subjective and time specific. Certainly, an impression can be gleaned from interviews and case studies of the sort carried out for this book. For example, each of the clubs discussed in Chapter 3 gave examples of initiatives that were designed to ensure the involvement of supporters in decisions and to provide mechanisms for communication and accountability. These included regular meetings with supporter groupings at PSV and FCK, liaison with the Supporters' Trust at Tottenham and web-based communication at Inter.[98] However, for the most part these interviews focused on directors and employees of the firm, with the attendant risk that interviewees might seek to manage the image presented. Furthermore, to be effective, stakeholder groups must accept the validity of these initiatives – inclusivity cannot be imposed.

One source that is of value in gathering an impression of the extent to which clubs are operating on an inclusive basis in the UK, is the annual survey of supporters and club officials carried out by the Football Governance Research Centre (FGRC) (Binns *et al.* 2002; Hamil *et al.*, 2001a). The report provides a comprehensive view of corporate governance in practice among British football clubs. It deals with a variety of issues – ranging from compliance with Companies Acts and the Combined Code on Corporate Governance through to issues concerned with communication and stakeholder involvement.[99] It identifies a variety of governance practices among clubs, some good, some bad. For example, the 2001 report notes that 'at some football clubs excellent governance practice admits supporter groups into a model of consensual management and this operates to the overall benefit of the club' (Hamil *et al.*, 2001a, p. 2). Overall, however, the authors' analysis of the position is not positive:

The general picture is one of club officials indicating the relative ease they have in disclosing information and maintaining dialogue with the fans' groups and shareholders, while the supporters view the picture in a far less positive light.

(Hamil *et al.*, 2001a, p. 2)

all the evidence suggests that general standards of corporate governance in football are poor with a lack of adequate internal and external control mechanisms.

(Binns *et al.*, 2002, p. 1)

The inclusive approach to business is both dependent on and vulnerable to the personal relationships that develop between different stakeholders and stakeholder representatives. Absence of more formalized governance structures creates an exacerbated risk that directors' interpretation of best practice and inclusivity may conflict with that of other stakeholders. This concern is also raised by Binns *et al.* (2002, p. 26) in the context of clubs in the UK. They describe the relationship between a club and its fans as having an inequality at its heart, the power imbalance between directors and other stakeholders. And so supporters can do little to force directors to listen to them or to demand accountability. However, while this may be an accurate presentation of the situation in the UK, it is important that we do not unjustifiably extend this analysis to clubs and companies in other countries, where broader, more consensual approaches are in evidence, in both business and society more generally.

Structural solutions

The challenge is to find mechanisms that encourage clubs to operate more inclusively and promote improved corporate governance. One approach may be structural. For example, clubs could adopt more inclusive ownership structures. One possibility is the formation of a mutually structured Supporters' Trust of the kind discussed in respect of Tottenham Hotspur. These have come to prominence in the UK in the last few seasons (see also Chapter 2).

From a supporters' perspective, trusts provide a collective structure that enables supporters to work together to influence behaviour and accountability within their club. The sum is worth more than the individual parts. From a club perspective, the presence of a trust, as perhaps a single point of contact, enables it to more easily manage its accountability, for example, enabling it to formalize *ad hoc* meetings and other communication initiatives. In the spirit of inclusivity, one would expect, therefore, clubs to recognize and work with such trusts where they are set up, as has been the case at Tottenham.

In its surveys, the FGRC comes down firmly in favour of supporters' trusts as being the way to achieve improved corporate governance in the UK. Caution is required, however, in interpreting the surveys and the resultant analysis. First, the sample of supporters surveyed is heavily skewed towards members of supporters organizations, with some 34.7 per cent (2002) actually being members of an existing supporters' trust. More fundamentally, the report authors (FGRC) are so intimately involved with the movement to promote supporters' trusts in the UK that inevitably concerns exist over the objectivity of the reports.[100]

Another formalized structure that has cultural relevance is dual-board structures, with a role for stakeholder representatives on the supervisory board. This would seem to have particular relevance in countries like the Netherlands and Germany where the governance process requires both supervisory and executive boards. Interestingly, in their work on the UK's privatized water industry, Letza and Smallman (2001) argue that in the management of the production of essential public goods, the protection of the interests of all stakeholders and effective corporate governance requires companies to operate a dual-board model.

With a dual-board structure, a clear distinction is drawn between different types of corporate governance activity. Tricker (1984) suggests that direction (formulation of strategy) and executive action are management functions, handled by an executive board, while the supervisory board is concerned with governance functions – supervision (monitoring and overseeing management performance) and account-ability (recognizing responsibilities to those making a legitimate demand for accountability). In view of this, a case can be made for involving supporters' representatives on the supervisory board, as this board is concerned with supporters' areas of concern.

The extent to which a case can be made for a supporter representative to sit on the unitary board of say a UK football club is more debatable. However, as of October 2002, two listed UK clubs – Aberdeen and Charlton Athletic – do have supporter directors, as do a further 19 UK league and non-league clubs (Binns *et al.* 202, p. 28), while *Supporters Direct* has consistently advocated supporter representation on the board. Arguably, however, this places too much emphasis on the individual elected (both when things go well and when things go badly) and is somewhat at odds with the fundamental principle of collectivity that underpins supporters' trusts. Concerns also exist about the extent to which the elected representative can have meaningful communication with the supporters' trust or other supporter groupings within the constraints of Company Law and possibly Stock Exchange rules, particularly where confidential information is being discussed. Other concerns include the risk of the supporter/director being captured; the risk of the supporter/director becoming alienated from the supporter grouping; the risk of the supporter/director being unrepresentative of the entire supporter grouping and the issue of what sanctions a supporter/director can apply should they feel they are being marginalized.[101]

Disclosure – encouraging best practice

An alternative to structural change as a way of advocating inclusivity and improving corporate governance is to focus on improving disclosure, i.e. persuading clubs to identify and communicate their approaches to governance and accountability. The aim of this disclosure-based approach would be to identify best practice in governance and accountability in the anticipation that it would motivate other clubs to seek to improve their behaviour. A parallel exists in UK financial reporting with regard to narrative reporting in company annual reports. The Accounting Standards Board (ASB) issued the Operating and Financial Review (OFR) in 1993 with the intention of encouraging best practice in narrative reporting. It is not, however, a mandatory accounting standard or required by law,[102] but is intended to have persuasive force. Since the OFR Statement was issued in 1993, the ASB note that there have been significant increases in both the quantity and quality of narrative reporting in annual reports (ASB, 2002).

In its 2002 report, the FGRC advocates setting up a code of good governance for football clubs and supporter groups, dealing both with good practice and legal obligations (Binns *et al.* 2002, p. 42). In England, there is already some evidence of a best practice approach emerging through the FA Premier League Annual Charter Reports (FAPL, 2002). The customer charter work is designed to provide a framework through which the FA Premier League and the clubs will better balance commercial interests and consumer needs. It aims to provide public accountability through a system of annual reporting and monitoring and to encourage best practice and self-regulation. In addition to reporting on the work of the FA Premier League and its member clubs in relation to things like community investment (see Chapter 2) and measures taken to deal with racism, it is also concerned with issues like consultation with stakeholders. For example, Exhibit 4.2 extracted from the Tottenham

Exhibit 4.2   Annual Charter Report – Tottenham Hotspur

TOTTENHAM HOTSPUR FOOTBALL CLUB

ANNUAL CHARTER REPORT 2001/02

This report reflects our work in relation to our 2001/02 Charter and to the agreed recommendations of the Football Task Force of 1988. Our charter is available on our website and on request from the Club.

. . .

CONSULTATION AND INFORMATION

This season our main focus was on improving our relationship with our supporter base. We began to involve the fans more in shaping future policies through meetings with supporter groups, comprehensive operational reviews, surveys and polls.

Meeting with Supporters

We met with Tottenham Hotspur Supporters' Trust on:

31 January 2002
3 April 2002
1 May 2002
15 July 2002

Our FA Premier League supporter panel took place on 2nd March 2002. Topics covered included merchandising, sponsors, catering and Club communication.

Ticket Office Reviews

The Tottenham Hotspur Supporters' Trust conducted a review of our ticket operations. We then appointed Deloitte Consulting to carry out a comprehensive independent Ticket Office Review. Following the two reports, we made a number of key changes. We created a loyalty scheme, sub-contracted call centres to help during busy periods, and installed an on-line reservations system to help with volume of calls. We are currently compiling a Ticket charter to ensure that supporters are aware of our policies.

Catering Feedback

We ran an open-ended poll on our website, inviting fans to write in with any comments or suggestions. As a result, our Catering Services Manager is working closely with the caterers to:

Structure staff training sessions
Have more senior managers on site
Increase stock levels
Erect shelving around the services areas (for fans to rest their purchases)
Change the product lines to improve the range and quality

Exhibit continued overleaf

Exhibit 4.2 *continued*

Disabled Supporters Poll

This season we wrote to every disabled supporter on our database to ask their opinion on our facilities and find out if they wanted to form a Disabled Supporters Association. The two main issues were demand for on-site match day parking (which we are currently trying to source for next season) and an agreement that a number of fans do want to form a Disabled Supporters Association.

Website Design Poll

We conducted a website design poll to enable the fans to tell us how they would like to improve our website, and as result we received over 100 useful responses. Two main concerns were raised: the download time of our website, and the speed with which the site was updated. We tackled both these issues by launching a brand new website on 25 July which had a faster download time and clearer links to our information.

Source: FAPL (2002, p. 317)

Hotspur Annual Charter Report sets out its communication initiatives in the 2001/02 season.

The key thing about the Charter Report is that to be of value it must focus on application. It must deal not only with principles and initiatives, but also outcomes. To that end, the type of information set out for Tottenham Hotspur is an example of good practice.

At a Europe wide level, another regulatory initiative that could be similarly used to encourage increased disclosure and best practice is the UEFA Club Licensing System (UEFA, 2002a). Due to be introduced from season 2004/05, the licensing system has a variety of objectives to improve quality standards in European football, including improvement of clubs' economic and financial capacities, through the installation by clubs of appropriate financial tools, as well as the adaptation of clubs' sporting, administrative and legal infrastructures to current requirements. The system could easily be modified to require a club to provide evidence of the approaches and initiatives adopted to recognize and involve its supporter base. In keeping with the spirit behind the introduction of the licensing system – that different associations should interpret the UEFA document in ways that reflect the particular characteristics of their country – it would be expected that stakeholder involvement and accountability would be achieved in different ways dependent on the club and the country, reflecting the pervasive financial, social and cultural conditions.

5   Communicating the Business of Football

The financial development of football in the last decade or so and the subsequent need for sound financial management have markedly increased interest in the financial affairs of football clubs and greater demands for financial accountability, both from football clubs' stakeholders and from governing bodies. The expectations placed on football clubs are no longer of a purely sporting nature. Most significant of future developments is likely to be the implementation by national associations of UEFA's Club Licensing System from season 2004/05.[103] Initiated by UEFA in 1999, it sets out licensing criteria for clubs in five areas: sporting, infrastructure, personnel/administrative, legal and financial. The financial criteria include the following objectives:

- Improvement of the economic and financial capability of the clubs, increasing their transparency and credibility, and placing the necessary importance on the protection of creditors.
- Assuring that the clubs have an adequate level of management and expertise.

(UEFA, 2002a, p. 7)

The financial criteria may be seen as the most demanding aspect of the licensing system and perhaps in recognition of this are being introduced in a phased manner. In this chapter the focus is on the availability and communication of financial information and the related issue of accountability. Its aims are first, to identify sources of financial information about football clubs, and second, to offer some particular points of guidance on the interpretation of that information.

The annual report and accounts

The most logical starting point for those interested in financial information about football clubs is likely to be the annual report and accounts. In the UK this is relatively straightforward as all major clubs are structured as limited liability companies and thus are required to prepare an annual report and accounts for their shareholders. If you are not a shareholder of a particular club, there are three possible ways of obtaining a copy of the annual report and accounts. First, several clubs now make their annual report and accounts available electronically on their website (see following section). If not, a request to the Company Secretary requesting a copy may be fruitful. Many clubs respond positively and quickly to requests; but others do not. If that fails, the annual report and accounts of any limited company can be obtained for a small fee from the Registrar of Companies at Companies House in either Cardiff for English and Welsh companies or Edinburgh for Scottish registered companies. In addition, Companies House also make the reports available electronically through its website (www.companieshouse.gov.uk). Accounts must be filed with the Registrar of Companies within 10 months of the end of the relevant accounting period for private limited companies and within 7 months for public limited companies.

The consultants, Deloitte & Touche Sport, provide detailed summaries of the annual reports of English and Italian clubs, accompanied by extensive statistical work and analysis in their Annual Reports of Football Finance (see, for example, Deloitte & Touche, 2002a). The accountants, PricewaterhouseCoopers (PWC), produce similar reports on Scottish clubs, although paradoxically, despite being based on publicly available information, the PWC report is not publicly available (see, for example, PricewaterhouseCoopers, 2002). Reporting and analysis of the results of Stock Exchange listed football clubs is also found in the press, both specialist publications like *Soccer Investor* and mainstream national newspapers (see the section on 'The Press' later in this chapter).

In other countries the availability of annual reports and accounts is less clear-cut. Differing legal structures and regulatory requirements can make it difficult for non-shareholders to obtain copies. Copies are available for listed clubs like Juventus and Borussia Dortmund. A club like Brøndby from Denmark also makes its annual report available on its website while others will respond positively to a request for information. However, it is fair to say that financial information about many European clubs is not conveniently available, and for some it is not apparently available at all. Under the first phase of the implementation of the UEFA Club Licensing System, from season 2004/05 clubs will be required to submit audited annual financial statements as well as unaudited interim financial statements to the relevant licensing authority (e.g. the FA, the SFA, the KNVB). In addition, clubs will be required to demonstrate that they have no outstanding football debts such as unpaid transfer fees or amounts due to their employees (UEFA, 2002a, 10.5.1, p. 85). While noting that meeting the criteria for this phase does not allow licence applicants to meet the objectives of the club licensing manual, nevertheless UEFA believes that 'it constitutes an enormous overall improvement in financial transparency and quality throughout the UEFA family' (UEFA, 2002a, p. 86). No mention is made in the UEFA document of public access to these statements. However, it is hoped that UEFA's wish for transparency will also encompass improved communication and accountability to all interested stakeholders.

For limited liability companies in the UK, the annual report and accounts include the primary financial statements (balance sheet, profit and loss account and cash flow statement), supplementary notes to the accounts, auditors' report and various narrative statements, such as an Operating and Financial Review (OFR), a Chairman's Statement and a report on Corporate Governance.

Since 1990, accounting standards in the UK have been set by the Accounting Standards Board (ASB), and this has resulted both in an increase in the number of Standards with which companies are required to comply and also an increased complexity therein. Many major companies – among them J. Sainsbury plc, Scottish Power plc and Stagecoach plc – have responded to the risk of information overload, by distributing only a summary set of financial statements accompanied by an Operating and Financial Review (OFR) to their shareholders. (The importance of the OFR as a means of stakeholder communication in football clubs is discussed in the section 'Narrative communication' later in this chapter. See also section on 'Disclosure – encouraging best practice' in Chapter 4.) A note to shareholders accompanies the summary document explaining that a full set of financial statements is available on request. To date, despite the fact that it seems likely that many football club shareholders will not be financial or investment experts, no football club has taken the decision to circulate only summary financial statements to their shareholders, although a small number of clubs provide summary or annual reports highlights pages on their websites (see Table 5.1).

Mahony and Howard (2001) suggest that over the next decade many sports organizations will strive to take advantage of the great potential of the Internet. The company website has become an important way for major football clubs to communicate with their communities. Extremely high levels of usage are reported. For example, www.ManUtd.com averages eight and a half million page impressions per month from fans

Table 5.1   Electronic availability of financial information

Club	Information provided
English clubs	
Arsenal	–
Aston Villa	Business and Leisure section contains annual report and accounts 2000 and interim report 2002. The annual report 2001 is not available.
Bradford City	–
Charlton Athletic	–
Chelsea	Chelsea Village annual report and accounts 2002
Coventry City	–
Derby County	–
Everton	2002 accounts available
Ipswich Town	–
Leeds United	2001 Annual report and accounts available
Leicester City	In administration – no financial information available. Previously an Investor Relations page was provided along with annual report and accounts (2001 annual report, interim report and preliminary results), financial calendar, company and directors' profile and prospects.
Liverpool	2001 Annual report and accounts
Manchester City	–
Manchester United	Investor Relations site Financial Data (5 year summary, Results and Presentations and Reports). Annual reports (2002, 2001) can be downloaded in individual sections (e.g. Financial Statements, Corporate Governance section etc.) Share price data Financial news and events alerting service Shareholders site (with information on capital structure, dividends etc.)
Middlesbrough	–
Newcastle United	Preliminary results for the years ended 31 July 2002, 2001 Interim Results summary 2002, 2001 Plc AGM Questions and Answers 08/12/00 Board changes and director shareholding change.

Club	Information provided
Southampton	Link to external Share Prices site.
Sunderland	Annual report 2002. The Chairman's Statement, Operating Review and Financial Review for the 12 months to July 2002 can be separately accessed. Trading update and interim results also available as well as a Share Buying Guide (How to invest in your club) and Share Price Feed.
Tottenham Hotspur	Annual report and accounts 2002, 2001 and 2000, presentation accompanying the Annual report 2000, interim report 2001, 2000. Email contact to obtain hard copy of annual report. Buying Shares in Tottenham Hotspur plc guide. Link to latest share price and stock exchange information
West Ham United	–
Scottish clubs	
Aberdeen	–
Celtic	Annual report 2002 Highlights plus full annual report. Annual reports for 1999–2001 plus interim accounts. 2001 Pre AGM video and 2000 AGM Report and Video. Share price from 10 days previously.
Dundee	–
Dundee United	–
Dunfermline Athletic	–
Heart of Midlothian	2002 interim annual results. Annual report and accounts 2001 and 2000. Plus Question and Answers from the 2001 AGM
Hibernian	–
Kilmarnock	–
Motherwell	–
Rangers	Announcement of results plus comment from present and former Chairman. Link to extracts from the annual report (Profit and loss and balance sheet).
St Johnstone	–
St Mirren	–

Source: Dates accessed: 29 October 2002

throughout the world (Worldcom, 2002). In the wider corporate world, the Internet is increasingly being used as a supplementary method of disseminating information and it has become common for organizations to provide interested users with downloadable versions of their paper-based accounts on their website (Beattie and Pratt, 2001; Richardson and Scholz, 2000). Regulatory changes are also facilitating these developments. For example, the introduction of the Companies Act 1985 (Electronic Communications) Order 2000 allows UK companies, with the agreement of their shareholders, to deliver essential documents like annual reports, accounts, notices of general meetings etc. in electronic form. The Act also provides a legal framework that enables shareholders to appoint proxies and provide voting instructions automatically (Strätling, 2000). However, despite these changes, to date only a few more innovative companies are harnessing the potential of the new technology by providing value-added packages that allow users to obtain information in different forms or to access information which is more relevant to their needs such as information on social or environmental issues (Richardson and Scholz, 2000).

The extent to which the Internet is currently used by football clubs as a basis for electronic communication of financial information was tested by surveying the websites of the clubs in the top divisions in England and Scotland (see Table 5.1).

As can be seen from Table 5.1, nine of the 20 FA Premier League clubs and a further two of the 12 Scottish Premier League clubs provide electronic links to their most recent annual report. In the context of communicating with its stakeholders, and in particular with its non share-owning supporters, the provision of a club's annual report in this way substantially widens convenient access to information about its financial performance and position. In addition, a number of clubs (notably Manchester United, Newcastle United, Sunderland, Tottenham Hotspur, Celtic and Heart of Midlothian) provide additional financial information on their websites beyond the annual report.

Of the 11 British clubs providing electronic access to their full annual reports, nine are Stock Exchange listed companies, the exceptions being Everton and Liverpool. In addition, the six clubs identified as providing additional financial information are all Stock Exchange listed companies. As discussed in Chapter 3, Stock Exchange listed clubs tend to have more diversified ownership structures with the shares being widely held among a range of owners. Hence, in contrast with clubs that have more concentrated ownership, in addition to it being a legal requirement, the annual report can be an important means of communicating with dispersed shareholders. Furthermore, Stock Exchange listed companies exist in a more public business space in which there is greater scrutiny and interest in issues like corporate accountability and social responsibility from a range of interested stakeholders. Consequently the annual report may be seen by directors as a mechanism to communicate with, and to demonstrate accountability to, these wider stakeholder groups. In these circumstances it may be considered a rational managerial decision to provide wider and more convenient access to financial information as part of developing and managing the organization's stakeholder relationships (see Chapter 4).

Interpreting an interpretation?

Accounting is often described as the language of business. As a language it has an implicit communicative function (Gallhofer *et al.*, 2000). One product or output of accounting, the financial statements, are the means by which the financial position and performance of a particular organization is communicated to interested parties. However, although financial reporting is governed by numerous accounting standards as well as by company law, these regulatory requirements differ from country to country. While countries like Germany have rule-based systems of financial reporting, in other countries like the UK, financial reporting continues to rely more heavily on professional judgments and opinions and is far from being an objective or neutral activity.[104] Furthermore, despite moves towards harmonization of accounting standards, different systems and rules of accounting continue to apply in different countries.[105] For example, a study by Andersen SCORE in UEFA's 51 European member nations found that there are almost as many different accounting principles, as there are UEFA members (Faasch and Ebel, 2002). In view of this, UEFA's Club Licensing System recommends that each association should adopt a procedure based on the local principles of accounting (UEFA, 2002a), although this will obviously make meaningful financial comparison between clubs in different countries more difficult and less convenient.

In his critique of 'the language of business', Lavoie (1987) suggests that accounts are interpretations [of an organization's economic activities] and that reading accounts thus becomes a matter of interpreting an interpretation. Key information sources about the business of football such as the reports produced by organizations like Deloitte & Touche and PWC, along with reports in both mainstream and specialist press, seem to introduce another layer of interpretation in to this process. (The issue of interpreting the interpreter's interpretation is considered later in this chapter.) Notwithstanding the availability of these comprehensive data sources, some interested users may prefer to make their own interpretation of clubs' financial statements or to focus in greater depth on a particular club's financial position or performance. Alternatively users may require the analysis sooner than would be the case by waiting for the production of a summary report.[106] To assist with the interpretative process, in this section some of the more unusual or peculiar accounting policies prevalent in the accounts of football clubs are identified; policies which may not be found in other corporate financial statements. It does not, how ever, seek to provide a detailed analysis of accounting policies adopted by clubs. Readers interested in such issues should look at Chapter 4 of *The New Business of Football* (Morrow, 1999).

Accounting for players: the effects of the new transfer fee system

In the UK, where a club signs a player, in accordance with the relevant Financial Reporting Standard, FRS 10 *Goodwill and intangible assets* (ASB, 1997), it is required to recognize the cost of his registration (the transfer cost) as an intangible asset on its balance sheet.[107] This amount is then amortized (written off as an expense in the profit and loss account) over the length of the player's contract, the unamortized costs continuing to be shown as an intangible fixed asset on the balance sheet. Homegrown players are not recognized as assets as there is no past transaction or event, i.e. no purchase cost. FRS 10 also requires that intangible assets should be reviewed for impairment at the end of the first full year following the acquisition, and in other periods if events or changes in circumstances indicate that the carrying value may not be recoverable. Similar accounting policies exist in other European countries including Italy and Spain. Furthermore, the UEFA Club Licensing document notes that paid transfer costs can be capitalized separately as intangible assets in the balance sheet of the FLD (Financial Licensing Documentation) as intangible assets and written off on a straight-line basis over the contract period (UEFA, 2002a, p. 103).

The amounts recorded as assets have been dependent on the transfer fee paid by the purchasing club, those fees being determined through the operation of a (transfer) market. While in the past some economists have assumed that the transfer fee is established at the selling club's reservation price (Szymanski and Smith, 1997), recent empirical work lends credence to the view that transfer fees are in fact the outcome of a bargaining process (Dobson and Goddard, 2001, pp. 231–6). This process is dependent on the attributes of the player concerned as well as the characteristics of the buying and selling clubs. The evidence suggests that observed transfer fees in fact tend to exceed the selling club's reservation price, with the selling club being able to capture part of the differential between its reservation price and the buying club's maximum bid price.

After tortuous negotiations between UEFA, FIFA and the European Commission, a refurbished transfer system was introduced in season 2002/03 (Morris *et al.*, 2003). A significant question not answerable at this stage is what effect this will have on the levels of transfer fees. The preservation of in-contract transfer fees – which in England still account for 90 per cent of all transfers (Antonini and Cubbin, 2000) – by the new regime (albeit tempered by explicit rights of notice conferred on players) means that the transfer market, although of declining importance in relative commercial terms, will remain a crucial vehicle for vitally assisting playing success.

Where breach of contract occurs, the bargaining process is replaced by predictable and transparent compensation determined by reference to objective criteria such as the financial conditions of the current contract and any unamortized fee paid previously by the former club in respect of the same player (FIFA, 2001, Article 22). All other things being equal, therefore, the replacement of an uncertain bargaining process by preordained compensation rules might be expected to exert downward pressure on the level of transfer fees. The compensation criteria set out in Article 22 will apply only where a compensation amount has not been specifically provided for in the contract (FIFA, 2001). Accordingly one rational response by clubs may be to insert a clause into a player's contract specifying a minimum level of compensation payable in the event of a player unilaterally breaching his contract. Player contracts in countries like Spain already include a breach of compensation figure which applies to any transfer which takes place during the contract period (Porquera and Jurado, 2001).[108] Furthermore, the regulations say nothing about a mutual agreement between a player and his existing club to terminate his contract prematurely thus allowing him to join a new club. In this situation the new club may be happy to recompense the player for buying out his contract; to all intents and purposes a transfer fee (Simmons, 2001).

A likely consequence of the new transfer system is that it will result in the balance sheets of several clubs being depleted. Where compensation is payable, then in accordance with FRS 10, the club acquiring the player's registration will recognize that amount as an intangible asset, rather than as previously recording the asset at the market determined transfer fee. However, home-grown players and now also players who move clubs at the end of their contracts, will not be recognized as assets on clubs' balance sheets, instead being treated similarly to fixed-term-contract employees in other organizations. Until now football players have been the exception rather than the rule in terms of employees' services being recorded on corporate balance sheets. While debate about recognizing human resources as assets in the financial statements has a long history in the academic literature, to date regulatory bodies such as the ASB have shown scant enthusiasm for encouraging human resource accounting in practice.

One risk for clubs, flowing from depleted balance sheets, arises from the implementation of the UEFA Club Licensing System. Under the third phase criteria (to be implemented at some as yet unspecified time after the 2006/07 season), clubs will only be licensed to participate in UEFA's competitions such as the Champions' League if they are able to prove both that they were in a net asset or positive equity position at the end of the season, and expect to be in the same situation at the end of the current year (UEFA, 2002a, p. 99). In other words, the organization is required to demonstrate its solvency. At present, many clubs are only able to report positive net assets due to the amounts recognized on their balance sheets as intangible fixed assets in respect of players' registrations. Deloitte & Touche (2002a, p. 53) estimate that in total, player value represents 95 per cent of net assets across the English leagues, while the corresponding figure for the Scottish Premier League is 75 per cent.[109]

At present, therefore, there is a degree of comparability among clubs about how to record players acquired after the payment of a transfer fee or compensation payment. But within clubs there is a lack of consistency in that only those players acquired through the transfer market can be recorded as assets. To many this is illogical. Often a home-grown player can be as valuable to a club as a player acquired through the transfer market. For example, at Manchester United plc, while the cost of acquiring Juan Sebastian Veron is treated as an asset on its Balance Sheet, no asset existed in respect of David Beckham. The reason for this is the historical cost convention upon which financial reporting is based which requires an asset to have a purchase cost.

One option available to clubs seeking to improve the relevance of the financial information communicated to interested users is to disclose an estimated realizable or sales value of the first team squad by means of a note to the financial statements. For example, Leeds United has adopted this approach. The sell-on-value of Leeds United's playing squad was estimated at £198m in September 2001, by sports business consultant, Dr Bill Gerrard, of which players who graduated from its youth development programme represented £68m. By contrast the book value of the playing squad (i.e. the asset value on the balance sheet) was only £64m (Leeds United Annual Report 2001, pp. 12–13) (see also later section on 'Narrative communication').

Deferred income

Although, historically, football clubs were thought of as cash businesses, for major clubs this is no longer the case. Nowadays, gate receipts, which used to be received in cash every second Saturday, are likely to be received by the club at the start of the season in the form of advance season ticket sales. Other income sources like sponsorship money and television deals are also frequently paid in advance. Notwithstanding the inherent uncertainty and uncontrollability which accompanies these income sources in the long term, in the short term from an accounting point of view, what is significant is that these sums are payable in advance of the provision of a particular service, i.e. in advance of the football matches which will be played over the course of the forthcoming season(s).

For example, season tickets are usually payable in advance and are non-refundable. From a club's point of view, however, the service in the form of the provision of a football match still has to be provided to the supporter. In other words, the club has not yet fulfilled its part of the obligation. As such, revenue cannot be regarded as having been earned (and hence included in the profit and loss account) until the service has been provided. Thus revenue has to be deferred (effectively treated as a liability or obligation on the balance sheet) and recognized over the period in which the football matches take place. An example of the disclosure of deferred income in respect of Fulham is set out in Exhibit 5.1.

Borrowing and securitization

How a company is funded is described as its capital structure and in most cases it includes both equity (share) finance and debt finance (borrowings). In contrast to personal finance, many companies like to have some

Exhibit 5.1 Deferred income disclosure

Fulham Football Club (1987) Limited Annual Report 2000			
Balance Sheet (extract)		**2000**	**1999**
As at 30 June 2000		£	£
...			
Total assets less current liabilities		4,202,586	5,193,204
Creditors: amounts falling due after more than one year	13	(33,682,597)	(22,201,152)
Deferred income	14	(1,454,132)	(1,319,157)
Net Liabilities		(30,934,143)	(18,327,105)
...			
14. Deferred income			
Season ticket sales in advance		1,019,805	883,586
Commercial income and sponsorship		434,327	432,963
Football Trust Grant		–	2,608
		1,454,132	1,319,157

debt in their optimum capital structure. Because the interest cost of debt is tax deductible for corporations, debt financing may lower a company's cost of capital. However, too much debt exposure or financial leverage can, of course, leave a company's entire financial situation precarious if anything goes wrong.[110]

Historically, most football clubs have been net borrowers from the banks (Morrow, 1999). A survey of English and Scottish Premier League and English First Division club finance directors carried out in 2002 found that 52 per cent of clubs had increased their bank borrowing facility during the year and that the same percentage expected to use more than 90 per cent of their available amount during the forthcoming year (PKF, 2002). While borrowing itself may be a rational financing decision, clubs' exposure to short-term borrowings like overdrafts, however, is of concern. One problem is that overdrafts are repayable on demand. For example, PKF (2002) found that 43 per cent of clubs have their borrowing repayable on demand. A second problem is that overdrafts carry a higher cost (rate of interest) than longer-term funding. For example, PKF (2002) found that 70 per cent of clubs are borrowing at a variable rate of bank/debt finance, with many clubs being on a variable rate two per cent or more over base rate. Reliance on short-term borrowing can cause a particular problem where there is a mismatch between funding and investment, i.e. where short-term finance is being used to fund long-term operations such as stadium investment or medium-term investment like player acquisitions.

In the last few years, an apparently new kind of borrowing has appeared in the football industry – securitization. Several clubs, among them SS Lazio, Leeds United, Manchester City, Newcastle United and Real Madrid are publicized as having carried out securitizations. In simple terms, these transactions are loan vehicles designed to take advantage of the apparently predictable and secure income streams enjoyed by major football clubs.

These transactions involve a company borrowing funds secured not against a business asset that may have a low value for security purposes (like a football stadium, for example), but instead against a receivable or future income stream like gate receipts. Perhaps the first thing worth noting about these transactions is that they are not technically securitizations. Securitization is a process whereby finance is raised from external investors by enabling them to invest in packages of specific financial assets (Wilson *et al.*, 2001) – effectively tradeable financial instruments are issued against anticipated cash flows from various kinds of receivables (Weston, 2001). In the case of football clubs, the receivable that is being borrowed against has most commonly been gate receipts, with bondholders receiving interest payments out of these gate receipts. However, supporters, whether season ticket holders or match-day purchasers, are clearly not legally obliged to buy future tickets. As there is no sale of the receivable itself (because there could not be), consequently the transaction is not actually a securitization. Rather what is being borrowed against is likely future ticket receivables. In some securitizations this problem has been overcome by setting up a new company or special purpose vehicle (SPV). One such example is the 17 year, £55m securitization, carried out by Newcastle United in September 2000 secured against ticket and corporate hospitality income, which involved setting up a new company or SPV which took over a sub-lease of St James' Park and thus acquired the rights to ticket and hospitality revenue (Weston, 2002).[111]

A club entering into one of these securitization deals is effectively bringing forward future income streams into the current time period. Thus clubs may have both advantages and disadvantages. For many major clubs, future income streams from gate receipts are likely to be reasonably predictable and secure.[112] The more certain the predicted cash flow, then the higher the credit rating that will be ascribed to the transactions and the easier it is for the club to borrow over a longer time period. For example, securitization of football club revenues in England has been over 25 years in most cases. Where the club is using these funds to invest in longer-term assets like stadium redevelopment then this will also ensure better matching of assets and liabilities as the asset cost is effectively matched against the income (ticket sales) which will come from using that asset. In addition, there may be a cost of capital advantage where borrowing is arranged at a more attractive rate than if it was secured against a property asset carrying a low security value. It also diversifies the investor base and allows new sources of capital to be exploited. Finally, any inflation over the securitization period will also benefit the club, as the proportion of gate receipts required to service the debt will decrease (Deloitte & Touche, 2002a, p. 48).

Problems arise, however, where clubs use the securitization proceeds to fund either recurring expenditure like salaries or to fund short- to medium-term investment like player acquisitions. This type of behaviour is unsustainable as effectively a club is simply using future income to pay for current costs. For example, the 25 year, £60m securitization, carried out by Leeds United plc in September 2001 secured against ticket and corporate hospitality income was to recoup funds it spent buying players to enable it to mount a challenge for the FA Premier League (Weston, 2001). One risk here is of creating a vicious circle, where the players must be replaced when they leave (Weston, 2002). More fundamentally, while future gate receipts (or other income sources) might be considered reasonably secure at many clubs, the nature of the business, pressure for change in how football is structured and its dependence on sporting competition, means that they are far from certain. Perhaps the most pertinent example is that of Leicester City (see Exhibit 5.2).

In August 2001, the club secured £28m against future media revenues over 25 years. Unfortunately, the club was relegated from the FA Premier League to the Nationwide League at the end of season 2001/02, thus reducing its media revenues. To further compound its difficulties, the collapse of ITV Digital in the summer of 2002 rendered the Nationwide League's television deal worthless. As a result Leicester City's media revenues for league football were limited to parachute payments it was

Exhibit 5.2   Securitization disclosure

Notes to the Financial Statements
for the year ended 31 July 2001

---

22. POST BALANCE SHEET EVENTS

On 10 August 2001, the Group entered into a private placement bond with
Teachers Insurance and Annuity Association for £28m secured upon future
media revenues and the new stadium land and buildings. The bond will be used
as part of the funding for the new stadium.

Source: Leicester City plc, Annual Report & Accounts 2001, p. 32

due to receive from the FA Premier League for the first three years after
its relegation. The club was placed into administration in October 2002.

Leicester City's experience (plus more recently that of Leeds United) is
a salutary lesson to other clubs of the dangers of securitization. It is
difficult to avoid the conclusion that for other than a tiny number of
major clubs, the revenue flows on which football club securitization rely
are simply too uncertain and too risky to make this a credible financing
strategy.

Sale and leaseback of players

The 2002 Deloitte & Touche Annual Review of Football Finance notes
that 'given ... [difficult] market conditions, it is not surprising that
alternative techniques such as player finance and securitizations have
emerged and are increasing in popularity. Player finance techniques
(typical asset finance contracts for the value of players) are like a "sale
and leaseback" of the players' registration' (p. 47).[113] Despite being
described as balance sheet funding (p. 47), the funding is apparently quite
the reverse, being off balance sheet finance. Off balance sheet finance is
an emotive term which by its nature is difficult to define. To many it
conjures up the image of devious accounting, designed to mislead the
users of financial statements. It implies that certain things belong on the
balance sheet and those which escape the net are deviations from the
norm i.e. something that we might expect to belong on the balance sheet
but which is not included (Wilson *et al.*, 2001, p. 1233). To others,
however, it describes sound commercial practice, where for example
companies may engage in transactions which share with other parties the
risks and rewards associated with certain assets and liabilities or where

transactions are undertaken to minimize a company's tax liability. However, whatever the motivation behind these transactions, company's must reflect them in their accounts such that those accounts provide a true and fair view of the company's financial position and performance (Wilson *et al.*, 2001, p. 1233).

In these sale and leaseback transactions a club wishes to buy a player but either does not want to or perhaps cannot pay, the transfer fee outright. Instead, therefore, it takes out a non-obligatory, offshore mortgage for the purchase price with an intermediary finance house. The intermediary pays the full transfer fee to the selling club and then collects lease payments over the life of the player's contract from the buying club. Although the intermediary cannot hold the player's registration under Football Association rules, nevertheless it does have first call on the registration (in terms of security) and can enforce a sale if it does not receive payments in accordance with the original agreement.

None of this, however, is readily apparent to someone reading a company's financial statements. The borrowing instrument is designed in such a way to ensure that it need not be recognized as a liability on the borrowing company's balance sheet. Furthermore, despite the fact that the accounting standard, FRS 5 *Off balance sheet transactions* (ASB, 1994), has a general requirement to disclose transactions in sufficient detail to enable the reader to understand their commercial effects, irrespective of whether or not they have given rise to an asset or a liability, there is no evidence of disclosure of these types of transaction in football club financial statements.[114]

As a result the first public evidence of these borrowings may emerge only should a company get into financial difficulties. For example, when Bradford City entered administration in May 2002, its debts were £22m. By the time its list of creditors was issued in August 2002, this figure had risen to £36.5m, a difference attributed to off balance sheet third party funding of this kind (Banks, 2002a). As well as issues of disclosure and communication, it also raises questions about the Football Authorities' insolvency policy. At present, should a club be placed in administration, football debts such as outstanding player wages over a player's contract or outstanding transfer fees, are treated as super creditors and given preferential status (see Chapter 2). One requirement is that these debts must be extinguished before a club is permitted to take part in football competitions. A consequence of these sale and leaseback schemes is that the football nature of the debt is masked by the presence of the intermediary party and thus a club could in theory run up transfer debts which were not treated as football creditors.

Narrative communication

In addition to the financial statements, additional information is disclosed in the annual report and accounts in narrative form. The form of this disclosure varies. In the UK, the Operating and Financial Review (OFR) was introduced in 1993 with the intention of encouraging best practice in narrative reporting. It provides the directors with an opportunity to analyse and explain the main features underlying the results and financial position of their company. Although aimed at large listed companies, the Accounting Standards Board (ASB) encourages other companies, particularly those operating in specialized or competitive industries, to provide an OFR or something similar, adapted to their own circumstances.

Improvements in both the quantity and quality of narrative reporting in annual reports have been observed since 1993 (ASB, 2002). However, few football clubs include a stand alone OFR within their annual report. The 2001 annual reports of the top division clubs in England and Scotland included only four reports which were either titled as OFRs or which were OFRs in substance while being described differently (see Table 5.2). Perhaps this is not surprising: the OFR is not mandatory and in any event at that time was only put forward as best practice for larger listed companies, a category into which most clubs do not fall. Furthermore, several clubs do incorporate some of the matters dealt with in the ASB statement within other narrative sections of the annual report like the Chairman's Statement or the Chief Executive's Review.

It has been argued that one consequence of the emphasis on narrative communication is that it has highlighted the activities of spin or image management in the non-traditional (narrative) dimensions of corporate annual reports (Gallhofer *et al.*, 2000), a risk exacerbated by the fact these new sites of accounting discourse are subject to minimal audit scrutiny. Notwithstanding this criticism, however, it remains the case that narrative disclosure does provide an opportunity to communicate information which is not captured in the financial statements; information which may assist users to more fully understand the nature of a company and its future potential and which may help improve accountability. Furthermore, narrative disclosure can be designed to reflect the idiosyncrasies of individual companies.

One area in which several football clubs are now actively using narrative disclosure is in providing information about their community initiatives and involvement (see Chapter 2). Previously, it has been suggested that the clubs could make greater use of the narrative sections

Table 5.2 Youth development narrative disclosure

Club	Separate OFR	Disclosure type	Location/length
English clubs			
Arsenal	No	Youth development objective On field success Facilities	Chairman's report 3 paragraphs, L
Aston Villa	Financial Review	Progress of young players	Chairman's Statement 1 paragraph, L
Bradford City	No	–	N
Charlton Athletic	Yes	Youth development objective First team progression Youth academy plans Investment in existing facilities (£1.5m)	Chairman's Statement Review of Operations Review of Season 7 paragraphs, M
Chelsea	Yes	Importance of home grown talent Training academy planning issues and importance	Chairman's Statement 2 paragraphs, L
Coventry City	No	Youth team success Progression for first team	Chairman's Statement 1 paragraph, L
Derby County	No	Youth team success Youth academy/planning permission	Chairman's Report 3 paragraphs, L
Everton	No	Youth academy developments and activities First team progression 'Fun' football	Chairman's Statement 1½ pages, M
Ipswich Town	No	Emphasis on youth development New training centre facility	Chairman's Report 1 paragraph, L
Leeds United	Yes	Information on academy Success of youth policy First team progression Quantification of value of home-grown talent (£68m)	Chairman's Statement Introductory pages 2 pages including photograph, M
Leicester City	Financial Review	Youth Academy	Chairman's Report 2 paragraphs, L

Club	Separate OFR	Disclosure type	Location/length
Liverpool	Business Review	Development of training facilities Role of Academy	Business Review 2 paragraphs 1 page photographs, L
Manchester City	No	–	N
Manchester United	Financial Review	Youth development objective Investment in new football academy (£7.5m)	Chief Executive's review 1 paragraph, L
Middlesbrough	No	–	N
Newcastle United	No	Youth development focus Acquisition of academy site	Chairman's Statement 2 paragraphs, L
Southampton	Financial Review	Academy personnel issues Development of overseas relationships	Chairman's Statement 1 paragraph, L
Sunderland	Financial Review	Youth development objective Development of facilities (£50–£60m spent on Academy since 1996)	Chairman's Statement 3 paragraphs, L
Tottenham Hotspur	Yes	Youth development objective Capital investment in academy	Chairman's Statement Review of Activities 1 paragraph, L
West Ham United	No	Youth development programme (£4m investment pa) On field success Facility expansion	Chairman's Statement 2 paragraphs, L
Scottish clubs			
Aberdeen	No	Youth development objective Resource implications First team progression	Chairman's Statement 2 paragraphs, L
Celtic	No	Youth development funding and need for facility improvement Youth Academy proposals First team progression	Chief Executive's review 3 paragraphs, L
Dundee	No	–	N
Dundee Utd	No	–	N
Dunfermline Athletic	No	One line comment on youth development programme investment strategy	Chairman's Report L/N

continued overleaf

Table 5.2 continued

Club	Separate OFR	Disclosure type	Location/length
Heart of Midlothian	No	Youth development objective Youth team success	Chairman's Statement Head Coach's Statement 2 paragraphs, L
Hibernian	No	–	N
Kilmarnock	No	Progress of young players	Chairman's Statement 1 paragraph, L
Motherwell	No	Emphasis on development of home grown players	Chairman's Statement 1 paragraph, L
Rangers	No	Youth development programme First team progression	Chairman's Statement Football Report 2 paragraphs, L
St Johnstone	No	Progress of young players	Chairman's Statement 1 paragraph, L
St Mirren	No	–	N

Disclosure index: E = Extensive; M = Moderate; L = Limited; N = Nil
Source: Annual Reports, 2001

of their annual reports to provide information on things like the market valuation or estimated sales value of its playing squad and also on things like its investment in training and development activities; information which would provide a much fuller picture of the organization's position and of its future potential (Morrow, 1999, pp. 152–6). The extent to which clubs disclose information about their investment in training and development in their annual reports is set out in Table 5.2.

As Table 5.2 demonstrates few clubs provide much meaningful disclosure about this issue anywhere in their annual reports. Only three clubs were classified as providing moderate levels of disclosure: Charlton Athletic, Everton and Leeds United. Two of these clubs, Charlton and Leeds United, along with Manchester United, Sunderland and West Ham United, provided some quantification of aspects of their youth and development work, although in all cases, disclosure was limited to an isolated figure. In view of the fundamental importance of youth development to the future success of most clubs, both in footballing and financial terms, the quality of disclosure is very disappointing. Obliging clubs to disclose meaningful information on investment in youth development and training, perhaps as a condition of the Club Licensing System, would highlight best practice within the industry and would identify those clubs that were looking to the future. In addition to information on capital expenditure on items like youth academies and training facilities, clubs should also be able to provide information about revenue investment in youth development and training and other softer information. While much of this expenditure is long term and provides uncertain outcomes, nevertheless clubs should be able to provide meaningful quantitative information on things like the number of players in different age classifications at the club, the percentage who progress through the ranks to professional contracts, the number of coaching staff employed, expenditure on coaching staff and so on. Information of this nature would provide a much fuller picture of a club's position and of its future potential.

Interpreting the interpreter's interpretation

The professionals

As was mentioned earlier in this chapter, organizations like Deloitte & Touche and PWC are now important and regular providers of information about the business of football. In addition, in recent years other accounting and/or consulting organizations like KPMG (1998) and PKF (2002) have also produced reports on differing aspects of the football business. Deloitte & Touche, however, are clearly the market leaders in this area. As Touche Ross, its first report 'Survey of Football Club Accounts' was published in 1993 (Touche Ross, 1993). Its reports are comprehensive: a mixture of information collated from annual accounts and analysis, both statistical and narrative, and an essential source for anyone studying the business of football.

However, when using these and similar reports, it is important to bear in mind several caveats. First, the analysis provided in these reports is simply that organization's interpretation of an interpretation (the original annual report and accounts). In other words, as a user you are interpreting an interpreter's interpretation. Second, the analysis put forward by Deloitte & Touche or PWC is concerned solely with the business or financial dimension of football. In view of accounting's social purpose it is disappointing that little attention is given to football's wider social dimensions. Third, it must also be kept in mind what the purpose of these reports is. While the desire to secure football club business is likely to be one motivating factor, perhaps more important is the publicity that arises out of being associated with a commercially high profile sport like football. That the analysis or perspective adopted in the reports is market-focused is thus not surprising – the market is after all made up of clients and prospective clients.[115] Arguably, however, this club/client focus may lead to the reports being less critical or evaluative than one might expect. For example, notwithstanding the benefits of hindsight, it is somewhat surprising that in its 2002 report, Deloitte & Touche chose only to outline the advantages of securitization, without mention of the downside risks (2002a, p. 48), while the attendant risks of player finance techniques might also have been an area for comment (2002a, pp. 46–8).

Another source of information about the financial affairs of football clubs which has emerged in recent years are specialist trade or professional publications like *SportBusiness* and *Soccer Investor*. These publications provide coverage and analysis of financial and commercial issues in the football sector and reach a large number of people involved with the business of football.[116] Of particular interest in this chapter is the analysis of the annual accounting results of all listed European clubs, and many other UK clubs, regularly provided in *Soccer Investor*. These provide an accessible summary of a club's financial results, as well as related operating and market information. Exhibit 5.3 provides an example in respect of Sunderland plc.

The press

Sport, and in particular football, is a significant economic, social, cultural and political phenomenon, of which the primary means of consumption is the media (Crolley and Hand, 2002, p. 8). There is more media coverage of football than ever. Television coverage has increased substantially due to the introduction of satellite television stations like Sky into the market place. Extensive live coverage of football matches is now available in the UK both on television and on radio through stations like BBC Radio 5 Live and BBC Radio Scotland. In addition, a substantial quantity of talk-based football content is now available on television and radio. These programmes include discussion-based programmes like *Any Sporting Questions* on Radio 5 Live, phone-in programmes like Radio 5 Live's *606* or Reel Radio's *Reel Football Phone In* as well as comedy based programmes like Radio Scotland's *Off the Ball*. These talk-based football programmes are also found in many other European countries, most extensively in Italy (Burke, 1998, pp. 136–45). In addition to these traditional sources, new media sources like the Internet have become increasingly important. Substantial amounts of information are now available on official club websites and fan-based websites, as well as on general content providers like the BBC. Surveys indicate that 45 per cent of football supporters have Internet access at home, a figure well above the current national home connection figure (SNCCFR, 2000, p. 23). More significantly, of those supporters with Internet access, only 17 per cent make no use of Internet access for football information (SNCCFR, 2000, p. 23).

The longest standing relationship that football clubs have with any form of the media, however, is with newspapers (Vamplew, 1988, p. 56). Today football remains an important element of print media discourse (Crolley and Hand, 2002, p. 1). In recent years, newspapers have responded to a more competitive information provision environment by extending their sports coverage.[117] For example, in the UK, most Sunday and Monday general newspapers now include separate sports supplements. In several other European countries, most notably France, Italy and Spain,[118] the appetite for information about sport is even more pronounced and this is reflected in the publication of specialist daily sports newspapers. In France, *L'Equipe*, claims about two million readers a day and devotes about 40 per cent of its space to football; in Italy, there are three national sports dailies – *Gazetta dello Sport*, *Corriere dello Sport* and *Tutto Sport* – which devote about 70 per cent of their space to football; while in Spain there are four national sports dailies – *Marca*, *As*, *Sport* and *El Mundo Deportivo*. The best selling of these is *Marca*, and its daily sales of over 420,000 now exceed those of *El País*, Spain's most widely read, general daily newspaper (Crolley and Hand, 2002, pp. 4–5).

The high news value of sport, especially football, makes the sports-business-media nexus a compelling area for research (Boyle and Haynes, 2000, p. xi). In the remainder of this chapter the role of the print media in communicating information about the business of football will be considered, focusing both on the quantity of information provided and its quality.

Reporting business

In recent years there has been heightened media interest in business and financial affairs. This is reflected not only in increased circulation for specialist financial publications like *The Financial Times* (as well as the

Exhibit 5.3   Sunderland plc annual results 2002

POOR FORM PUTS SUNDERLAND IN RED

A poor performance on the pitch, as well as increased player amortisation and write-downs, pushed **Sunderland plc** into its first statutory loss as a public company.

A pre-tax loss of £2.79m was recorded for the twelve months ending 31 July 2002 compared with a profit of £3.01m the year before.

Turnover:

Turnover fell 5% from £46.02m to £43.83m. One contributory factor was a decline in gate receipts. While average attendance was only slightly down at 46,744 (2001: 46,832), the poor form on the pitch meant that the club had four fewer home cup games to benefit from, as well as four fewer away cup games.

Also the club's policy of reducing season ticket prices impacted on the level of gate receipts.

The poor performance on the pitch last season also negated the improved **Premier League** TV deal as the 17th position (2001: 7th) meant that Sunderland saw a £3m fall in its merit award. Therefore, despite the new **BSkyB** deal, TV income fell 2% from £18.3m to £17.98m.

The 9% climb in sponsorship, hospitality and royalty income was a result of the company adding to its sponsorship portfolio, while also enjoying the share of the improved league sponsorship deal with **Barclaycard**.

The club blamed the poor on-field performance on the 8% decline in retail and merchandising income to £3.17m (£3.43m).

Costs:

On the costs side, staff wages climbed 11% to £25.78m (£23.22m). This represented 59% (50%) of turnover.

This was a result of a number of acquisitions during the year – Jason McAteer, Bernd Haas, Lilian Laslandes, Claudio Reyna and Joachim Bjorklund.

Further acquisitions since the year-end has pushed the wage level to over £30m – around 66% of the expected turnover for next year should things remain as they are now.

Plc chairman **Bryan Sanderson** said that the 59% level was "still at a manageable level in a season of poor performance", but that it was "a performance measure that your board keeps under constant supervision".

All this meant that the operating profit before player trading was halved from £9.0m to £4.6m.

The acquisition of the above players during the year helped to push player amortisation costs to £7.1m (£5.91m). However, after sensing the fall in the transfer market during the summer and assessing the value given to some of its players the club decided to write-down £4.68m in player values (against £724,000 in 2001).

This led to a total amortisation charge of £11.8m (£6.6m).

Compared to the previous year, however, the club gained more from the sale of players with the departures of Don Hutchison (**West Ham United**), Alex Rae (**Wolverhampton Wanderers**) and Danny Dichio (**West Bromwich Albion**) all leading to a £5.2m profit on player disposals (£1.18m).

Sanderson said that the company would look to trim its squad size of 36 in the next transfer window.

Bernd Haas and Llilian Laslandes, who are both currently on loan abroad having failed to break into the first team, are just two of eight players viewed as targets to be sold.

With net interest of £831,000 this resulted in a pre-tax loss of £2.79m. The loss per share was 41.3p (35.2p earnings). The loss and the financial situation for the current financial year forced the company to forego a dividend payment (2001: 5p a share).

But, Sanderson said that the decision had not been taken lightly and the company was committed to restoring dividends on improvement of performance.

In the results, it was announced that former chief executive **Hugh Roberts** had returned to the post he had vacated earlier this year for personal reasons. He will be CEO to the club and an executive director of the plc.

The club has also changed its coaching team with the departure of manager **Peter Reid**, to be replaced by **Howard Wilkinson** and **Steve Cotterill**. Sanderson said that these two keeping the club in the PL was paramount to ensuring that the long-term investment in the club would not be put at risk.

Financial director **Peter Walker** said that a further £4m is due to be spent this year on the club's academy, which is due to be completed early next year with the completion of phase two of the project.

The club is currently appealing against a decision by **South Tyneside Metropolitan Borough** to refuse planning permission for proposed facilities as part of stage three.

Walker said that the club's cash position was affected by the later than usual sale of season tickets which included a three-stage interest free payments scheme. This was taken up by almost 50% of season ticket holders.

Net debt stood on 31 July 2002 at £21.2m (£9.9m), creating gearing of 69% (29%).

Looking ahead, Sanderson predicted that, with acquisitions during the financial year and after possibly totalling £25m, the loss for the year to 31 July 2003 would be "significantly higher" than 2002.

Sunderland results 12 mths to 31-7-02

£m	31/07/02	31/07/01	% change
Turnover	43.829	46.021	−4.8%
Operating expenses	−39.218	−37.056	5.8%
Operating profit pre-player amort'n	4.611	8.965	−48.6%
Player amort'n	−11.784	−5.905	−99.6%
Profit on disposal of players' contracts	5.214	1.182	−341.1%
Provision for permanent diminution in value of players contracts	–	−0.724	N/A
Net interest	−0.831	−0.507	N/A
Pre-tax profit	−2.79	3.011	−192.7%
Retained profit	−3.537	2.583	−236.9%
Dividend	–	5	N/A
Earnings per share (p)	−41.3	35.2	−217.3%

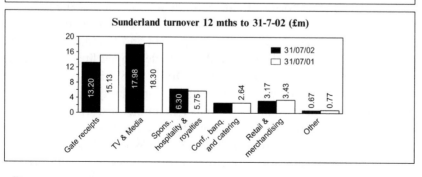

Sunderland turnover 12 mths to 31-7-02 (£m)

31/07/02 31/07/01

Gate receipts 13.20 / 15.13; TV & Media 17.98 / 18.30; Spons., hospitality & royalties 6.30 / 5.75; Conf., banq. and catering 2.64; Retail & merchandising 3.17 / 3.43; Other 0.67 / 0.77

Source: *Soccer Investor*, Weekly Issue 118

launch of new specialist titles like the Scottish-based daily *Business am*),[119] but also in the general boom in financial news in other newspapers. For example, broadsheet newspapers like *The Times* and *The Daily Telegraph* now have extensive business sections while much of the tabloid press has City pages or tip sheets.[120] The terms 'financial press' or 'financial journalism' are used to describe economic and business reporting as well as strictly financial coverage – in short, the world of money. In common with other 'worlds', the money world has developed its own practices, culture, language and jargon, often leaving that world incomprehensible to the layman. One role for the financial press, therefore, is to act as an interpreter: to bridge the comprehension gap. A particular problem for the financial press is the issue of market or customer; being targeted both at those in the money business and also at those who have an interest in the wider financial and economic scene and/or for whom the money business impinges on their personal lives (Brett, 1991).

The type of financial journalism that exists in the UK today can be traced to developments in the late nineteenth century. Until then financial journalism was characterized as factual, cold, even indolent, consisting of little more than lists of prices and data with no comment or explanation. The development of 'New Financial Journalism' emphasizing financial intelligence rather than facts, replicated developments occurring at that time in the British press more generally. The coverage of financial news was consequently transformed and extended in response to the increased supply of, and demand for, useful financial intelligence, both on stock markets and on corporate activity (Porter, 1998).[121] Interestingly the newspaper reporting of business is an area that has been largely neglected by the academic community. Given that media studies have emphasised the importance of mass communication, Parsons (1989, p. 3) argues that it is unsurprising that forms of elite communication such as the financial press have been neglected. Some literature does exist on the reporting of macro-economic issues such as inflation (Gavin and Goddard, 1998) but here too authors note with surprise the underdeveloped literature on the media and the economy. In other areas Dreier (1982) has examined the complex relationship between the business community and the media while Gallhofer and Haslam (1991) have examined historical aspects of the reporting of business, investigating press reporting of questionable accounting practices in Germany during World War I. However, there is little evidence in the literatures of either media studies or accounting and finance of contemporary studies on topics such as how the media report on the publication of accounting information or take-over speculation.

Reporting the business of football

Are Leeds bankrupt? Will there be 600 footballers out of work at the end of the season? Yawn, yawn. Every newspaper now employs a specialist on football finance, which keeps them off the street, so we're getting more and more of such stories.

(Hunter Davies, *New Statesman*, 18 March 2002, p. 58)

Football is more and more featured in the financial press. *The Financial Times*, at the start of season 2001/2, had a special football pullout – previously the FT wouldn't have touched football with a barge pole.

(John Reid, 2001, *Reclaim the Game*, p. 16)

Back in March 2000, in the days when football's business profile was more prominent that it had been before or since, the stock market capitalization of Manchester United plc exceeded £1bn for the first time.[122] While breaking through barriers always captures a certain amount of interest in the financial markets, this breakthrough still left Manchester United plc, perhaps the world's premier football business, well outside the corporate top division. Its market capitalization placed it at 191st position in the FT All-Share Index, while a trebling of its share price would have been required to enable it to challenge those companies at the bottom end of the FTSE 100 index.[123] Nevertheless, United breaking through the £1bn barrier was reported in newspapers as diverse as *The Financial Times, The Daily Mail* and *The Sun*.[124]

By any conventional measure of business size, however, in a UK context Manchester United is the exception rather than the rule. For example, the combined market capitalization of the other listed British clubs on the day Manchester United broke through the £1bn barrier was less than £700m. Most football clubs remain small businesses in absolute terms with turnover and, where applicable, market capitalization being insignificant in comparison to companies in other business sectors reported in the financial press. Furthermore, making profits in the football sector remains the exception (see, for example, Deloitte & Touche, 2002a; PricewaterhouseCoopers, 2002).

Despite this, growing interest in business aspects of football is evident across the media spectrum. For example, the City of London's bible, *The Financial Times* has had a weekly sports page and journalists specializing in the coverage of financial issues in sport since March 1997. Several other broadsheet newspapers have journalists with an expert knowledge of the business side of the industry reporting in their sports pages. Perhaps the longest standing example of this is the *Daily Telegraph* columnist, Mihir Bose, whose specialism includes sports business stories. Other examples include David Conn's *Inside Football* report in *The Independent*, and Ian Bell's columns in the *Sunday Herald*. Even the tabloid market is beginning to show some interest, with the *News of the World* retaining Simon Banks, a qualified accountant and financial journalist as its football [business] consultant.[125] Arguably, however, the publicity and comment that football receives as a business arises not from its significance as a business, but rather from its wider social interest.

Issues of quantity

As discussed above, newspapers remain a key source of information for football supporters. As football has become more business centric, demand for information might be expected to extend to matters of a financial nature. Supporters, although not necessarily having financial expertise, may nevertheless have a keen and a legitimate interest in the financial affairs of the clubs in which they are stakeholders (see Chapters 3 and 4). Arguably this interest becomes more pronounced when a club is in financial difficulties or where it has adopted the most business-like structures, e.g. becoming a Stock Exchange listed company. A number of football clubs now have several thousand individual shareholders; many of whom have invested out of a sense of loyalty and attachment to their club and are likely to have no direct shareholdings in any other companies. Consequently, they may often be unfamiliar both with the type of information provided by listed companies and of how to interpret it. For many supporters, newspapers may thus be an obvious place to turn for such guidance.

Empirical evidence of the quantity of football business information provided in the press can be readily established. To provide a broad overview of the level of disclosure, a sample of newspapers was comprehensively surveyed for football business coverage during one randomly selected week. Football business was broadly defined to include any item that dealt both with football and a related financial, business or economic dimension in the same coverage. Coverage of transfer stories, however, whether actual or speculated, was excluded from the survey.[126]

The survey ran for seven days beginning on Tuesday 15 January 2002. Tuesday was selected as the start day to allow the week's coverage to end with Monday's reporting of the weekend's football matches and other activities, although it is not expected that these will include business matters. The papers surveyed are set out in Table 5.3. As explained in the notes to the table, several of these newspapers are either Scottish-based

Table 5.3   Newspapers surveyed

Weekday		Sundays	
Broadsheets	**Tabloids**	**Broadsheets**	**Tabloids**
The Herald*	*The Sun*[‡]	*The Sunday Times*[‡]	*The Mail on Sunday*[‡]
The Scotsman*	*The Daily Mail*[‡]	*The Sunday Herald**	*The Sunday Mail**
The Daily Telegraph[‡]	*The Daily Record**	*Scotland on Sunday**	
The Times[‡]		*The Observer*[‡]	
The Independent			
The Guardian			

*   Scottish-based newspapers.
[‡]   Scottish versions of national (UK) newspapers.

newspapers or are Scottish editions of UK (London) newspapers. By extension, therefore, the stories being reported have a greater focus on the Scottish market place.

The study is concerned with two main issues, which have relevance beyond the actual coverage of this particular week: first, to identify which newspapers actually cover football business-type stories, and second, within those newspapers, to identify where that coverage is located.

Content analysis – week beginning Tuesday 15 January 2002

Eighty-three different pieces of coverage were identified in respect of some 16 separate football business stories. Perhaps unsurprisingly in view of the newspapers sampled, coverage was dominated by two main stories, both of which were Scottish-focused: first, coverage of political and economic issues arising from Scotland's proposed bid to host the European 2008 Football Championships (30 items of coverage); and second, the financial and sporting implications arising from the Scottish Premier League's (SPL) proposal to set up its own TV station (21 items of coverage). A summary of the findings is set out in Table 5.4. Full details are provided in Appendix 1.

Arguably, neither of the top two stories in this week is typical of newspaper reporting of the business of football. In particular the Euro 2008 bid story is clearly focused on issues of macro rather than microeconomics. However, even within the coverage of this story, there was discussion of finance issues at the level of individual clubs. For example, there was discussion of whether limited companies such as Aberdeen or Hibernian should receive public money to assist them in

Table 5.4 Reporting the business of football – items reported week beginning Tuesday 15 January 2002

News story	Newspaper type			Location				
	Total	Broadsheet	Tabloid	News	Editorial	Sport	Business	Column
Coverage of political and economic issues arising from Scotland's proposed bid to host the European 2008 Football Championships.	30	17	13	12	5	8	–	5
The financial and sporting implications arising from the SPL's proposal to set up its own TV station	21	13	8	3	1	10	2	5
Niall Quinn's decision to donate his testimonial proceeds to charity	6	5	1	4	1	1	–	–
The ownership and financial position of Dundee United: the return of Jim McLean as Chairman	5	2	3	–	–	5	–	–
Issues arising from the redevelopment/financing of Wembley Stadium.	4	4	–	–	–	4	–	–
Financial difficulties at East Fife	4	2	2	–	–	4	–	–
Financial difficulties at Celtic	3	3	–	–	–	3	–	–

Financial difficulties in the Football League	1	1	–	–	–	–	–	1
Financial difficulties at York City	1	1	–	–	–	–	–	1
The search for alternatives to TV cash	1	1	–	–	–	1	–	–
The business of Rushden and Diamonds	1	1	–	–	–	1	–	–
Proposed co-operative purchasing venture among Scottish clubs	1	–	1	–	–	1	–	–
IG Spread Betting profits	2	2	–	–	–	–	2	–
Argentina's financial crisis – implications for football clubs	1	1	–	–	–	1	–	–
Hampden debentures – Champions' League tickets	1	1	–	–	–	1	–	–
Bonds to guarantee financial commitments	1	1	–	–	–	1	–	–
TOTAL	83	53	30	19	7	41	4	12

developing their grounds in order to make them suitable to host matches in the 2008 European Championships.

The 30 items reported on this story were well distributed within the different sections of the newspapers. The wider political and social significance of the story is reflected in the fact that 12 of the items were located in the news sections, while editorials were partly devoted to the issue on a further five occasions. Interestingly, given that only five of the 15 newspapers surveyed were tabloids, proportionately there was greater coverage in the tabloids than in the broadsheets, although unsurprisingly the broadsheets covered the item in more detail. It is also interesting to note that this story was clearly seen as a news story by the tabloids, with only one report being located in the sports pages.

Coverage of the SPL's proposed in-house television channel was also extensive. Although primarily located in the sports sections, again coverage was also found in the News sections as well as in Editorials and Columns. It is interesting to note that this story also found its way into the business sections. The only other sports business story to be reported in the business sections in this particular week was some very modest coverage of the negative effect that David Beckham's last minute strike for England against Greece in the 2002 World Cup qualifier had on the profits of spread betting company, IG index.

One explanation for the lack of coverage in the business sections of papers may be that the financial press (bespoke financial titles as well as the financial/business pages of newspapers) is aimed at an elite audience (Parsons, 1989). Those interested in football, whether on or off the field, may be perceived as not being an elite and hence are less well catered for. However, less conspiratorially, it seems likely that is also reflects the narrow types of story normally reported in the financial press – things like company results, takeovers, expansions and so on. Many of the football business stories identified in Table 5.4 fall outside these areas. Furthermore, in other weeks such as during football's 'financial reporting' season, it is routine to find the business pages commenting on the annual results of listed clubs.

Indeed, perhaps what is more interesting about these conventional financial stories in respect of football clubs is the fact that, unlike similar stories for non-footballing companies, they are often reported on in more than one section of a newspaper. Nowhere was this more evident that in BSkyB's bid to take over Manchester United in 1999. One interpretation is that while these are business-type stories, the reason they are reported arises not from their business or financial significance but rather from the wider social significance of football and football clubs. Paradoxically, it can be argued that football clubs like Manchester United, Newcastle United and Celtic, have played a part in popularizing free market capitalism, continuing a trend started during the Thatcher government's privatization programme, where the sale of BT in 1984 marked the first time a share issue had received major coverage in the non-City pages of newspapers (Parsons, 1989, p. 209).

Issues of quality

While increased coverage of the financial aspects of football in the media is indisputable, quantity need not equate to quality. An alternative approach to commenting on the quality of reported information, involving the use of a detailed case study, was utilized by Boyle *et al.* (2002), and the remainder of this section draws heavily on that work. This research focused on the 1998 putative take-over of Celtic (a club then controlled by its majority shareholder, Fergus McCann) by a high profile consortium including the ex-Celtic star, Kenny Dalglish, and the rock singer Jim Kerr. Since taking over the club in 1994, McCann had consistently stated that he would stay for five years and would then offer his shares in the first instance to existing shareholders, season ticket holders and other Celtic supporters. As he reached the end of his tenure, the club had over 10,000 shareholders and 50,000 season ticket holders, making it the fifth best supported football club in the world.

The research involved a detailed survey of stories reported in the press about the putative takeover, followed by interviews with several of the journalists involved in reporting the bid as well as some of those involved with the public relations on both sides of the bid. In summary, the research illustrated how public interest in sport, and its attendant news value, can actually illuminate aspects of how financial news is produced and reported in the print (and broadcast) media. Within this, however, various issues emerged concerning qualitative aspects of how the business of football is reported.

A key problem identified was the cult of the celebrity. In this case it was clear that much of the media (both print and other forms) were very closely linked with celebrities involved in the bid. This building up of links with high profile celebrities is a common feature of sports journalism (Boyle and Haynes, 2000). Here it evidenced itself in the way in which many journalists focused on the emotional appeal of the bidders: unashamedly, and without producing evidence to substantiate their claims, proclaiming 'King Kenny [Dalglish]' as the fans' favourite (Boyle *et al.*, 2002). One consequence of the celebrity linkage was the apparent reluctance of many journalists to damage those links by critically appraising the facts, financial and other, behind the supposed bid. Relatedly, a problem with football business stories is that often they are reported as stories about football businessmen. Here this problem was exacerbated by the fact that unlike many others directors in the football business, Fergus McCann had never courted the media, while at the same time his manner and personality had certainly not endeared him to many in the media. One consequence of this personalization is that sports business reporting simply becomes embedded in its subject rather than illuminating it (Rowe, 1991).

This cult of the football celebrity also causes problems in other ways, in particular an unwillingness among some sports journalists to recognize that football business stories cannot be reported in the same way as more conventional football stories. One example is the preference among some sports journalists for relying on traditional sources, often former players/ managers, to provide 'expert' analysis, irrespective of whether the issue under discussion relates to their area of expertise. One such example arose following Celtic's 1999/2000 Scottish Cup defeat by Inverness Caledonian Thistle. Writing in *The Scotsman*, in a piece headed 'Defeat costly for investors as Celtic shares take a dive', journalist Allan Wright quoted the former Celtic manager and player, Billy McNeill, as saying 'obviously they [the plc board] must be worried about that amount of money being wiped off the club's resources' (Wright, 2000, p. 37).

This quote is illustrative of many inadequacies in the reporting of the business of football. While it is likely that the directors of any plc will be concerned about adverse share price movements it is wrong to assert that these movements have an effect on 'the club's resources'. In fact the company's resources are unaffected directly by movements in its share price.[127] The price is determined by the supply and demand for those shares in the Stock Exchange, and importantly in the context of thinly traded shares in football clubs, by market makers adjusting the prices at which they will trade those shares (Morrow, 1999, pp. 93–107). In communicating reality, the journalist has constructed reality (Hines, 1988), introducing spurious concern about one of the key interests of football supporters, namely the availability of funds.

A particular problem with the reporting of the football business has been the lack of knowledge of financial matters among many sports journalists. Financial expertise has traditionally been outside the experience and training of most journalists (Rukeyser, 1983). At the time of Manchester United's 1991 share float, one of the club's advisers, Glenn Cooper, commented that:

You had for the first time the crossover between sports journalists and City journalists. The sports journalists were writing for the first time about City matters and the City journalists were writing for the first time about sporting matters. By and large both made a complete cock-up of it.

(cited in Bose, 1999)

Boyle *et al.* (2002) did not find evidence of universal improvement in this respect. Hugh Keevins, then chief sportswriter at one of Scotland's leading tabloid newspapers, *The Sunday Mail*, observed that 'football writers are going into this [area] completely blind and we misunderstand and misinterpret' (Boyle *et al.*, 2002, p. 168). What is concerning for those trying to glean information about clubs from the press is not that journalists lack the financial knowledge to fully understand this growing area of the industry, but rather that this does not stop them reporting on it. Several examples were reported in the paper of inaccurate and partial reporting of technical matters. These dealt with matters as fundamental as whether or not the consortium could afford the bid and who would ultimately become the owners of the club (Boyle *et al.*, 2002). A significant structural difference was identified between the broadsheets and the tabloids, in that it was common in the broadsheets for journalists with an expert knowledge of the business side of the industry to appear in their sports pages. This was less likely to happen in the tabloids for the simple reason that there are fewer, if any, journalists with business expertise to be found in the tabloids.

Consequently, reliance is placed on other sources. For example, Boyle *et al.* (2002) identified an increasingly important role for professional financial intermediaries such as PRs, who were able to influence media coverage by providing easy copy to under pressure journalists, trying to produce stories that help sell newspapers in a highly competitive environment. Even perhaps of greater concern from the perspective of those seeking credible financial information, is the possibility of journalists basing their views on what they are told by the information providers themselves. This can lead to a collusion of sorts when the topic under discussion involves complex financial dealing and issues beyond the journalistic competence of football reporters. One example of this type of coverage was *The Daily Record*'s reporting in March 2000 of a proposed rights issue by Rangers plc. Its back page headline was the unambiguous '*£100m*', accompanied by the byline: '*Rangers chief unveils the deal that puts Scottish football in the shade*' (31 March 2000, p. 80). The inside back pages were also devoted to the story, with the paper

Exhibit 5.4   Reporting the proposed Rangers rights issue

WHERE THE MONEY COMES FROM	WHERE THE MONEY WILL GO
• £53m from a new share issue in the club	• £50m to clear off Rangers' debt
• £20m from season ticket holders and corporate deals	• £20m to buy new players for next season
• £20m from a new TV deal	• £10m to build Rangers' new youth academy
• £10m from floating Rangers FC on stock exchange	• £20m of cash at the bank

Source: *The Daily Record*, March 31, 2000, 79

helpfully providing an income and expenditure box to explain where the money was coming from and how it would be used (see Exhibit 5.4).

Close inspection, however, reveals that these numbers simply do not substantiate the back page headline claim. First, only two of the apparent inflows – the rights issue and the flotation – would actually contribute new capital or funds. Furthermore, the journalist is apparently confusing the possibility of raising funds in these ways with a certain outcome – some years later, for example, Rangers has still not floated on the Stock Exchange. Second, the other sources of income are of course recurring income sources. Yet the expenditure side does not include recurring expenditure such as player wages, arguably the reason why the club ran up debts of £50m in the first place. All told it is a rather meaningless piece of journalism. Yet many readers, with little expertise in matters of corporate finance, may well have taken the headline and its byline at face value.

One sports journalist, *The Herald*'s Chief Sports Writer, Graham Spiers, then writing for *Scotland on Sunday* and *The Guardian*, commented on the sway of key decision makers in the Scottish game, using the £100m rights issue to illustrate his case. Speaking of the influence Rangers' Chairman, David Murray, appeared to exert over sections of the Scottish press, he observed that:

Murray has a great knack of being a puppeteer of newspapers. When you read some versions of what he is doing at Rangers, the impression is gleaned that he has almost become the sports editor of certain tabloids. He tosses financial figures into the air which are dutifully reproduced, usually with a grand sense of inflation which allows the arithmetic to be pumped up a bit. Last week, for instance, at Murray's obvious behest, the Rangers rights issue, which might have trouble reaching its £53m goal was effortlessly translated by one paper into a £100m beanfeast for Ibrox.

(*Scotland on Sunday*, 2 April 2000)

Driven by a content-hungry media, there appears little sign that the importance of the business of sport is set to diminish. Furthermore, as clubs have adopted more business-like structures, there is evidence of increased demands from one of football's key stakeholders, the supporters, for improved accountability and transparency in clubs' business activities. One challenge faced by sports desks will be their willingness to add business expertise to their personnel, as this part of the football industry becomes increasingly important. There is some evidence that this is happening with almost all of the broadsheet newspapers now retaining at least one journalist whose remit includes reporting about the business of sport. In the tabloid press, however, it seems more likely that no similar expansion will take place and instead celebrity driven stories will increase as the commercial importance of the sports star continues to grow (Andrews and Jackson, 2001).

Conclusion

'Football? Bloody hell!'

(Alex Ferguson, Camp Nou, Barcelona, May 1999)

With these words Alex Ferguson, the latest in a long line of Scottish managers including Matt Busby, Bill Shankly and Jock Stein, who emerged from Scotland's industrial heartlands of the 1950s and 1960s, greeted the triumph of Manchester United, arguably the world's most business-oriented football club, in the 1999 Champions' League final. Football has changed since the days when Ferguson was an apprentice welder in the shipyards on Glasgow's River Clyde. Certainly the communities and people of Glasgow, Manchester and elsewhere have changed too. But was football more 'the people's game' in the 1950s and 1960s than it is now? Was United's 1999 triumph greeted any less enthusiastically or passionately than its 1968 European Cup victory under Busby? Did the 1968 triumph really mean more to 'the people'?

Football's business significance arises from the game's enduring social and communal appeal. But its lasting allure does not mean that football and its people will not continue to change. The test is to ensure that future changes, whether concerned with league structures, organizational form, communication or whatever, reflect the wishes and aspirations of as many of football's people as possible. Certainly, seeking inclusivity in contemporary football is a challenge. It is also an opportunity.

At the present time there is no evidence to suggest that clubs, however structured or organized, will lose their pivotal role in football in the future. Already, examples exist in different countries of clubs that operate in ways that can be described as inclusive. Many clubs are working to improve communication with supporters and with communities and to ensure that communication is a two-way dialogue rather than a dialogue of the deaf. This involvement and cooperation is likely to be beneficial, not only in ensuring better understanding of the role of clubs as social institutions, but also from a financial or business perspective – a club involving and including in its decision making and planning the community which is the major contributor to its revenue is entirely wise and rational. Furthermore, such involvement may help to reduce the financial expectations gap which often exists between supporters and directors. Fuller disclosure of information and heightened communication will enable supporters to understand better the operating and financial risks faced by club directors and managers.

Best practice is to be encouraged, of course. But when it really matters, it is inescapable that while some of football's communities have sufficient power to look after their own interests unaided, other communities or stakeholders – often those whose objectives are likely to encompass social concerns – are powerless. This is why governing bodies must take a leading and proactive role. At one level this must take the form of leading debate about fundamental issues of policy – such as, say, the structure of competitions or the distribution of income therein – rather than being seen to react to pressure or circumstances. More pragmatically, it also about putting in place an infrastructure for clubs that formalizes best practice in terms of communication, accountability and stakeholder involvement. UEFA's club licensing system, though seen as bureaucratic and unwieldy by some, is a step in the right direction. In addition to setting criteria to do with, for example, sporting issues and financial issues, an opportunity exists to extend these criteria to encompass social or societal dimensions. For example, in keeping with developments in areas like corporate social responsibility, clubs should be required to provide statements or reports on community involvement or supporter communication; reports which would deal not only with policy and aspiration, but importantly also with action.

Challenges also exist for football's communities. Like it or not, business involvement in football is irreversible. The challenge for supporters and others is to harness football's business dimensions for the good of its social role. Being run in a business-like way need not equate to being run for the benefit of business people. Beyond that it also means engaging in debate about the direction of football, being open to discussion and change on issues ranging from league reconstruction and income distribution through to more mundane things like club locations. Football supporters must seek to influence changes in football, rather than being left only to react to them.

Football can be viewed as a cooperative activity: an activity that relies on the coming together of financial capital, human capital and social capital. These capital providers are unlikely ever to share identical objectives. Nevertheless, if there is an institutional framework that encourages co-operation and if there is a willingness on the part of different constituencies to co-operate, then inevitably there will be increased opportunities for goal congruence and for outcomes that result in more winners than losers. What is required is continuing reinterpretation of how contemporary football clubs interact and affect their communities, both economically and socially. Modernization and strengthening of the relationship between clubs, supporters and communities can position football for the challenges ahead. Football changes, people change: but football can remain 'the people's game'.

Appendix 1: Football Business Coverage

Coverage of political and economic issues arising from Scotland's proposed bid to host the European 2008 Football Championships

	Day/Date (Jan 2002)	*Section*	*Details*
Newspaper (Broadsheet)			
The Scotsman	Wed 16	News	Front page headline 'Euro 2008 will create 7,000 jobs' (p. 1, $1/4$ page) 'Euro Bid could still be a winner' (p. 6, $1/2$ page)
		Editorial	'Why Scotland should go for Euro 2008 goal' (p. 13, $1/6$ page)
The Herald	Wed 16	Sport	'Delay may end Scots Euro Bid (p. 29, $1/12$ page)
The Daily Telegraph	Wed 16	Sport	'Scots may lose chance to bid for Euro 2008' (p. S2, $1/6$ page)
The Independent	Wed 16	Sport	'Scotland's Euro 2008 bid at risk' (p. 22, $1/10$ page)
The Times	Wed 16	Sport	'It's now or never for Scots' 2008 Bid' (p. 1,715 words)
The Herald	Thurs 17	Sport	'UK Sport pledge to support Euro bid', (p. 36 [back], $1/12$ page)
The Scotsman	Thurs 17	News	'Euro 96 director urges executive to back Scots bid for championship' (p. 1, $1/6$ page)
		Editorial	'Scotland and Euro 2008', (p. 5, $1/4$ column)

	Day/Date (Jan 2002)	Section	Details
The Scotsman	Fri 18	News	'UK Sport steps in to boost Euro 2008 hopes' (p. 11, $\frac{1}{8}$ page)
The Scotsman	Sat 19	Sport	'Tactics open to question as 2008 bid caught flat-footed' (p. 5, $\frac{1}{2}$ page)
		Column	'Sorry but Scots can't budget for going solo' (p. 5, $\frac{1}{3}$ page)
The Sunday Herald	Sun 20	Sport	'Football's fourth estate must get behind Scotland's bid' (p. 9, $\frac{1}{4}$ page)
The Observer	Sun 20	News	'McConnel blow to Euro 2008' (p. 1 [front], $\frac{1}{4}$ page)
		Column	'We're up for the Cup' (p. 23, $\frac{1}{4}$ page)
The Scotsman	Mon 21	Editorial	'Euro 2008 still a winner' (p. 13, $\frac{1}{12}$ page)

Newspaper (Tabloid)

	Day/Date (Jan 2002)	Section	Details
The Daily Record	Tues 15th	News	'Political Football', (pp. 8,9, $1\frac{1}{2}$ pages)
		Editorial	'Your choice' ($\frac{1}{4}$ column)
The Daily Mail	Tues 15th	Sport	'Euro bid is harmed by Executive indecision' (p. 80 [back], $\frac{1}{8}$ page)
The Daily Record	Wed 16	News	Front page exclusive '60% Say No to Scots Euro 2008' (p. 1, $\frac{1}{8}$ page, p. 8, $\frac{1}{4}$ page) 'The high price of being a lowly soccer nation' (p. 16, $\frac{1}{2}$ page)
The Daily Mail	Wed 16	News	'Game plan for Euro 2008 in turmoil as McConnel wavers' (p. 18, $\frac{1}{3}$ page)
The Daily Record	Thurs 17	News	'Pay up £100m to get Euro 2008' (p. 2, $\frac{1}{3}$ page)

	Day/Date (Jan 2002)	Section	Details
The Sun	Thurs 17	News	'Euro 2008 will mean 7000 jobs' (p. 7, $^1/_{12}$ page)
The Daily Record	Fri 18	Editorial	'Euro bid more than a game', (p. 8, $^1/_8$ page)
The Sun	Fri 18	News	'Jack snubs Euro 2008 Money bid' (p. 9, $^1/_8$ page)
The Daily Record	Sat 19	News column	'Let's put our money where our mouth is' (p. 13, $^1/_2$ page)
The Sunday Mail	Sun 20	Column (Wilson)	'Don't miss Euro goal' (p. 32, $^1/_{16}$ page)
The Daily Record	Mon 21	Sport column	'It's time to kick Euro 2008 into touch Jack' (p. 3, 1 page)

The financial and sporting implications arising from the SPL's proposal to set up its own TV station

Newspaper (Broadsheet)

The Herald	Wed 16	News	Front page lead 'Breakaway TV channel planned by Scots clubs' (p. 1, $^1/_4$ page)
		Editorial	'SPL makes TV its new goal' (p. 15, $^1/_8$ page)
The Scotsman	Wed 16	Sport	'SPL set to go it alone on TV deal' (p. 24 [back], $^1/_6$ page)
The Daily Telegraph	Wed 16	Sport	'Top clubs switched on by TV plan', (p. S2, $^1/_{12}$ page)
The Times	Wed 16	Sport	'SPL chiefs agree to dedicated TV channel' (p. 1, 158 words)
The Scotsman	Thurs 17	Sport column	'SPL TV deal looks like pie in the sky ' (p. 22 [back], $^1/_6$ page)
The Herald	Thurs 17	News	'Analysts urge caution over SPL channel' (p. 10, $^1/_6$ page)
The Herald	Sat 19	Sport	'Do not adjust your set' (interview with John Boyle '(p. 3, $^1/_2$ page)

	Day/Date (Jan 2002)	Section	Details
Scotland on Sunday	Sun 20	Sport	'Scottish clubs hopeful that Sky is not the limit as they bid to beef up their television revenues' (p. 10, $\frac{1}{4}$ page)
The Sunday Herald	Sun 20	Sport column	'SPL's television dreams distinctly out of focus' (p. 7, $\frac{1}{4}$ page)
The Sunday Herald	Sun 20	News	'SMG and Kirsty Wark in bid for SPL channel' (p. 10, $\frac{1}{6}$ page)
The Sunday Times	Sun 20	Business	'City lines up to kick off SPL TV' (p. 3 [Business], $\frac{1}{8}$ page)
The Sunday Times	Sun 20	Business	'Scottish agenda – SPLTV plan just might pull off the shock of the season' (p. 8, [Business], $\frac{1}{12}$ page)

Newspaper (Tabloid)

	Day/Date (Jan 2002)	Section	Details
The Daily Record	Wed 16	Sport	'Armchair fans get a tellyful' (pp. 48[back], 44, $\frac{1}{4}$ page)
The Daily Mail	Wed 16	Sport	'SPL set to sell their own TV right' (pp. 80 [back], 78, $\frac{1}{4}$ page)
The Sun	Wed 16	Sport	'SPL Fantasy Channel' (p. 52 [back], $\frac{1}{8}$ page)
The Daily Mail	Fri 18	Sport Column	'SPL correct to go down TV channel' (p. 92, $\frac{1}{6}$ page)
The Daily Record	Fri 18	Sport column	'SPL's channel can work – but it will be tough' (p. 75, $\frac{1}{3}$ page including photograph)
The Sun	Sat 19	Sport	'SPL TV to get great reception' (p. 64, $\frac{1}{10}$ page)

	Day/Date (Jan 2002)	Section	Details
The Daily Record	Sat 19	Sport	'SPL TV in battle against the clock' (p. 66, $1/10$ page)
The Sunday Mail	Sun 20	Sport column	'Placing big bets on telly gamble' (p. 84, $1/3$ page)

Issues arising from the redevelopment/financing of Wembley Stadium

Newspaper (Broadsheet)

The Guardian	Wed 16	Sports	'Wembley team to be cut' (p. 29, $1/6$ page)
The Herald	Wed 16	Sports	'Troubled Wembley appoint new board' (p. 32, $1/8$ page)
The Guardian	Wed 16	Sports	'Crozier stays in Wembley team' (p. 28, $1/16$ page)
The Independent	Wed 16	Sports	'New focus for Wembley '(p. 22, $1/12$ page)

Financial difficulties at East Fife FC

Newspaper (Broadsheet)

The Scotsman	Wed 16	Sports	'Debts forces out East Fife boss' (p. 23, $1/16$ page)
The Herald	Wed 16	Sports	'Frustrated Clarke quits East Fife' (p. 28, 3 short paragraphs)

Tabloid

The Daily Record	Wed 16	Sports	Resignation of East Fife manager (p. 43, 50 words)
The Daily Mail	Wed 16	Sport	Resignation of East Fife manager (p. 79, 50 words)

IG index spread betting profits

Newspaper (Broadsheet)

The Times	Tues 15	Business	'City Diary: Painful kick' (p. 22, one paragraph plus small photo).

	Day/Date (Jan 2002)	Section	Details
The Guardian	Wed 16	Finance	'Net result: Beckham goal hits IG profit' (p. 21, $1/16$ page plus photo $1/6$ page)

The ownership and financial position of Dundee United: the return of Jim McLean as Chairman

Newspaper (Broadsheet)

The Herald	Thurs 17	Sport	'McLean says he'll sue old United board' (p. 33, $1/4$ page)
The Scotsman	Thurs 17	Sport	'Unmuzzled Mclean shoots from the hip' (p. 20, $1/2$ page)

Newspaper (Tabloid)

The Daily Mail	Thurs 17	Sport	'Terrier McLean aims to put the bite on £4m debt' (p. 82, full page)
The Daily Record	Thurs 17	Sport	'Betrayed: treat of legal action as McLean claims old board lied' (p. 64, $2/3$ page)
The Sun	Thurs 17	Sport	'I've been wearing a muzzle for last few weeks and it doesn't suit me' (pp. 54,55, 1 page)

Proposed co-operative purchasing venture among Scottish clubs

Newspaper (Tabloid)

The Daily Record	Thurs 17	Sport	'Clubs to shop as co-op' (p. 62, $1/12$ page)

Financial difficulties at Celtic plc

Newspaper (Broadsheeet)

The Herald	Fri 18	Sport	'Celtic's "missing"millions were used to repay the Co-operative bank loan' (p. 38 [back], $1/8$ page)

	Day/Date (Jan 2002)	Section	Details
The Herald	Fri 18 *(cont.)*		'Why Celtic are staring at a financial abyss with little hope of escape' (p. 34, 1 page including photographs)
The Guardian	Sat 19	Sport	'Lack of funds a cause for O'Neill concern', (p. 17, $^1/_6$ page)

Niall Quinn's decision to donate his testimonial proceeds to charity

Newspaper (Broadsheeet)

The Sunday Times	Sun 20	News	'Footballer to give £1m testimonial to charity' (pp. 1, 2 [front], $^1/_6$ page, $^1/_4$ page)
The Sunday Times	Sun 20	Sport	'Thanks a million', (p. 13 [Sport], 1 page)
The Scotsman	Mon 21	News	'Footballer's gift to charity restores the image of the beautiful game' (p. 7, $^1/_8$ page)
The Independent	Mon 21	News	'Football's other face: A player pledging £1m to charity', (p. 3, $^2/_3$ page)
The Independent	Mon 21	Editorial	'Casting out greed' (p. 3 [Review], $^1/_{16}$ page)

Newspaper (Tabloid)

The Sun	Mon 21	News	'One Quinn in a million' (p. 13, $^1/_2$ page)

Other stories

Newspaper (broadsheet)

Financial difficulties at York City

The Independent	Fri 18	Sport Column (Conn)	'Chairman's threat leaves the future of York in doubt' (p. 20, $^2/_3$ page including photograph)

Day/Date (Jan 2002)	Section	Details

Financial difficulties in the Football league

The Daily Telegraph	Fri 18	Sport Column (Bose)	'Football League plan new regional system with play-offs as clubs fear the effects of economic instability' (p. S4, $2/3$ page including photograph)

Argentina's financial crisis

The Daily Telegraph	Fri 18	Sport	'Crisis as football clubs fear the backlash from Argentina's bankruptcy' (p.S5, $1/8$ page)

The business of Rushden and Diamonds

The Times	Sat 19	Sport	'Griggs realistic in his attempts to achieve the max' (p. 31, $1/6$ page)

Bonds to guarantee financial commitments

The Independent	Sat 19	Sport	'Bond idea may save league clubs from collapse', (p. 26, 532 words)

Hampden debentures – no CL final

Scotland on Sunday	Sun 20	Sport	'Anger over Hampden debentures' (p. 2, $1/16$ page)

The search for alternatives to TV cash

The Observer	Sun 20	Sport	'Cash-hit clubs warned beware of branding' (p. 7, $1/4$ page)

Newspapers sampled

	Tues	Wed	Thurs	Fri	Sat	Sun	Mon
Herald	✓	✓	✓	✓	✓		✓
Scotsman	✓	✓	✓	✓	✓		✓
Daily Telegraph	✓	✓	✓	✓	✓		✓
Times	✓	✓	✓	✓	✓		✓
Independent	✓	✓	✓	✓	✓		✓
Guardian	✓	✓	✓	✓	✓		✓
Sun	✓	✓	✓	✓	✓		✓
Daily Mail	✓	✓	✓	✓	✓		✓
Daily Record	✓	✓	✓	✓	✓		✓
Sunday Times						✓	
Sunday Herald						✓	
Scotland on Sunday						✓	
Mail on Sunday						✓	
Sunday Mail						✓	
Observer						✓	

Notes

1 For a more detailed consideration of the link between resources and performance in elite Scottish football see Murphy (1999b). Over the period 1946–99, Murphy found that the performance gap between the top and bottom clubs was narrowing, but that the likelihood that the Championship would be won by either Celtic or Rangers was increasing.

2 Sometimes complex economic analysis is unnecessary. Half way through season 2001/02, a 5-year-old girl was taken to see her first ever football match, Celtic v Hibernian, at Celtic Park. Before the first half was over, with the score at 2–0 in favour of the home team, her question succinctly summed up Scottish football's problems: '*Daddy, why are they only using one of the nets?*' Furthermore, one Scottish newspaper, *The Sunday Herald*, is now publishing a hypothetical weekly league table entitled 'Life Without the Old Firm' which sets out what the SPL would look like without Celtic or Rangers matches.

3 For analysis of the nature of this rivalry see, for example, Bradley, 1998; Finn, 1991a, b; Murray, 1984, 1998.

4 For further discussion on the competitive imbalance in the SPL and its consequences, see *Soccer Investor* (2002e).

5 The teams were Milan, Inter, Juventus, Bayern Munich, Borussia Dortmund, Werder Bremen, Real Madrid, Barcelona, Atlético Madrid, Manchester United, Liverpool and Arsenal. The data only run from 1991 for England, as English clubs were banned from European competition for the previous given years (Hoehn and Szymanski, 1999).

6 In the UK, the OFT (Office of Fair Trading) challenged the lawfulness of the Premier League selling collective rights on behalf of its member clubs. However, the challenge was rejected by the Restrictive Practices Court, which took the view that these arrangements did not operate against the public interest. The Court accepted that the collective arrangements helped promote competitive balance between clubs within football, which was recognised as beneficial to the public interests (Cave, 2000).

7 Spanish clubs have been permitted to negotiate television rights individually since 1996/97 for seasons until 2002/03. One consequence has been an overall increase of 408 per cent for all clubs' television revenues. Real Madrid's deal with Canal Satellite Digital is worth €43m pa on average while Barcelona's deal with Via Digital is worth €43.8m pa on average (Allen, 2001).

8 The strength of this apparent relationship as a predictive tool is questioned by Gerrard (2002). He notes that the authors' reliance on one regression statistic (R^2) combined with use of long term averages and a sample made

up of clubs of very different size makes the goodness-of-fit between wage expenditure and league position unsurprising.

9   Having topped the table during the season, Ipswich Town ultimately finished 5th in the FA Premiership in season 2000/01, thus qualifying for the UEFA Cup. However, the club was subsequently relegated to the Nationwide League at the end of the following season. In Italy Chievo spent several weeks at the summit of Serie A during season 2001/02, resulting in qualification for the 2002/03 UEFA Cup.

10 Proof of the financial difficulties caused by relegation was provided in February 2003 when Ipswich Town was granted a temporary administration order by the High Court to allow it to restructure its debts (*Soccer Investor*, 2003).

11 Much has been made in the press and elsewhere of the introduction of so-called wage caps by G14 clubs (from season 2005/06) as well as in the English Nationwide League (see, for example, 'Europe's elite agree to salary cap', *The Guardian*, 6 November 2002, 28; 'English clubs vote for salary cap', *The Scotsman*, 22 November 2002, 32). While salary caps were first introduced in the USA by the NBA in season 1984-85 (see, for example, Staudohar, 1999), what is being proposed in football is little more than voluntary wage restraint, with clubs agreeing to restrict their annual payments to employees to a specified percentage of turnover (70 per cent in the case of the G14 clubs, initially 60 per cent dropping to 50 per cent in the case of the Nationwide League). While this initiative is welcome, it is also evidently overdue. Besides, to many involved in business, it is scarcely credible that these organizations should have allowed a situation to develop such that they were obliged to publicize as a good news story a financial management initiative which is little more than economic common sense.

12 The G14 group of clubs is an economic interest grouping set up to look after the interests of some of Europe's top clubs. Its original membership was 14 clubs; AC Milan, Ajax, Barcelona, Bayern Munich, Borussia Dortmund, Inter Milan, Juventus, Liverpool, Manchester United, Olympique Marseille, Paris St Germain, Porto, PSV Eindhoven and Real Madrid. It was expanded in 2002 by the admission of four new members: Arsenal, Bayer Leverkusen, Olympique Lyonnais and Valencia.

13 One persuasive voice has been that of Alan Leighton, then Vice Chairman of Leeds United plc (see, for example, 'Power hungry with fewer mouths to feed', *The Independent on Sunday*, 8 December 2002, p. 15).

14 Although, it should be noted that this was part of a contractual structure that many viewed as being unfair, with young talented players being locked into contracts which not only often carried low or very basic terms, but also were often for very long time periods.

15 The coefficient is dependent on the performance of teams in the European Cups during a five year period. During that period each team gets two points for a win and one point for a draw. From 1999 on these points are

halved for qualification matches: one point for a win and half a point for a draw. One bonus point is allocated for reaching the quarter final, the semi final and the final. Reaching the first round of the Champions League yields one bonus point. The UEFA coefficients are calculated by taking an average, based on the total number of points divided by the total number of teams of each country (UEFA, 2002b).

16 UEFA is solely responsible for exploiting the commercial rights to the UEFA Champions' League (UEFA, 2002b, para. 24.05). These include media contracts, advertising rights, merchandising and licensing rights (Annex VII, para. 2.1). Gate receipts are retained by the home club (para. 24.04).

17 In a discussion on UEFA's failure to consult it about modifications to be made to the Champions' League, the G14's website notes that its members 'request that the distribution of proceeds, both for the Champions League and the UEFA Cup, maintain the privileges of the 5 largest leagues.' www.g14.com accessed 11 December 2002.

18 However, it is also worth remembering that many of the same clubs that are now disadvantaged by the UEFA Champions' League system – clubs like Celtic, Rangers, PSV Eindhoven and Ajax – have acted in not dissimilar ways domestically, either pushing for breakaway leagues such as the SPL or for the abandonment of collective television deals (Netherlands), changes motivated by their desire to secure a greater share of domestic income at the expense of some or all of their domestic competitors.

19 Current ethical requirements indicate that 15 per cent (or 10 per cent in the case of limited companies) would be an unduly large proportion of gross income to earn from one client.

20 For example, in the late 1980s Tottenham Hotspur made unsuccessful attempts to diversify its business away from core football activities, getting involved in sportswear, women's fashion and ticketing.

21 All the deals arranged between clubs and Stream for 2002/03 were for the same amount as season 2001/02 (AS Roma – €37.2m; SS Lazio – €32m; Parma – €24.8m; Bologna – €13.4m and Udinese €12.9m). Similarly, the deals arranged between Torino (€8m) and Reggina (€7m) and the broadcaster Telepiu for 2002/03 were the same as the 2001/02 deals (*Soccer Investor*, 2002a).

22 According to the Sir Norman Chester Centre for Football Research (SNCCFR, 2002), football is now available on almost every night of the week, with some estimates putting the volume of football available at the weekend at 70 hours.

23 See, for example, 'Clubs need more say in League', *The Financial Times*, 15 October 1998, p. 2; 'UEFA response to proposed Super League', *The Mirror*, 3 October 1998, p. 39; 'UEFA moves to head off Atlantic league', *The Guardian*, 8 February 2001, p. 32 or 'Atlantic League heading for UEFA Collision', *Sunday Business*, 4 February 2001, p. 47.

24 Although it must be noted that the G14 has made clear its refusal to create a competition outside official structures, i.e. other than under the auspices of UEFA (www.g14.com).

25 Arguably, the decision to allow Manchester United to take part in the inaugural World Club Championship in January 2000, rather than the FA Cup, suggests that some clubs are already considered as trans-national organizations.

26 See, for example, 'Celtic Director fans Atlantic League flames' (www.sportbusiness.com, 1 March 2001) or 'Atlantic league or bust' (www.sportbusiness.com, 25 April 2002).

27 Sportsound, BBC Radio Scotland, 3 August 2002.

28 See, for example, 'UEFA in cool response to North Atlantic Cup project', *The Independent*, 5 August 2002, p. 9, or 'North Atlantic League cup? Give us a break', *The Daily Record*, 5 August 2002, p. 3.

29 See, for example, 'Digger: Secret talks boost hopes of a breakaway', *The Guardian*, 31 August 2002, Sport, 11.

30 While a similar discussion could be had about say Dutch clubs participating in the German Bundesliga, the argument is more advanced in the UK, primarily due to the fact that although Scotland and England are separate footballing nations, politically of course, the nation state is the United Kingdom.

31 For example, the first Old Firm match televised live throughout the UK on Sunday 6th October 2002 drew an audience of 3.4 million, equivalent to 35 per cent of the viewing audience. By comparison, only 1.7 million people watched Sky's live coverage of England's friendly with Portugal in September 2002 ('3.4m TV viewers', *The Daily Mail*, 8 October 2002, p. 85).

32 Clubs in several European countries receive media income arising from their domestic league being broadcast overseas. In addition, major clubs like Manchester United and Barcelona derive substantial income from merchandise sold overseas.

33 Further indication of the possibility of a legal challenge has come from political sources, with Toine Manders, a Dutch Liberal Democrat and Reform MEP, asking the European Commission to investigate whether UEFA is acting as a monopoly in thwarting attempts to set up a cross-border league and is in breach of European trust laws (Chaudhary, 2001).

34 See numerous newspapers in October and November 2001. See also Harding (2003).

35 Rosen and Sanderson (2001) provide a good example of the importance of technology to explain the difference between sportstars' rents with those of teachers, suggesting that when teachers start to use the Internet and other media like distance learning to teach large numbers of students at the one time, then teachers will be rewarded similarly to sportstars.

36 Within a market for superstars, Lucifora and Simmons (2003) note that several factors would be expected to moderate the extreme earnings of football players compared to other entertainers: first, that supporters

normally support a team and not individual players and relatedly that their judgement of people playing for an opposing team may not be objective; second, the nature of team sports means that it may be difficult to separate out an individual's contribution; third, supporters may have preferences for different styles of play and fourth, in football each match is different and supporters value live performances (on television or in the stadium) more than video replays. (See also section on 'Supporters', in particular the classification set out in Figure 2.1.)

37 Administration is a procedure that places a company under the control of an insolvency practitioner and the protection of the court, in order to achieve one or more of the statutory purposes. The effect of an Administration Order is that there is an immediate moratorium which effectively precludes any action by any creditor without leave of the court or the consent of the administrator (Section 11, Insolvency Act 1986)

38 The full list of super-creditors includes amounts due under players' contracts, amounts owed to other clubs and amounts due to the FA, the Football League and Football Trust, the PFA, the Inland Revenue and HM Customs & Excise.

39 See, for example, Elliot (2000), Horrie (2002b) and Simpson (2002).

40 British football's recent history is replete with supporter-led campaigns, the purpose of which has been to save their particular club.

41 The 30 clubs were: (England) Arsenal, Aston Villa, Bradford City, Chelsea, Coventry City, Derby County, Everton, Leeds United, Leicester City, Liverpool, Manchester United, Middlesbrough, Newcastle United, Sheffield Wednesday, Southampton, Sunderland, Tottenham Hotspur, Watford, West Ham United and Wimbledon; (Scotland) Aberdeen, Celtic, Dundee, Dundee United, Heart of Midlothian, Hibernian, Kilmarnock, Motherwell, Rangers and St Johnstone.

42 This underlining is often located in the community sections of club web pages and/or in the case of many English clubs, customer charters, as required by the FA Premier League, which are provided in electronic form on club sites. However, as communities change, so too do websites. Hence some of these pages are likely to change and develop.

43 Under Schedule 7(3)-(5) of the Companies Act 1985, UK companies are required to disclose any cash donations above a nominal amount of £200 in their Annual Reports.

44 No research has been carried out as part of this project into the community involvement of clubs outside the UK. However, one project, which is worthy of note, is the Inter Futura project at Inter Milan. It aims to reach out to children in under-privileged areas. The project combines soccer with education, using Inter as an incentive to motivate the children in their education. It is a global project, which has been in places as diverse as Bosnia, Brazil and Palestine (interview with Jefferson Slack, Inter Active CEO, January 2002).

45 Recent evidence from the United States suggests that from a sporting perspective supporters are wise to encourage clubs to stay in their existing stadiums. In a study of professional baseball, basketball and ice-hockey games between 1987 and 2000, it was found that teams that moved stadiums lost 24 per cent of their home advantage. While this effect is most likely due to the lack of familiarity players have with their new ground, it was also suggested that players in the new ground are unlikely to have the same territorial passion of a team that has played at the same ground for years (Sample, 2003).

46 Hammam subsequently re-emerged as Chairman and owner of Cardiff City.

47 It has been questioned whether Koppel ever substantiated his claims that Wimbledon made genuine efforts to find a suitable ground in Merton or adjoining boroughs (Kelly, 2002). Indeed, he even offered backing to Plough Lane residents on the grounds that football supporters were undesirable neighbours. In a survey of its members carried out by the Football Fans Census, only 13 per cent agreed or strongly agreed that 'enough alternative solutions were explored by the club before deciding to move to Milton Keynes' (www.footballfanscensus.com)

48 In the United Kingdom, franchising normally refers to business format franchising popularized by companies like McDonald's and Shell. This involves the granting of a licence by one person (the franchiser) to another (the franchisee), which entitles the franchisee to trade under the trade mark/trade name of the franchiser and to make use of an entire package, comprising all the elements necessary to establish a previously untrained person in the business and to run it with continual assistance on a predetermined basis (www.british-franchise.org). This is quite separate from its meaning in the context of professional sport in the United States of America.

49 The FA commission rejected the claim that the Milton Keynes decision represented football's first franchise case, but the term was embraced enthusiastically by Wimbledon's partner in Milton Keynes, Pete Winkelman (White, 2003). The results of the survey of its members carried out by the Football Fans Census is interesting on this subject, with the respondents split. In response to the question, 'Do you think this move signals the start of franchising in English football?', 16 per cent said Definitely; 38 per cent said Probably; 34 per cent said Unlikely; 6 per cent No Way and 7 per cent Don't Know (www.footballfanscensus.com).

50 In other words to seek Pareto improvements, wherein a change is potentially good as long as the improvement in welfare of those who gain from a change is more than sufficient to compensate for those who lose.

51 Pareto-optimality is an evaluative principle according to which the community becomes better off if one individual becomes better off and none worse off (Albert and Hahnel, 1990).

52   Debate about organizational objectives has not, however, been restricted to football clubs. One of the issues considered in the UK's Company Law Review Consultation document was described as the 'scope' issue – 'in whose interests should companies be run' (Company Law Review Steering Group, 2000).

53   Growth in television income is one indicator of this increase. The annual rights fee for the 1988 four year deal between the old English First Division and ITV was £11.0m. This grew to £42.8m for the 1992 five year deal between the FA Premier League and BSkyB, and grew further to £167.5m for the 4 year deal that started in 1997 (Morrow, 1999, p. 5). See also Table 1.10.

54   The administrative offices issue depository shares that give certificate holders the right to attend and speak at shareholders' meetings and to call for extraordinary meetings. They have no votes; voting rights attached to shares can only be exercised by administrative offices. Furthermore, often the boards of these companies appoint themselves. This type of system therefore provides corporate management with the ability to entrench itself (Becht and Mayer, 2001, p. 32).

55   The International Accounting Standards Board is committed to developing, in the public interest, a single set of high quality, understandable and enforceable global accounting standards that require transparent and comparable information in general purpose financial statements (IASB, 2001).

56   For example, in the UK – The Cadbury Report (1992), The Combined Code (1998), The Company Law Review Steering Group (2000); in France – The Vienot Report (1999); in Denmark, The Nørby Committee (2001).

57   Other organizational forms that are common include partnerships, which are particularly prevalent among smaller businesses and among providers of professional services, and mutually structured organizations, which are common in sectors like financial services.

58   Interestingly a bid for ENIC's shares was made on 10 March 2003 by Kondar Limited, a private equity vehicle, whose sole director is Tottenham Chairman, Daniel Levy. The deal which valued ENIC at £40.3m reflected the ENIC directors' recognition of the likely need to invest further cash to fund and protect the value of its football investments and that such investment would be inappropriate without offering shareholders a cash exit at a fair price (see, for example, 'Cash bid to take ENIC private', *The Financial Times*, Companies and Finance, 11 March 2003, p. 23).

59   An association is defined in Article 2.26 of the Dutch Civil Code as being a corporate body with members, which aims to meet the needs of its members.

60   A foundation is defined in Article 2.258 of the Dutch Civil Code as a corporate body with no members, which aims to achieve a particular purpose as set out in its statutes with funds allocated to that end.

61 The first of these was Feyenoord's 2–1 victory over Celtic in the 1970 European Cup; the last being the same club's 2002 UEFA Cup victory over Borussia Dortmund.

62 See, for example, Giulianotti (1999, pp. 10–14).

63 This structure remains common among Dutch clubs today, most prominent among them being Feyenoord. However, moves have begun to alter this structure, which it is argued, restricts the competitiveness of clubs in the contemporary football business and which it is argued is not understood by anyone outside the organization (www.feyenoord.nl).

64 While Philips presently continues as PSV's main sponsor, it also has involvement with other sporting events. For example, at one level it was an official partner (global sponsor) of the 2002 World Cup in Seoul, at another it is the main sponsor of the European University Football League (press releases, www.philips.com).

65 In common with many European clubs, PSV has a hierarchical business partnership structure. At the top is the head sponsor, Philips, followed by 11 official business partners (including Bavaria NV, Canal Plus and Daimler Chrysler Nederland), seven official sponsors such as KPMG, seven official suppliers, 45 organizations that have 'business room en apartment', and 288 members of its Business Club (*PSV Business Yearbook 2001–2002*).

66 The PSV–PAOK Thessaloni UEFA Cup match in November 2001, was the first Dutch game to be shown on the Internet, and was watched by 16,000 people (interview with Fons Spooren, December 2001).

67 One of PSV's main competitors in the Dutch league, Feyenoord, carried out a comprehensive survey of 1,200 of its supporters, in which they were asked about their professions, and their usage of things like the Internet and mobile phones. The data collected allows them to improve their leveraging of their supporters, through, for example, being able to tell potential advertisers what the profile of their target audience is (Lambton, 2001).

68 Among other things, the new government has cut budgets to reduce public spending, particularly in the areas of civil society, human rights and overseas aid (Smith, 2002).

69 For example, SIF Fodbold Support was floated in the summer of 1989 to raise funds for active operation in the player market (Company information, Copenhagen Stock Exchange www.xcse.dk).

70 Company information, Copenhagen Stock Exchange, www.xcse.dk, accessed 30 May 2002.

71 Notwithstanding the importance of the decision to be taken by club members the unanimity among the members is unsurprising within the context of Danish associational culture. In fact, according to Ibsen (2001) 'it is expected that decisions are made in agreement and efforts are made to avoid decision-making procedures with indications of inequality or disagreement (for example, ballots)'.

72   The decision to run the club as an entertainment business was made explicitly, with Østergaard declaring publicly that he was going to run the club as 'FC Entertainment' (Brandt and Jyllands-Posten, 2002).

73   FCK's listing on the Copenhagen Stock Exchange in 1997 resulted in it having more than 6,500 shareholders (Brandt and Jyllands-Posten, 2002). By 2001, approximately 25 per cent of the shares in Parken are still owned by small supporter investors (interview with Dan Hammer, October 2001).

74   The gesture was also compensation for the fact that the FCK players did not acknowledge the supporters after the game, instead heading straight for the dressing rooms (interview with Anders Larsen, October 2001).

75   Per capita GDP 2000 (based on current purchasing power parities): Italy $25,100; UK $24,500; France $24,400; EU average $24,400 (OECD, 2002).

76   The takeover bid fronted by the then Fiat and Juventus owner, Gianni Agnelli for Italian conglomerate Montedison, was seen by some as the end of the *salotto buono*, as Montedison was controlled by Mediobanca, the Milanese merchant bank that had previously exercised substantial and unchallenged control over much of Italian industry (Edmondson, 2001). Agnelli died in January 2003.

77   Another example of the role of football in Italian society is the fact that the Italian national broadcaster, RAI, was reported to be considering taking legal action against FIFA for reimbursement for damages sustained by the company following the elimination of the Italian team from the World Cup due to inadequate refereeing (Gerlis, 2002a).

78   Italian clubs have won the European Champions' Cup on ten occasions, the Cup Winners Cup on six occasions and the UEFA Cup on nine occasions.

79   The Parmalat Finanziaria company acquired a 45 per cent holding in Parma in 1989. The President and CEO of Parma Calcio, Stefano Tanzi, is the son of Parmalat Finanziaria Chairman, Calisto Tanzi. Two other family members, Francesca Tanzi and Paolo Tanzi are also directors of Parma Calcio. The founding Tanzi family owns 51 per cent of Parmalat Finanziaria (www.parma.it).

80   However, it should also be noted that the failure of eight smaller Serie A clubs to secure television deals in the summer of 2002, resulted in Italy's major clubs (Inter, Juventus, Lazio, Milan, Parma and Roma) agreeing to forfeit about £4m (€5.8m) of their own television income in order to subsidize a collective agreement.

81   However, it should be noted that the Italian government has expressed its intention to review completely the tax system for individuals, with an anticipated top rate of income tax of 33 per cent coming into force in 2006. It is estimated that such a change would reduce the gross cost of labour for a club like Juventus by about €10m per annum (Banca IMI, 2002, p. 8).

82   By contrast, Szymanski and Kuypers (1999, p. 29) noted that 'the absence of a powerful relationship between changes in position and changes in profits is one of the most important regularities in the business of football. It implies that there is no simple formula that relates financial success to success on the pitch.'

83   However, sustainability can also becomes an issue even at a club like Inter, which might be considered to be one of the clubs acting as an upward force on player salaries. For example, it was reported that some of Inter's then top players – Reboca, Ronaldo and Vieri – had offered to take a 5 per cent pay cut to help the club through a period of financial difficulty (*Scotland on Sunday*, 14 July 2002, Sport, p. 10).

84   However, this is clearly an area that would benefit from some extensive empirical work.

85   Changing organizational structures in German football clubs are also of interest. Deutsche Fussball Bund (DFB) statutes previously stated that only teams that have a licence granted by the DFB could play in the *Bundesliga* and that such licences would only be granted to traditionally structured clubs (Dykes, 2000, p. 131). In October 1998, under pressure from its member clubs, the DFB changed its rules to allow publicly listed companies to take part in the Bundesliga championship. The resolution passed by the DFB allowed clubs to convert their professional activities into public limited companies (*Aktiengesellschaft* [AG]), limited liability companies (*Gesellschaft mit beschränkter* [GmbH]) or limited partnerships with share capital (*Kommanditgesellschaft auf Aktien* [KgaA]), provided that the original club (*Komplementär*) retained control (50 per cent plus one share) of the voting equity of the joint stock company. Recent evidence about the changing organizational structure of German football clubs is provided by Wilkesman and Blutner (2002) who for season 2000/01 provide a classification of German clubs as follows: 1) classical membership club structure defined as a registered society by the German Civil Code (e.g. FC Bayern München); 2) public limited company with supervisory board also defined as a registered society (e.g. FC Schalke 04) and 3) a jointstock company (e.g. BVB Dortmund GmbH & Co. KgaA).

86   This notion of stakeholder power and accountability arising out of the interaction of the political system and the media draws on Hellwig (2000, pp. 122–5).

87   For example, the rationale behind the Juventus Initial Public Offering (IPO) was to generate funds to acquire and develop its Delle Alpi stadium (see Chapter 3 – Italy).

88   The emergence of the *Supporters Direct* initiative can be seen as one response to unfettered market control of clubs precisely in the areas of ownership and governance (see, for example, Hamil *et al.*, 2001b) (see also Chapter 2). It is also worth noting that independent supporters

associations have long existed to contest other accepted notions of how a
football club should operate (Brown, 1998).

89   Recent press reports have concentrated on the stake building of Cubic
     Expression, a company linked to Irish multi-millionaires, JP McManus
     and John Magnier. It has become the major shareholder in the company,
     with a stake of 10.37 per cent (see, for example, 'Ferguson's allies up their
     stake in club', *Sunday Herald*, Sport, 9 March 2003, p. 9, or previously,
     'Man Utd shares net Edwards £22m', *The Independent*, Business, 29 May
     2003, p. 19). Other reports have focused on the share buying of Malcolm
     Glazer, owner of reigning Super Bowl American Football Champions,
     Tampa Bay Buccaneers and an investment firm linked to the chairman of
     Dutch TV Company Endemol and Dermot Desmond, a major shareholder
     in Celtic plc (see, for example, 'US Tycoon's stake building sparks Man
     Utd bid fever', *The Independent*, Business, 3 March 2003, p. 17). Perhaps
     more surprisingly, the club has also recently been linked with a proposal to
     convert it into a mutually structured organization owned by its supporters
     (see, for example, 'Secret move to hand Manchester United over to its
     fans', *The Sunday Times*, Business, 22 December 2002, p. 1).

90   However, as discussed in Chapter 3 (Denmark) recent political moves to
     the right may result in these traditions being transformed.

91   For example, an analysis of proxy votes cast at corporate meetings found
     that only 4.04 per cent of votes lodged at meetings are against management
     (Webb *et al.*, 2001).

92   Shleifer and Vishny (1997) argue that shareholders are in fact the
     stakeholders *least* able to influence management, as their investment has
     been sunk, and hence they require the greatest protection from expropria-
     tion by management.

93   Secondary trading volume figures are provided weekly by *Soccer Investor*.

94   The importance of being able to identify oneself as a supporter, in particular
     to members of a reference group (such as a fan club or a group denominated
     by their space in the stadium), was also noted by De Ruyter and Wetzels
     (2000). In response to the open question included in their questionnaire,
     several respondents indicated that they would buy the club's stock only if
     physical evidence would be issued in order to put it on the wall (p. 403).

95   For example, at time of BSkyB's bid for Manchester United, the focus of
     much supporter discontent was the then Chairman, Martin Edwards.
     However, at that time, Edwards held only 14 per cent of the shares, with
     the ownership of the club being highly dispersed. While his decision to
     recommend the bid to shareholders partly explains the hostility towards
     him, arguably it also reflected his public profile and identification as the
     public face of Manchester United plc, and the supporters' need for *someone*
     – as opposed to *something* like the dispersed ownership structure – to be
     held to account.

96   Cameron (1994), however, notes that Sugar's memories of supporting
     Tottenham Hotspur as a boy are somewhat vague, being unable to

remember the names of his side's famous FA Cup and League winning team of the 1960s.

97   Of course, as mentioned previously in this chapter the importance of personality is not new in football. For example, in the UK many businessmen became involved with football clubs because they saw it as a way of raising their profile in the community and of enhancing their status (Birley, 1985, p. 39; Crampsey, 1986, p. 21).

98   Other initiatives are actively encouraged by some leagues and associations or highlighted in club customer charters. Some examples include Supporter Liaison Forums, Fan Forums and Supporter Open Days.

99   For example, clubs were asked about things like providing access to the share register and its policy on questions at the AGM, while supporters were asked about things like how effective the club is in communicating with them and the effectiveness with which the club's Customer Charter is publicized to them (Binns *et al.*, 2002).

100 'The report from the Football Governance Research Centre at Birkbeck, University of London, was commissioned by Supporters Direct ... Supporters Direct [until 2003 based at Birkbeck College, University of London] was launched in 2000 to give legal and other assistance to supporters who want to play a greater role in the running of their clubs, including through the establishment of shareholder trusts' (Hamil *et al.*, 2001a, p. vii). Among the report's recommendations and suggestions? That 'supporter groups ... endeavour to "realise" their stake in the club by acquiring a shareholding and using shareholder rights ... [and that] the supporter trust, and in particular the supporter trust formed as an Industrial and Provident Society, is the way to achieve this' (p. 2) (Hamil *et al.*, 2001a, p. 2).

101 For example, it is worth noting that the supporter representative at Aberdeen, although a founder member of the Aberdeen Supporters' Trust, does not represent the Trust on the board, but rather was appointed to represent all supporters of the club.

102 However, the Government's White Paper on Company Law Review (DTI, 2002) proposes that large public and very large private companies should be required by law to prepare an OFR.

103 The UEFA club licensing manual is designed as a working document, compiled to help the national associations implement the guidelines and requirements of the UEFA club licensing system into a national club licensing system (UEFA, 2002a, p. 8).

104 This point was reinforced in 2002 as various corporate accounting scandals came to light, primarily but not exclusively in the United States. Some have argued that the structure of accounting and auditing in the UK makes such accounting scandals as, or more, likely in the UK than in the US (Mitchell and Sikka, 2002).

105 The International Accounting Standards Board is committed to developing, in the public interest, a single set of high quality, understandable and

enforceable global accounting standards that require transparent and comparable information in general purpose financial statements (IASB, 2001). However, it is not until 2005 that all EU-listed companies will be expected to use International Accounting Standards for their consolidated financial statements. At present the situation remains one of divergence in accounting standards.

106   Summary reports are usually not available until at least 12 months after the end of the relevant accounting period.

107   Prior to the introduction of FRS 10 in 1997, a wide variety of accounting policies were adopted by clubs in accounting for transfer fees (Morrow, 1995, 1999). The consequences of this discretionary accounting policy choice in respect of accounting for transfer fees and intangible asset recognition in the football industry are considered in Rowbottom (2003).

108   For example, the buy-out fee in Rivaldo's contract with Barcelona was £106 million. See 'Football in crisis over transfer deadline', *The Times*, 22 September 2000.

109   The problem of financial reporting failing adequately to reflect corporate assets is not, of course, unique to football clubs. For example, a large proportion of the assets of 'new economy' companies or research and development-based companies are also intangible in nature. See, for example, Vance (2001).

110   The existence of debt within a football club's capital structure is something which is often misunderstood or misinterpreted by the press, with debt almost inevitably being equated to financial difficulties.

111   Securitizations have been used in other areas of the entertainment business. The first-ever securitization of future royalties from rock music compositions took place in February 1997 with the sale of $55m of bonds backed by a catalogue of songs, compositions and copyrights on David Bowie's music (*The Financial Times*, 'David Bowie music backs bond issue', 5 February 1997, p. 38).

112   For example, an analysis of attendance records at Newcastle United over a 100 year period found that only during world wars had attendances been insufficient to cover loan covenants (Moller, 2000).

113   Despite the absence of disclosed information about these transactions, Deloitte & Touche's 2002 Annual Review of Football includes an estimate of the amount of funding (£120m) that had been raised by English clubs through these techniques. Interestingly, its report carries no critical analysis of these techniques or of the risks involved therein.

114   It is worth noting that UK GAAP, the bible of generally accepted accounting practice in the UK (Wilson *et al.*, 2001) has an extensive section on sale and leaseback (pp 1364–73), which suggests that there are so many variants that one would require inside knowledge to understand what was going on.

115   It should be noted that until 2002, Deloitte & Touche had made its annual reports available free of charge to students and educational establishments.

116 *Soccer Investor* claims to reach over 7,000 people working within the football industry including top clubs in 36 countries, marketing companies, lawyers, player management agencies, public relations companies and media companies.

117 See, Crolley and Hand (2002, pp. 1–15) for an overview.

118 Germany has a similar model to the UK, with football mainly being covered by mainstream newspapers (Crolley and Hand, 2002, p. 4).

119 *Business am*, Scotland's first national daily newspaper for more than one hundred years, was launched in September 2000. Unfortunately, however, its owners, Bonnier Media, closed it down in December 2002.

120 See Brett (2000, pp. 363–78), for an overview of the financial media in the UK.

121 The number of 'Finance and Investment' titles listed in the British and Irish Press Guide grew from 19 in 1874 to 109 by 1914, with a corresponding increase in the financial coverage to be found in other newspapers over the same period (Porter, 1998).

122 Stock market capitalization is the number of shares in issue in a company multiplied by its current share price.

123 Since its £1bn valuation, along with most other listed football clubs Manchester United plc's valuation and share price has fallen markedly. Two years later (11 March 2002) its market valuation was only £335.75m; by 14 November 2002 it had fallen further to £258.5m.

124 See, for example, 'Man Utd brakes through £1bn barrier: Football in favour – Old Footsie favourites make way for the new economy in shake up of market indices', *Financial Times*, 9 March 2000, Companies and Finance, p. 26; 'Billionaires United on course to rule the world', *Daily Mail*, March 9, 2000, pp. 92, 96; 'Man United worth £1 bn', *The Sun*, March 9, 2000.

125 Banks is also the author of *Football's Going Down* (Banks, 2002b).

126 Methodologically, of course, to provide a representative picture of the volume of football business reporting taking place, coverage in many more weeks would need to be considered. Study of disclosure in only one week leaves one open to the valid criticism that the week selected may not be representative of coverage more generally. Nevertheless, the survey provides an indication of the extent of coverage.

127 Indirectly, there may be an effect on a club's future resources. For example, should the club wish to raise capital in the future by means of a rights issue to existing shareholders, the price at which the rights issue is made (and hence the amount that is raised) will be affected by the current share price.

References

Albert, M. and Hahnel, R. (1990), A *Quiet Revolution in Welfare Economics*. (Princeton: Princeton University Press).

Allen, R. (2001), 'Mounting Debts Reign in Spain', *Football Business International*, Issue 1, September, 26–28.

Andrews, D.L. and Jackson, S.J. (2001), *Sports Stars: The Cultural Politics of Sporting Celebrity*. (London: Routledge).

Antonini, P. and Cubbin, J. (2000), 'The Bosman Ruling and the Emergence of a Single Market in Soccer Talent', *European Journal of Law and Economics*, vol. 9, no. 2, pp. 157–73.

Arnold, A. and Beneviste, I. (1987), 'Wealth and Poverty in the English Football League', *Accounting and Business Research*, vol. 17, no. 67, pp. 195–203.

ASB (1994), FRS 5 *Off Balance Sheet Transactions*. (London: The Accounting Standards Board).

ASB (1997), FRS 10 *Goodwill and Intangible Assets*. (London: The Accounting Standards Board).

ASB (2002), *Revision of the Statement 'Operating and Financial Review'*. (London: The Accounting Standards Board).

Baimbridge, M., Cameron, S. and Dawson, P. (1996), 'Satellite Television and the Demand for Football: A Whole New Ball Game', *Scottish Journal of Political Economy*, vol. 43, no. 3, pp. 317–33.

Bale, J. (2000), 'The Changing Face of Football: Stadiums and Communities', *Soccer and Society*, vol. 1, no. 1, 91–101.

Bale, J. (2002), 'New Football Stadia', *Soccer Review 2002*, pp. 53–7.

Banca IMI (2002), *Juventus Research Document*. (at www.borsaitalia.it/media/star/db/pdf/9129.pdf).

Banks, S. (2002a), 'Football Catches Enronitis', *Spiked Life, 12 September*. (at www.spiked-online.com).

Banks, S. (2002b), *Football's Going Down*. (Edinburgh: Mainstream).

Bannerman, C. (1997), *Against All Odds: The Birth of Inverness Caledonian Thistle*. (Inverness: Inverness Thistle and Caledonian FC plc).

Beattie, V. and Pratt, K. (2001), *Business Reporting: Harnessing the Power of the Internet for Users*. (Edinburgh: The Institute of Chartered Accountants of Scotland).

Becht, M. and Mayer, C. (2001), 'Introduction', in *The Control of Corporate Europe*, Barca, F. and Becht, M. (eds) (Oxford: Oxford University Press), pp. 1–45.

Bell, C., Benjamin, M. and Gumble, W. (2003), *'The Capital Crimes': Wimbledon/AFC Wimbledon, Barnet, Enfield/Enfield Town*. (Heswall: Hurrah Books).

Bellos, A. (2002), *Futebol: The Brazilian Way of Life*. (London: Bloomsbury).

Benjamim, A. (2002), 'Still less than half a percent', *The Guardian, Society*, 25 November. (at http://society.guardian.co.uk/givinglist/story/0,10994, 847359,00.html).

Bennie, D (1995), *Not Playing for Celtic: Another Paradise Lost*. (Edinburgh: Mainstream).

Bianchi, M., Bianco, M. and Enriques, L. (2001), 'Pyramidal Groups and the Separation between Ownership and Control in Italy', in *The Control of Corporate Europe*, Barca, F. and Becht, M. (eds) (Oxford: Oxford University Press), pp. 154–188.

Binns, S., Hamil, S., Holt, M., Michie, J., Oughton, C., Shailer, L. and Wright, K. (2002), *The State of the Game: The Corporate Governance of Football Clubs 2002*. Research paper 2002/03 for Supporters Direct. (London: Football Governance Research Centre).

Birley, D. (1995), *Land of Sport and Glory: Sport and British Society, 1887–1910*. (Manchester: Manchester University Press).

Bose, M. (1999), *Manchester Unlimited*. (London: Orion Business Books).

Boyle, R., Dinan, W. and Morrow, S. (2002), 'Doing the Business? The Newspaper Reporting of the Business of Football', *Journalism: Theory, Practice and Criticism*, vol. 3, no. 2, pp. 161–81.

Boyle, R. and Haynes, R. (2000), *Power Play: Sport, the Media and Popular Culture*. (Harlow: Longman).

Bradley, J. (1998), '"We Shall Not Be Moved"! Mere Sport, Mere Songs?', in *Fanatics! Power, Identity & Fandom in Football*, Brown, A. (ed.) (London: Routledge), pp. 203–18.

Brandt, H. and Jyllands-Posten (2002), 'Topping the Charts', *Soccer Analyst*, vol. 3, no. 2, pp. 27–30.

Brett, M. (1991), *How to Read the Financial Pages*. (London: Business Books).

Brett, M. (2000), *How to Read the Financial Pages: A Simple Guide to the Way Money Works and the Jargon*. (London; Random House Business Books).

Brook, K. (2002), 'Trade Union Membership: An Analysis of Data from the Autumn 2001 LFS', *Labour Market Trends*, vol. 110, no. 7, pp. 343–54.

Brown, A. (1998), 'United We Stand: Some Problems with Fan Democracy', in *Fanatics! Power, Identity & Fandom in Football*, Brown, A. (ed.) (London: Routledge), pp. 50–67.

Brown, A. (2000a), 'European Football and the EU: Governance, Participation and Social Cohesion – Towards a Policy Research Agenda', *Soccer and Society*, vol. 1, no. 2, pp. 129–50.

Brown, A. (2000b), 'The Football Task Force and the Regulator Debate', in *Football in the Digital Age: Whose Game is it Anyway*, Hamil, S., Michie, J., Oughton, C. and Warby, S. (eds) (Edinburgh: Mainstream), pp. 248–61.

Buckland, S. (1999), 'SPFA Alarm as 270 Players Confront Dole', *The Scotsman*, 24 June, p. 32.

Burke, G. (1998), *Parma: Notes from a Year in Serie A*. (London: Victor Gollancz, Cassel).

Burns, J. (1999), *A People's Passion*. (London: Bloomsbury).

Cadbury Report, The (1992), *Report of the Committee on the Financial Aspects of Corporate Governance (Chaired by Sir Adrian Cadbury)*. (London: Gee & Co.).

Caiger, A. and Gardiner, S. (eds) (2000), *Professional Sport in the EU: Regulation and Re-regulation*. (The Hague, Netherlands: T C M Hasser Press).

Caiger, A. and Gardiner, S. (2001), 'Re-regulating Professional Sport in the European Union', *Sports Law Bulletin*, March/April, pp. 10–12.

Cameron, C. (1994), 'Net Loss', *Management Today*, October, pp. 86–8.

Campbell, A. (2000), 'In the Shop Window', *The Sunday Herald*, 17 December, p. 7.

Campbell, D. (2000), 'Atlantic Plan is Best Sunk', *The Mirror*, 18 December, p. 20.

Campbell, D. (2001), 'For Sale: One Used Player', *The Observer*, 27 May, p. 9.

Campbell, D. (2002a), 'Spent Forces', *Observer Sport Monthly*, 5 May. (at www.observer.co.uk/osm/story/0,6903,708240,00.html).

Campbell, D. (2002b), 'European Football Revolution: The Blueprint', *The Observer*, Online extra, 3 February. (at http://www.observer.co.uk/sport/story/0,6903,644285,00.html).

Campbell, L., Gulas, C. S. and Gruca, T. S. (1999), 'Corporate Giving Behaviour and Decision-Maker Consciousness', *Journal of Business Ethics*, vol. 19, pp. 375–83.

Carlin, W. and Mayer, C. (1998), 'Finance, Investment and Growth', *University College London Discussion Papers in Economics, Paper 98–09*.

Carlin, W. and Mayer, C. (2000), 'How do Financial Systems Affect Economic Performance?', in *Corporate Governance*, Vives, X. (ed.) (Cambridge: Cambridge University Press), pp. 137–68.

Carr, P., Findlay, J., Hamil, S., Hill, J. and Morrow, S. (2001), 'The Celtic Trust', *Soccer and Society*, vol. 1, no. 3, pp. 70–87.

Cave, M. (2000), 'Football Rights and Competition in Broadcasting', in *Football in the Digital Age: Whose Game is it Anyway*, Hamil, S., Michie, J., Oughton, C. and Warby, S. (eds) (Edinburgh: Mainstream), pp. 180–90.

Chaudhary, V. (2001), 'Call for European Inquiry on Atlantic League', *The Guardian*, 1 February, Sport, 31.

CIA (2001), *The World Factbook 2001*. (Central Intelligence Agency). (at www.cia.gov/cia/publications/factbook/index.html).

CJEC (1995), *Judgement of the Court – Union Royale Belge des Sociétés de Football Association ASBL v Bosman. Case C-4415/93. 15 December.* (Court of Justice of the European Communities).

Clarke, R. (2002) *The Future of Sports Broadcasting Rights*. (London: SportBusiness Group).

Coalter, F. (2000), *The Role of Sport in Regenerating Deprived Urban Areas.* (Edinburgh: Scottish Executive Central Research Unit).

Cohen, N. and Guerrera, F. (2002), 'ENIC may be Forced to Cut Football Stakes', *The Financial Times*, 28 June, p. 24.

Combined Code, The (1998). (London: The London Stock Exchange).

Company Law Review Steering Group, The (2000), *Modern Company Law for a Competitive Economy: Developing the Framework* (Consultation document). (London: Department of Trade and Industry).

Conn, D. (1997), *The Football Business – Fair Game in the '90s?*. (Edinburgh: Mainstream).

Conn, D. (2002a), 'Barnsley's Fall is Ominous Sign for Game at Large', *The Independent*, 12 October, Sport, p. 7.

Conn, D. (2002b), 'Volunteers Left High and Dry as Clubs Look to Administrators', *The Independent*, 26 October, Sport, p. 7.

Cowie, C. and Williams, M. (1997), 'The Economics of Sports Rights', *Telecommunications Policy*, vol. 21, no. 7, pp. 619–34.

Cowton, C. J. (1987), 'Corporate Philanthropy in the United Kingdom', *Journal of Business Ethics*, vol. 6, pp. 553–58.

Crampsey, R. A. (1986), *The Economics of Scottish Professional Football*. (Glasgow: Scottish Curriculum Development Service).

Cresswell, P. and Evans, S. (2000), *The Rough Guide to European Football*. (London: Rough Guides).

Crolley, L. and Hand, D. (2002), *Football, Europe and the Press*. (London: Frank Cass).

Crowther, P. (2000), 'The Attempted Takeover of Manchester United by BSkyB', in *Football in the Digital Age: Whose Game is it Anyway*, Hamil, S., Michie, J., Oughton, C. and Warby, S. (eds) (Edinburgh: Mainstream), pp. 64–70.

Culyer, A. J. (1975), *The Economics of Social Policy*. (London: Martin Robertson).

De Jong, A., Kabir, R., Marra, T. and Röell, A. (2001), 'Ownership and Control in the Netherlands', in *The Control of Corporate Europe*, Barca, F. and Becht, M. (eds) (Oxford: Oxford University Press), pp. 188–207.

Dean, J. (2001), 'Public Companies as Social Institutions', *Business Ethics: A European Review*, vol. 10, no. 4, pp. 302–10.

Deloitte & Touche/Lega Calcio (1999), *Italian Football 1997/98: An Economic, Financial and Organizational Analysis*. (Milan: Deloitte & Touche/Lega Calcio).

Deloitte & Touche (2001a), *Il Calcio Italiano 2000 Analisi Economico – Finanziaria*. (Milan: Deloitte & Touche Sport).

Deloitte & Touche (2001b), *Deloitte & Touche Annual Review of Football Finance*. (Manchester: Deloitte & Touche).

Deloitte & Touche (2002a), *Deloitte & Touche Annual Review of Football Finance*. (Manchester: Deloitte & Touche).

Deloitte & Touche (2002b), *Comparative Review of Sports Finances*. (Manchester: Deloitte & Touche).

Demirag, I., Sudarsanam, S. and Wright, M. (2000), 'Corporate Governance: Overview and Research Agenda', *British Accounting Review*, vol. 32, pp. 341–54.

Demsetz, H. and Lehn, K. (1985), 'The Structure of Corporate Ownership: Causes and Consequences', *Journal of Political Economy*, vol. 93, no. 6, pp. 1155–77.

De Ruyter, K. and Wetzels, M. (2000), 'With a Little Help from My Friends – Extending Models of Pro-social Behaviour to Explain Supporters' Intentions to Buy Soccer Club Shares', *Journal of Economic Psychology*, vol. 21, pp. 387–409.

DGI (2002), Danske Gymnastik og Idraesforeninger. (at www.dgi.dk/forside/ sprog/engelsk.htm).

Dobson, S. and Goddard, J. (2001), *The Economics of Football*. (Cambridge: Cambridge University Press).

Dreier, P. (1982), 'Capitalism Versus the Media: An Analysis of an Ideological Mobilization Among Business Leaders', *Media, Culture and Society*, vol. 4, no. 2, pp. 111–32.

DTI (Department of Trade and Industry) (2002), *Modernising Company Law White Paper*, Command Paper CM5553-1. (London: HMSO).

Duke, V. (2002), 'Local tradition versus globalization: Resistance to the McDonaldization and Disneyization of Professional Football in England', *Football Studies*, vol. 5, no. 1, pp. 5–21.

Dykes, S. (2000), Commercialization and Fan Participation in Germany', in *Football in the Digital Age: Whose Game is it Anyway*, Hamil, S., Michie, J., Oughton, C. and Warby, S. (eds) (Edinburgh: Mainstream), pp. 129–35.

Dyson, J. (1992), *Accounting for Non-Accounting Students*. (London: Pitman)

EC Treaty, The (1997), *Treaty Establishing the European Community*. (Luxembourg: Office for Official Publications of the European Communities).

Edmondson, G. (2001), 'A Hostile Bid that's Dandy for Italy', *BusinessWeek* online, 16 July. (at www.businessweek.com/magazine/content/01_29/ b3741141.htm).

EIU (2001), Country Profiles (The Economist Intelligence Unit). (at www. economist.com).

Elliot, L. (2000), 'Kick-off for Mutuality Fightback', *The Guardian*, City, p. 27.

Ethics Standards Board, The (2002), *Setting the Agenda for Ethics*. A Consultation Paper, May. (London: The Accountancy Foundation Limited).

Europa (2001), Activities of the European Union – Summaries of Legislation. *Sport: Introduction*. (at http://europa.eu.int/scadplus/leg/en/lvb/l35001.htm).

European Commission (1999), *Report From The Commission to The European Council With a View to Safeguarding Current Sport Structures and Maintaining the Social Function of Sport Within the Community Framework (The Helsinki Report)*, Com 644 final. (Brussels: Commission of the European Communities).

European Commission (2002), *Communication from the Commission Concerning Corporate Social Responsibility: A Business Contribution to Sustainable Development*, Com. 347 final (Brussels: Commission of the European Communities).

Faasch, T. and Ebel, M. (2002), 'Feature – UEFA Club Licensing System', *Soccer Investor*, Issue 94, 8 May, p. 13.

FAPL (2002), *The FA Premier League Annual Charter Reports Season 2001/02*. (London: The FA Premier League).

Ferguson, C. and McKillop, D. (1997), *The Strategic Development of Credit Unions*. (Chichester: Wiley).

Ferris, K. (2003) 'Tottenham pull out of Wimbledon friendly', *Independent Online*. (at www.iol.co.za).

FIFA (2001), *FIFA Regulations for the Status and Transfer of Players*. (Buenos Aires/Zurich: Federation Internationale de Football Association).

Fincham, P. (2003), 'Hornet Fans Deal with the Sting of the Premiership Dream', *Supporters Direct Newsletter*, Issue 9, pp. 8–9.

Finn, G. P. T. (1991a), 'Racism, Religion and Sectarianism: Irish Catholic Clubs, Soccer and Scottish Identity – I The Historical Roots of Prejudice', *International Journal of Sports History*, vol. 8, no. 1, pp. 72–95.

Finn, G. P. T. (1991b), 'Racism, Religion and Sectarianism: Irish Catholic Clubs, Soccer and Scottish Identity – II Social Identities and Conspiracy Theories', *International Journal of Sports History*, vol. 8, no. 3, pp. 370–97.

Finney, N. (2000), 'The MMC's Inquiry into BSkyB's Merger with Manchester United plc', in *Football in the Digital Age: Whose Game is it Anyway*, Hamil, S., Michie, J., Oughton, C. and Warby, S. (eds) (Edinburgh: Mainstream), pp. 71–80.

FIR (1982), *English Football League Clubs – Status and Performance*. (London: Financial Intelligence and Research).

Football Task Force (1999), *Football: Commercial Issues*. A Report submitted by the Football Task Force to the Minister for Sport.

Foster, K. (2000), 'Can Sport be Regulated by Europe? An Analysis of Alternative Models', in *Professional Sport in the EU: Regulation and Re-regulation*, Caiger, A. and Gardiner, S. (eds) (The Hague, Netherlands: T C M Hasser Press), pp. 43–64.

Foster, K. (2002), 'UEFA Rules OK? European Law's Impact on Football', *Soccer Review 2002*, pp. 31–6.

Freeman, R. (1984), *Strategic Management: A Stakeholder Approach*. (Pitman: Boston).

Gallhofer, S. and Haslam, J. (1991), 'The Aura of Accounting in the Context of a Crisis: Germany and the First World War', *Accounting, Organizations and Society*, vol. 16, no. 5/6, pp. 487–520.

Gallhofer, S., Haslam, J., Morrow, S. and Sydserff, R. (2000), 'Accounting, Transparency and the Culture Of Spin: Re-Orientating Accounting Communication in the New Millennium', *Pacific Accounting Review*, vol. 11, no. 2, pp. 97–111.

Gavin, N. T. and Goddard, P. (1998), 'Television News and the Economy: Inflation in Britain', *Media, Culture and Society*, vol. 20, no. 3, pp. 451–70.

Gerlis, S. (2002a), 'FIFA Faces Legal Battle', *SportBusiness.com*, 21 June. (at www.sportbusiness.com/news/?news_item_id = 147255).

Gerlis, S. (2002b), 'Juventus Profit Expected', *SportBusiness.com*, 10 April. (at www.sportbusiness.com/news/index?news_item_id = 145875).

Gerrard, B. (2002), 'The Economics of Football: A Review of the Current State of Play', *European Sport Management Quarterly*, vol. 2, no. 2, pp. 167–72.

Giulianotti, R. (1999), *Football: A Sociology of the Global Game.* (Cambridge: Polity Press).

Giulianotti, R. (2002), 'Supporters, Followers, Fans, and Flâneurs', *Journal of Sport and Social Issues*, vol. 26, no. 1, pp. 25–46.

Glautier, M. W. E. and Underdown, B. (1997), *Accounting Theory and Practice.* (London: Pitman).

Glendinning, M. (2000), 'Atlantic League Takes Shape', *Sport Business*, Issue 52, 1 December, p. 7.

Glendinning, M. (2002), 'Italian Clubs Face Harsh Facts', *SportBusiness.com*, 24 July. (at www.sportbusiness.com/news/fandc?region = global& page%5fno = 1&news_item_id = 147772).

Goodwin, B. (1988), *Spurs: A Complete Record 1882–1988.* (Derby: Breedon Books Sport).

Gourley, P. (2001), 'Hopes of Atlantic League are Sinking', *Business am*, 6 August.

Greenfield, S. and Osborn, G. (2001), *Regulating Football: Commodification, Consumption and the Law.* (London: Pluto Press).

Hague, E. and Mercer, J. (1998), 'Geographical Memory and Urban Identity in Scotland: Raith Rovers FC and Kirkcaldy', *Geography*, vol. 83, no. 2, pp. 105–16.

Hamil, S. (1999a), 'Corporate Community Involvement: A Case for Regulatory Reform', *Business Ethics: A European Review*, vol. 8, no. 1, pp. 14–25.

Hamil, S. (1999b), 'A Whole New Ball Game: Why Football Needs a Regulator', in *The Business of Football: A Game of Two Halves*, Hamil, S., J. Michie and C. Oughton (eds) (Mainstream: Edinburgh), pp. 23–39.

Hamil, S., Michie, J. and Oughton, C. (eds) (1999), *A Game of Two Halves? The Business of Football.* (Edinburgh: Mainstream).

Hamil, S., Michie, J, Oughton, C. and Shailer, L. (eds) (2001a), *The State of the Game: The Corporate Governance of Football Clubs 2001.* Research Paper 2001/02 for Supporters Direct. (London: Football Governance Research Centre).

Hamil, S., Michie, J., Oughton, C. and Warby, S. (eds) (2000), *Football in the Digital Age. Whose Game is it Anyway?* (Edinburgh: Mainstream).

Hamil, S., Michie, J., Oughton, C. and Warby, S. (eds) (2001b), *The Changing Face of the Football Business: Supporters Direct.* (London: Frank Cass).

Harding, J. (2003), 'PFA TV Monies Dispute', *Soccer Review 2002*, pp. 15–19.

Harverson, P. (2000), 'English Clubs Play Better Money Game', *The Financial Times*, 18 August, 13.

Harvey, J., Law, A. and Cantelon, M. (2001), 'North American Professional Team Sport Franchises Ownership Patterns and Global Entertainment Conglomerates', *Sociology of Sport*, vol. 18, no. 4, pp. 435–57.

Haynes, R. (1995), *The Football Imagination.* (Aldershot: Avebury).

Hellwig, M. (2000), 'On the Economics and Politics of Corporate Finance and Corporate Control', in *Corporate Governance*, Vives, X. (ed.). (Cambridge University Press: Cambridge), pp. 95–136.

Hill Zimmer, M. and Zimmer, M. (2001), 'Athletes as Entertainers: A Comparative Study of Earnings Profiles', *Journal of Sport and Social Issues*, vol. 25, no. 2, pp. 202–15.

Hines, R. (1988), 'Financial Accounting, In Communicating Reality, We Construct Reality', *Accounting, Organizations and Society*, vol. 13, no. 3, pp. 251–61.

Hoehn, T. and Szymanski, S. (1999), 'European Football: The Structure of Leagues and Revenue Sharing', *Economic Policy*, April, pp. 204–40.

Holt, M. (2003), 'The Next Phase: Trusts Branch out to the Community', *Supporters Direct Newsletter*, Issue 9, January, pp. 12–13.

Home Office (1990), *The Hillsborough Stadium Disaster: Inquiry by the Rt. Hon. Lord Justice Taylor, Final Report*, Cmd. 962. (London: HMSO).

Hore, M. (2002) 'The "Super Creditor" Rule: Creditors Must Agree Rule Change', *Accountancy Age*, 18 June. (at www.accountancyage.com/Comment/1129556).

Hornby, N. (1992), *Fever Pitch*. (London: Victor Gollancz).

Horrie, C. (2002a), *Premiership: Lifting The Lid On a National Obsession*. (London: Simon & Schuster).

Horrie, C. (2002b), 'Death of a TV dream: Footie Goes Back to Drawing Board', *The Observer*, Business, 28 April, p. 5.

IASB (2001), *International Accounting Standards Board Mission Statement*. (London: International Accounting Standards Committee Foundation). (at www.iasc.org.uk).

Ibsen, B. (2001), *Daily Life in Danish Associations – Not So Altruistic After All*. (Vingsted, Denmark: Sports Intelligence Unit). (at http://www.play-the-game.org/articles/1997/culture/daily_life.html).

Ibsen, B. (2002) *Voluntary Work in Sport*. Speech to the sports directors from the member states of EU at a meeting in Copenhagen, Schæfergården, October 23. (at www.ifo-forsk.dk/qBI2002_1.htm0-4).

ICAS (2002), 'President's Comment: Quaere Verum – Seek the Truth', *The CA Magazine*, August, p. 64.

IFC (2002), *The Independent Football Commission Annual Report 2002*. (Middlesbrough: The Independent Football Commission).

Jacobsen, C. (2001), *Factsheet Denmark: Body, Culture and Sport* (Copenhagen, Denmark: The Royal Danish Ministry of Foreign Affairs). (also available at www.um.dk/english/faktaark/fa22/fa22_eng.asp).

Jarvie, G. (2003), 'Communitarianism, Sport and Social Capital', *International Review for the Sociology of Sport*, vol. 38, no. 2, pp. 139–53.

Jarvie, G. and Burnett, J. (2000), *Sport, Scotland and the Scots*. (Edinburgh: Tuckwell Press).

Jensen, M.C. and Meckling, W.H. (1976), 'Theory of the Firm: Managerial Behaviour, Agency Costs and Ownership Structure', *Journal of Financial Economics*, vol. 3, pp. 305–60.

Jones, I. (1998), *Football Fandom: Football Fan Identity and Identification at Luton Town Football Club*. (Unpublished PhD thesis, University of Luton).

Kelly, G. (2002), 'Franchise Football is Not in The Interests of Genuine Fans', at www.wisa.org.uk.

King, A. (1997), 'New Directors, Customers and Fans: The Transformation of English Football in the 1990s', *Sociology of Sport Journal*, vol. 14, pp. 224–40.

King, A. (1998), *The End of the Terraces: the Transformation of English Football in the 1990s*. (Leicester: Leicester University Press).

KPMG (1998), *European Super League: results of a survey carried out by MORI on behalf of the KPMG Football Unit, March*. (KPMG/Soccer Investor Ltd.).

Lambton, D. (2001), 'Clubs Bank on Retail Therapy', *Football Business International*, Issue 2, December, pp. 10–14.

La Porta, R., Lopez-de-Silanes, F. and Shleifer, A. (1999), 'Corporate ownership around the world', *Journal of Finance*, vol. 54, no. 2, pp. 471–517.

Lavoie, D. (1987), 'The Accounting of Interpretations and the Interpretation of Accounts: The Communicative Function of "The Language of Business"', *Accounting, Organizations and Society*, 12, pp. 579–604.

Leeds, M. and von Allmen, P. (2002) *The Economics of Sports*. (Boston: Addison Wesley).

Letza, S. and Smallman, C. (2001), '*Est in aqua dulci non invidiosa voluptas*. In Pure Water There is a Pleasure Begrudged By None: On Ownership, Accountability and Control in a Privatised Utility', *Critical Perspectives on Accounting*, vol. 12, pp. 65–85.

Lloyd, J. (2002), 'The Whole of Italy in His Hands', *New Statesman*, vol. 15, no. 62, pp. 22–5.

Lords Hansard (2002), Volume 637, Part 163, 3 July, Column 326, Football Clubs.

Lucifora, C. and Simmons, R. (2003), 'Superstar Effects in Sport: Evidence from Italian Soccer', *Journal of Sports Economics*, vol. 4, no. 1, pp. 35–55.

Mahony, D. F. and Howard, D. R. (2001), 'Sport Business in The Next Decade: a General Overview of Expected Trends', *Journal of Sport Management*, vol. 15, pp. 275–96.

Malcolm, D., Jones, I. and Waddington, I. (2000), 'The People's Game? Football Spectatorship and Demographic Change', *Soccer and Society*, vol. 1, no. 1, pp. 129–43.

Mann, C. (2002), 'Premiership Teams Face £400m Drop in Income', *The Business*, 11/12 August, p. 6.

Manning, L. (2002), 'Capping Players' Wages Will Help Keep Clubs Afloat', *The Times*, 24 October, Business, p. 38.

Martin, J. N. (1979), *Daly's Club Law*. (London: Butterworths).

Martin, R. (2002), 'Real Nationwide League Can Save All Our Clubs', *The Mirror*, 8 August, pp. 62, 64.

Mayer, T. (1960), 'The Distribution of Ability and Earnings', *Review of Economics and Statistics*, vol. 42, pp. 189–95.

Meier, K. (1979), 'We Don't Want to Set the World on Fire: We Just Want to Finish Ninth', *Journal of Popular Culture*, vol. 13, pp. 289–301.

Michie, J. (1999), *New Mutualism: A Golden Goal?* (London: The Co-operative Party).

Michie, J. and Ramalingam, S. (1999), 'Whose Game is it Anyway? Shareholders, Mutuals and Trusts', in *A Game of Two Halves? The Business of Football*, Hamil, S., Michie, J. and Oughton, C. (eds) (Edinburgh: Mainstream).

Mitchell, A. and Sikka, P. (2002), *Dirty Business: The Unchecked Power of Major Accountancy Firms*. (Basildon: Association for Accountancy & Business Affairs)

Mitrano, J.R. (1999), 'The "Sudden Death" of Hockey in Hartford: Sports Fans and Franchise Relocation', *Sociology of Sport*, vol. 16, no. 2, pp. 134–54.

Moerland, P. (1995), 'Corporate Ownership and Control Structures: An International Comparison', *Review of Industrial Organizations*, vol. 10, pp. 443–64.

Moller, S. (2000), 'Securitization – A Safe Bet For Your Assets', *The Treasurer*, September, pp. 40–2.

Monks, R.A.G. and Minow, N. (2001), *Corporate Governance*, 2nd edn. (Cambridge, MA: Blackwell).

Monopolies and Mergers Commission (1999), *British Sky Broadcasting Group plc and Manchester United plc: A Report on the Proposed Merger*. Cmnd 4305. (London: The Stationery Office).

Moorhouse, H.F. (1994), 'From Zines Like These? Fanzines, Tradition and Identity in Scottish Football', in *Scottish Sport in the Making of the Nation*, Jarvie, G. and Walker, G. (eds) (London: Leicester University Press).

Morris, P., Morrow, S. and Spink, P. (1996), 'EC Law and Professional Football: Bosman and its Implications', *Modern Law Review*, vol. 59, no. 6, pp. 893–902.

Morris, P., Morrow, S. and Spink, P. (2003) 'The New Transfer Fee System in Professional Soccer: An Interdisciplinary Study', *Contemporary Issues in Law*, vol. 5, no. 4, pp. 253–81.

Morrow, S. (1995), 'Recording the Human Resource of Football Players as Accounting Assets: Establishing a Methodology', *Irish Accounting Review*, vol. 2, no. 1, pp. 115–32.

Morrow, S. (1999), *The New Business of Football: Accountability and Finance in Football*. (Basingstoke: Macmillan now Palgrave).

Morrow, S. (2000), 'Football clubs on the Stock Exchange: An inappropriate match?', *The Irish Accounting Review*, vol. 7, no. 2, pp. 61–90.

Morrow, S. (2001a), 'Atlantic League or North Atlantic Drift?', *Singer and Friedlander's Seasonal Review 2000–01*, pp. 43–5.

Morrow, S. (2001b), 'Winning way to put a cap on players' soaring salaries', *Business am*, 26 January 2001, p. 35.

Morrow, S. and Hamil, S. (2003, forthcoming), 'Corporate Community Involvement by Football Clubs: Business Strategy or Social Obligation?'.

Mortimer, T. and Pearl, I. (2000), 'The Effectiveness of the Corporate Form as a Regulatory Tool in European Sport: Real or Illusory?', in *Professional Sport in the EU: Regulation and Re-regulation*, Caiger, A. and Gardiner, S. (eds) (The Hague, Netherlands: T C M Hasser Press), pp. 217–36.

Murphy, P. (1999a), 'Banking on Success: Examining the Links Between Performance and the Increasing Concentration of Wealth on English Elite Football', *Singer and Friedlander's Football Review 1998–99 Season*, pp. 37–44.

Murphy, P. (1999b), 'For Richer, for Poorer North of the Border', *Singer and Friedlander's Football Review 1998–99 Season*, pp. 45–9.

Murray, B. (1984), *The Old Firm: Sectarianism, Sport and Society in Scotland.* (London: John Donald Publishers).

Murray, B. (1998), *The Old Firm in the New Age.* (Edinburgh: Mainstrean).

Nash, R. (2000), 'The Sociology of English Football', *Football Studies*, vol. 3, Part 1, pp. 49–62.

Neale, W.C. (1964), 'The Peculiar Economics of Professional Sports', *Quarterly Journal of Economics*, vol. 78, no. 1, pp. 1–14.

Nice European Council (2000), *Presidency Conclusion Annex IV, Declaration on the Specific Characteristics of Sport and its Social Function in Europe, of Which Account Should Be Taken in Implementing Common Policies.*

Nicolson, S. (2002), 'Old Firm "Heading For Defeat" in Europe', *Business am*, 7 October, p. 6.

Nixon, N. (2000) *Singin' the Blues* (Lockerbie: Terrace Banter, ST Publishing).

Nørby Committee, The (2001), *Corporate Governance in Denmark – Recommendations For Good Corporate Governance in Denmark.* (Copenhagen: The Nørby Committee's Report).

OECD (1999) *OECD Principles of Corporate Governance.* (Paris: Organization for Economic Co-operation and Development).

OECD (2002) *National Accounts of OECD Countries – GDP per capita 2001.* (at www.oecd.org/pdf/M000180 00/M00018518.pdf).

Oosterwijk, F. (2002), 'Houdt Philips nog van PSV?', *Johan*, no. 7, July, pp. 117–50.

O'Sullivan, N. (2000), 'Impact of Board Composition and Ownership on Audit Quality', *British Accounting Review*, vol. 32, no. 4, pp. 397–414.

Oughton, C., Hunt, P., Mills, C. and McClean, M. (2003), *Back Home: Returning Football Clubs to their Communities.* (London: Mutuo).

Pagano, M., Panetta, F. and Zingales, L. (1995), 'Why do Companies Go Public? An Empirical Analysis', *Manuscript*, Graduate School of Business, University of Chicago.

Parrish, R. (2000), 'Reconciling Conflicting Approaches to Sport in the European Union', in *Professional Sport in the EU: Regulation and Re-regulation*, Caiger, A. and Gardiner, S. (eds) (The Hague, Netherlands: TCM Hasser Press), pp. 21–42.

Parrish, R. (2002), 'Football's Place in the Single European Market', *Soccer and Society*, vol. 3, no. 1, pp. 1–21.

Parsons, W. (1989), *The Power of the Financial Press.* (Aldershot: Edward Elgar).

Paterson, C. (2002), *Field of Dreams – Live the Dream*, Football Aid promotional literature. (Edinburgh: Football Aid).

Peasnell, K., Pope, P.F. and Young, S. (2001), 'Managerial Equity Ownership and the Demand for Outside Directors', *International Developments in Corporate Governance Conference Proceedings*, 14 December, Cardiff Business School.

Pendry, Lord (2003), 'Placing Football at the Heart of the Community', *Supporters Direct Newsletter*, Issue 9, January, p. 13.

Perkins, S. (2000), 'Exploring Future Relationships Between Football Clubs and Local Government', *Soccer and Society*, vol. 1, no. 1, pp. 102–13.

Plunkett, J. (2002), 'Sky Steps into ITV Football Breach', *The Guardian*, Media, 5 July. (at http://media.guardian.co.uk/digitaltv/story/0,12184,750093,00.html).

PKF (2002), *Financing Football – the New Reality*. (PKF/AccountancyAge).

Porquera, J. and Jurado, A.L. (2001), 'Adapting to the Ruling: A New Scenario in the Players' Market', *Paper presented at the European Football Finance Conference*, Milan.

Porter, D. (1998), 'City Editors and the Modern Investing Public: Establishing the Integrity of the New Financial Journalism in Late Nineteenth Century London', *Media History*, vol. 4, no. 1, pp. 49–60.

Price Waterhouse (1997), *Converging Cultures: Trends in European Corporate Governance*. (London: Price Waterhouse).

PricewaterhouseCoopers (2002), *The PricewaterhouseCoopers Financial Review of Scottish Football 2000/01*. (Edinburgh: PWC).

PSV (2001), *Jaarverslag PSV NV Seizoen 2000/2001*.

Quirk, J. and Fort, R.D. (1997), *Pay Dirt: The Business of Professional Team Sports*. (Princeton, New Jersey; Princeton University).

Radnedge, K. (1998), *The Complete Encyclopaedia of Football*. (London: Carlton Books).

Ratliff, J. (2002), 'Major Events and Policy Issues in EC Competition Law 2001', *International Company and Commercial Law Review*, vol. 13, no. 2, pp. 60–79.

Reade, R. (2000), 'Football in the Community', *Singer & Friedlander Review 1999/2000 Season*, pp. 5–7.

Reid, J. (2001), *Reclaim the Game: Ten Seasons of the Premier League Swindle*. (London: The Socialist Party).

Richardson, V.J. and Scholz, S. (2000), 'Corporate Reporting and the Internet: Vision, Reality and Intervening Obstacles', *Pacific Accounting Review*, vol. 11, no. 2, pp. 153–9.

Roberts, J. and Scapens, R. (1985), 'Accounting Systems and Systems of Accountability – Understanding Accounting Practices in their Organizational Contexts', *Accounting, Organization and Society*, vol. 10, no. 4, pp. 443–56.

Rosen, S. (1981), 'The Economics of Superstars', *American Economic Review*, vol. 71, December, pp. 845–98.

Rosen, S. and Sanderson, A. (2001), 'Labour Markets in Professional Sports', *The Economic Journal*, vol. 111, pp. F47–68.

Rosner, D. (1989), 'The World Plays Catch Up', *Sports, Inc.*, 2 January, pp. 6–13.

Rothmans (2002), *Rothmans Football Yearbook 2002–2003*, Rollin, G. and Rollin, J. (eds) (London: Headline).

Rowbottom, N. (2003), 'The Application of Intangible Asset Accounting and Discretionary Policy Choices in the UK Football Industry', *British Accounting Review*, vol. 34, no. 4, pp. 335–56.

Rowe, D. (1991), 'That Misery of Stringer's Clichés: Sports Writing', *Cultural Studies*, vol. 5, January, pp. 77–90.

RSA (1995), *Tomorrow's Company: The Role of Business in a Changing World*. (London: The Royal Society for the Encouragement of Arts, Commerce and Manufactures).

Rukeyser, I. (1983), *What's Ahead for the Economy?* (New York: Simon & Schuster).

Rutterford, J. (1993), *Introduction to Stock Exchange Investment*. (Basingstoke: Macmillan – now Palgrave).

Sample, I. (2003), 'Moving Stadium Dents Team Performance', *New Scientist*, 27 January.

Schindler, C. (1999), *Manchester United Ruined My Life*. (London: Headline).

Scottish Parliament Official Report (2001), Credit Unions Debate. Session 1, vol. 11, no. 6, col. 658, Thursday 15 March.

SER (2001), *The Functioning and Future of the Structure Regime*, Abstract O1/O2E. (The Hague, Netherlands: SociaIl Economische Raad/Social and Economic Council).

Shaw, B. and F.R. Post (1993), 'A Moral Basis for Corporate Philanthropy', *Journal of Business Ethics*, vol. 12, pp. 745–51.

Shleifer, A. and Vishny, R.W. (1997), 'A Survey of Corporate Governance', *Journal of Finance*, June 1997, vol. 52, no. 2, pp. 737–83.

Simmons, R. (2001), 'Making Sense of the FIFA/UEFA Proposals to Reform the Football Transfer System', *Singer & Friedlander Review 2000–2001 Season*, pp. 8–12.

Simpson, S. (2002), 'Fans Take Stake in Future of Football', *The Herald*, 23 April, p. 7.

Sinclair, A. (1995), 'The Chameleon of Accountability: Forms and Discourses', *Accounting, Organizations and Society*, vol. 20, no. 2/3, pp. 219–37.

Sloane, P. (1971), 'The Economics of Professional Football: The Football Club as a Utility Maximiser', *Scottish Journal of Political Economy*, June, pp. 121–46.

Smith, Sir John (1997), *Football – its Values, Finances and Reputation*, Report to the Football Association by Sir John Smith.

Smith, S. (2000), 'A Club in the Community: Using Football as an Educational Tool', *Singer & Friedlander Review 1999/2000 Season*, pp. 8–11.

Smith, S. (2002), 'Copenhagen Flirts with Fascism', *The Guardian*, 5 June, p. 16.

SNCCFR (1997), *FA Premier League Fan Surveys 1996/97 General Sample Report*. (University of Leicester: Sir Norman Chester Centre for Football Research).

SNCCFR (2000), *FA Premier League National Fan Survey 2000 Summary Report*. (University of Leicester: Sir Norman Chester Centre for Football Research).

SNCCFR (2002), *Fact Sheet 8: British Football on Television*. (University of Leicester: Sir Norman Chester Centre for Football Research).

Soccer Investor (2001a), 'French Clubs Take Case to EC', Issue 76, 28 December, pp. 1–2.

Soccer Investor (2001b), 'Juve Shares to Start Trading on Dec 20', Issue 75, 18 December, p. 12.

Soccer Investor (2001c), 'Italian Football Sinks into Financial Blackhole', Issue 69, 6 November, p. 10.

Soccer Investor (2001d), 'Canal Plus Reportedly Seeks PSG Exit as French Clubs Await New Law', Issue 32, 20 February, p. 12.

Soccer Investor (2002a), 'Italian League Start Date in Doubt', Issue 109, 20 August, pp. 1, 2

Soccer Investor (2002b), 'New-look French League Sets Off', Issue 107, 6 August, p. 12.

Soccer Investor (2002c), 'Collective €702m Loss for Serie A Clubs', Issue 105, 23 July, p. 12.

Soccer Investor (2002d), 'Almost 30% of Serie A Players Earning over 21m Euros a Year', Issue 99, 11 June, p. 9.

Soccer Investor (2002e), *The Old Firm's Contribution to Scottish Football*. (London: Soccer Investor).

Soccer Investor (2002f), 'Progress on Milan and Turin Stadia', Issue 93, 30 April, p. 9.

Soccer Investor (2002g), 'Serie A Makes 133m Euros Loss in 2000–01, Issue 91, 16 April, p. 12.

Soccer Investor (2002h), 'Lazio Considering £60m Securitization', Issue 84, 26 February, p. 7.

Soccer Investor (2002i), 'French D1 Clubs €135m in Debt', Issue 81, 5 February, p. 7.

Soccer Investor (2003), 'Ipswich Goes Into Administration', Issue 134, 18 February, pp. 1–2.

Solnik, B. (1996), *International Investments*. (Reading, MA: Addison Wesley).

Staudohar, P.D. (1999), 'Salary Caps in Professional Team Sports', in *Competition Policy in Professional Sports*, Jeanrenaud, C. and Kesenne, S. (eds) (Antwerp: Standard Editions), pp. 71–90.

Stephen, K. (2003), 'Capital Clubs Look to Keep Fans Informed', *The Herald*, 24 June, p. 34.

Stewart, G. (1986), 'The Retain and Transfer System: An Alternative Perspective', *Managerial Finance*, vol. 12, no. 1, pp. 1–5.

Strätling, R. (2001), 'General Meetings: A Dispensable Tool for Corporate Governance of Listed Companies', *International Developments in Corporate Governance Conference Proceedings*, 14 December, Cardiff Business School.

Sunday Herald (2002), 'PFA Warns on Wages Caps', November 24, Sport, 5.

Szymanski, S. and Kuypers, T. (1999), *Winners and Losers: The Business Strategy of Football*. (London: Viking).

Szymanski, S. and Smith, R. (1997), 'The English Football Industry: Profit,

Performance and Industrial Structure', *International Review of Applied Economics*, vol. 11, pp. 135–53.

Taylor, R. (1992), *Football and Its Fans: Supporters and their Relation with the Game, 1885–1985*. (Leicester: Leicester University Press).

Thynne, I. and Goldring, J. (1981), 'Government "Responsibility" and Responsible Government', *Politics*, vol. 16, no. 2, pp. 197–207.

Touche Ross (1993), *Survey of Football Club Accounts*. (Manchester: Touche Ross & Co.).

Tower, G. (1993), 'A Public Accountability Model of Accounting Regulation', *British Accounting Review*, vol. 25, no. 1, pp. 61–86.

Tricker, R.I. (1984), *Corporate Governance: Practices, Procedures And Powers in British Companies and their Boards of Directors*. (Aldershot: Gower).

UEFA (2002a), *UEFA Club Licensing System – Season 2004/05. Version 1.0 E – March*. (Nyon, Switzerland: UEFA).

UEFA (2002b), *Regulations of the UEFA Champions League 2002/2003*. (Nyon, Switzerland: UEFA).

UKCH (2001), *Religious Trends No. 2 2000/2001*. (London: Christian Research).

Vamplew, W. (1988), *Pay Up and Play the Game: Professional Sport in Britain 1875–1914*. (Cambridge; Cambridge University Press).

Vamplew, W., Coyle, J., Heath, J. and Naysmith, B. (1998), 'Sweet FA: Fans' Rights and Club Relocations', *Occasional Papers in Football Studies*, vol. 2, no. 2, pp. 55–68.

Vance, C. (2001), *Valuing Intangibles: A Discussion Paper*. (London: The Institute of Chartered Accountants in England and Wales).

Vienot Report, The (1999), *Recommendations of the Committee on Corporate Governance chaired by Mr Marc Vienot*. (Paris: Association Française des Enterprises Privées AFEP/Mouvement des Enterprises de France Medef).

Vives, X. (2000), 'Corporate Governance: Does it Matter?', in *Corporate Governance*, Vives, X. (ed.) (Cambridge: Cambridge University Press), pp. 1–21.

Waddell, G. (2001), 'Football: We've Killed the Game; Murray Blames Decline on the Old Firm', *Sunday Mail*, 2 December, pp. 75–6.

Waddington, I., Malcolm, D. and Horak, R. (1998), 'The Social Composition of Football Crowds in Western Europe', *International Review for the Sociology of Sport*, vol. 33, no. 2, pp. 155–69.

Wann, D. and Branscombe, N. (1990), 'Die-hard and Fair-Weather Fans: Effects of Identification on BIRGing and CORFing Tendencies', *Journal of Sport and Social Issues*, vol. 14, pp. 103–17.

Watson, N. (2000), 'Football in the Community: What's the Score?', *Soccer and Society*, vol. 1, no. 1, pp. 114–25.

Weatherhill, S. (2000) 'Resisting the Pressures of "Americanization": The Influence of European Community Law on the "European Community Model"' in *Law and Sport in Contemporary Society*, Greenfield, S. and Osborn, G. (eds) (London: Frank Cass), pp. 156–81.

Webb, R., McKinnon, R. and Beck, M. (2001), 'Problems and Limitations of Institutional Participation in Corporate Governance', *International Developments in Corporate Governance Conference Proceedings*, 14 December, Cardiff Business School.

Westerbeek, H. and Smith, A. (2002), *Sport Business in the Global Marketplace.* (Basingstoke: Palgrave).

Weston, R. (2002), 'Treading an Uneasy Path? The Securitization of Gate Receipts', *Proceedings of the Academy of Commercial Banking and Finance*, vol. 2, no. 1, pp. 49–52.

Weston, R. (2001), 'Exploring the Boundaries of Securitization', 30th Annual Conference of Economists, 23–27 September, University of Western Australia. (Economics Society of Australia), pp. 1–16.

White, J. (2003), 'Pitch battle', *The Guardian*, 11 January.

Wilkesman, U. and Blutner, D. (2002), 'Going Public: The Organisational Restructuring of German Football Clubs', *Soccer and Society*, vol. 3, no. 2, pp. 19–37.

Williams, J. and Perkins, S. (1998), *Ticket Pricing, Football Business and Excluded Football Fans.* (Leicester: Sir Norman Chester Centre for Football Research).

Williams, J., Hopkins, S. and Long, C. (2001), *Passing Rhythms: Liverpool FC and the Transformation of Football.* (Oxford: Berg).

Wilson, M., Davies, M., Curtis, M. and Wilkinson-Riddle, G. (2001), *UK and International GAAP: Generally Accepted Accounting Practice in The United Kingdom and Under International Accounting Standards.* (London: Butterworths Tolley).

Worldcom (2002) *United They Stand.* (at www.worldcom.com/ca/products/internet/uuhost/customers/manutd.pdf20

Wright, A. (2000), 'Defeat Costly for Investors as Celtic Shares Take a Dive', *The Scotsman*, 10 February, p. 37.

Wynne, D. (2001), 'What is the Trust', *Tottenham Hotspur Supporters' Trust Website.* (at www.tottenhamtrust.com/viewarticles.asp?id = 5).

Index

Key: **bold** = extended discussion; e = exhibit; f = figure; n = note; t = table

Aberdeen 6t, 64t, 81t, 132t, 141, 149t, 163t, 173
Aberdeen Supporters' Trust 205(n101)
AC Milan, *see* Milan (AC Milan)
accountability 3, 58, 75, 77, 88, 89, 129, 137–45, 147, 151, 161, 181, 183
  Italy 123, 124, **126–7**
  personification 134, 204(n95)
accounting
  effects of new transfer fee system **152–5**, 206(n107)
  information 170
  'language of business' 151
  scandals 205(n104)
  see also financial information
accounting standards 151, 205–6(n105), 206(n114)
Accounting Standards Board (ASB) 142, 147, 154, 161
accounts **145–51**
administration/insolvency 46–7, 159, 160, 195(n10), 198(n37)
administrative offices 76, 200(n54)
advertising 93, 196(n16), 201(n67)
AEK Athens 83, 84
AFC Wimbledon 70
Agnelli family 115, 117, 118, 202(n76)
Ajax 12t, 12, 92, 96, 195(n12), 196(n18)
AKER RGI (Norwegian company) 69
Aktiengesellschaft (AG) 203(n85)

Alternative Investment Market (AIM) 80
amortization 152, 168e, 169e
Amshold Limited 83t, 83n
Amsterdam Stock Exchange 91
Amsterdam Treaty: Declaration on Sport (1997) 37
Anderlecht 22–3
Andersen (consultants) 122
Andersen SCORE 151
annual reports 57–9, 62, 64, 66, 142, **145–51**, 161, 164, 206(n115)
  cash donations 198(n43)
  disclosure 65t
Annual Review of Football Finance (Deloitte & Touche Sport) 146, 159, 206(n113)
Argentina 175t, 192
Arsenal 8, 8t, 47, 63, 194(n5), 195(n12)
  community initiatives 66
  concentrated ownership 132t
  disclosure 64t
  financial information (electronic availability) 148t
  ownership 81t
  stadiums 72
  UEFA Champions League market pool league tabl
  youth development narrative disclosure 162t
As (Spanish national sports daily newspaper) 167
assets (intangible) 152, 154, 206(n107), 109)
association (*vereniging*) 91, 200(n59)

224

Aston Villa, 63, 64t, 81t, 148t, 162t
Athletic News 80
Atlantic League 8, 33–4, 196(n23)
Atlético Madrid 10t, 194(n5)
auditing 27, 147, 196(n19),
 205(n104)
Auxerre 11t

Baillie, J. 54
balance sheets 152–5
 book value of playing squad 155
 Fulham FC (1999–2000) 156e
 home-grown players 154
Bale, J. 53, 68
banks 76, 90, 134, 156
Banks, S. 172, 207(n125)
Bannerman, C. 72
Barcelona 10t, 10, 56, 74, 194(n5),
 206(n108)
 G14 club 195(n12)
 membership organization 126
 merchandising 197(n32)
 television deal with Via
  Digital 194(n7)
 UEFA Champions League market
  pool league table 25t
Basle 83
Bavaria NV 201(n65)
Bayer Leverkusen, 10t, 11, 25t,
 195(n12)
Bayern München 1, 10t, 11, 25t, 74,
 194(n5), 195(n12), 203(n85)
BBC 14t, 167
 Radio Five Live 166
 Radio Scotland 166
Becht, M. 116
Beckham, D. 154, 176, 190
Belgium 22–3
Bell, I. 172
Bellos, A. 68
Berlusconi, S. 117, 127
Besloten Vennootschap (BV) (private
 limited company) 90–1, 92
best practice 3, 140, **142–4**, 161, 165,
 183

Bianchi, M. 115
 et al. (2001) 115, 209
Binns, S. 140, 141
 et al. (2002) 140, 141, 209
Birkbeck College (London) xi, 51,
 205(n100)
Birmingham City 81t
Blackburn Rovers 8, 17, 81t, 125
Blutner, D. 203(n85)
Boavista 25t
Boldklubben 1903 (B1903) 67,
 104–5, 110
Bologna 196(n21)
Bolton Wanderers 81t
bonds 157, 159e, 175t, 192,
 206(n111)
Bonnier Media 207(n119)
Bordeaux 11, 11t
borrowing **155–9**
 overdrafts 'repayable on
  demand' 156–7
 press misinterpretation 206(n110)
Borussia Dortmund 10t, 25t, 146,
 194(n5), 195(n12), 201(n61)
Bose, M. 75, 172, 179
Bosman, J–M. 37, 39, 44
Bosnia 198(n44)
Bowie, D. 206(n111)
Boyle, J. 187
Boyle, R. xi, 177, 179
 et al. (2002) 177, 179, 209
Bradford City 64t, 148t, 160, 162t
Bradley, J. xii, 194(n3)
brands 35, 49
Brazil 68, 198(n44)
breach of contract 153
Brejinho 68
Bremner, B. 51
Brett, M. 207(n120)
Brøndbyernes IF FO (Brøndby) 5,
 103t, 146
 fan culture 104, 113
 financial statements
  (1996–2001) 104t
 listed company 104

Brooklyn Dodgers 71
Brown, A. 27, 38, 42, 48, 54
BSkyB 14t, 31, 168e, 176, 200(n53),
    204(n95)
  Sky 28, 166, 197(n31)
  Sky Sports 29t
BT 177
Buchan, M. 13
Buchler, D. 87
Bundesliga 14t, 15t, 197(n30),
    203(n85)
Burnden Leisure 81t
Busby, Sir Matt 182
Business am (2000–2) 170, 207(n119)
business ethos **136–8**
business organizations 78, 200(n57)
business and society **128–44, 203–5**
  structural rationale 128–31
'business structure' 84–5
BVB Dortmund GmbH & Co KgaA
    203(n85)

Cadbury Report (Sir Adrian Cadbury)
    200(n56), 209
Cameron, C. 204
Camp Nou 1, 126
Canal Plus 14t, 201(n65)
Canal Satellite Digital 194(n7)
Cardiff City 199(n46)
Carlin, W. 133̇4
Carlton 18
Caspian (Leeds United) 81t
Catalonia 56
catering 143e, 169e
CCI, *see* corporate community
    involvement
Celta Vigo 10t
Celtic 6t, 6, 23, 39, 56, 63n, 178,
    194(n2), 196(n18), 201(n61)
  disclosure 64t, 65t
  financial information (electronic
    availability) 149t
  financial information (website
    availability) 150
  helps to popularize capitalism 177

  ownership 81t
  putative takeover (1998) 177
  rescued (1994) by F. McCann 106
  UEFA Champions League market
    pool league table 25t
  youth development narrative
    disclosure 163t
  see also Old Firm
Celtic Charity Fund 57, 59e, 65t
Celtic plc 57, 58e, 174t, 190–1
Celtic Supporters' Association 55
Celtic Trust 55
Centros case 40
chairman's statement 147, 161, 162–4t
charitable donations 55, 61, 62, 63t,
    174t
charitable organizations/trusts 62, 63
Charlton Athletic 81t, 141, 148t,
    162t, 164
Chelsea 8t, 27, 64t, 148t, 162t
Chelsea Village 81n, 148t
chief executive officers 86, 169e
chief executive's review 161, 163t
Chievo 9t, 16, 195(n9)
Cirio Finanziari 117
Cirio Holding 117
Cirio del Monte 117
civic pride 1, 132
civil society 201(n68)
club: 'array of meanings' 74
club charters 60e, 65t, 198(n42),
    205(n98–9)
co-operative purchasing venture
    (Scottish clubs) 175t, 190
Combined Code 139, 200(n56), 210
commercialization 48–9
common bond 53
communication 3, 88, 89, 138, 139,
    143e, **145–81**, 183, **205–7**
community **55–73**, 77, 182, 183, 184
companies
  cash donations 198(n43)
  dual–board structures 141
  freedom of movement in EU 40
  private 135

Companies Act (1985) 198(n43)
Companies Act 1985 (Electronic
   Communications) Order
   2000 150
company boards 77
company directors 60
company law 57, 134, 139, 142, 151,
   200(n52), 205(n102)
Company Law Review Steering
   Group (2000) 200(n56), 210
competition 124
competition policy (EU) **36–9**
competitive balance 5, 20, 35
   impact of television income 16,
      194(n8)
concentrated sporting success **5–12**,
   13, 16
conglomerates: media and
   entertainment 31
Conn, D. 47, 172
Conservative Party (Denmark) 102
consultation **41–2**, 70
Cooper, G. 178
cooperation 114, 131, 183
Copenhagen Stock Exchange 101–2,
   104, 105, 108, 113, 114, 202(n73)
corporate community involvement
   (CCI) 57, **60–6**, 69
corporate governance 3, 14, 75,
   76–7, 126, 137–40, 203(n88)
   code proposed 142
   Denmark 102
   FCK **113–14**
   insider system of control 136
   Italy 115–16, 117, 119
   PSV Eindhoven **96–8**
   reports 77, 200(n56)
   structural solutions **140–2**
   Tottenham Hotspur **88–90**
corporate hospitality 93, 114, 157,
   158, 169e, 202(n74)
corporate management: ability to
   entrench itself, 200(n54)
corporate social responsibility 57,
   58, 183

corporate structures 80
   rationale **128–31**
Corriere dello Sport 167
Coventry City 64t, 148t, 162t
Coventry City Football Club
   (Holdings) Ltd 81n
Cragnotti, S. 83, 117, 125, 135
credit union movement 53–4
creditors 145, 160
cricket 105
Crolley, L. 207(n117)
Crommert, J. van de 97f
cross–border leagues/competitions
   32, 34, 40, 197(n33)
cross–border moves 69
Crozier, A. 189
Crystal Palace FC 68
Cubic Expression 204(n89)
cult of celebrity 177–8, 181
culture 130–1, 140, 144
customer markets 133
Customer Relationship Marketing
   (CRM) 100
customers 77, 89
Czech Republic 83

Daily Mail 173t, 186, 188, 189, 190,
   193
Daily Record 173t, 179, 180e, 186, 187,
   188, 189, 190, 193
Daily Telegraph 170, 172, 173t, 185,
   187, 192, 193
Daimler Chrysler
   Nederland 201(n65)
Dalglish, K. 177
Daly's Club Law 74
Danish People's Party 102
Danish SAS Ligaen 108
Danske Bank 106, 107t
Davies, H. 171
de Jong, A. 91
   et al. (2001) 91, 211
de Ruyter, K. 133, 204(n94)
debts 22, 147, 160, 180
deferred income 155, 156e

Delle Alpi stadium 121, 203(n87)

Deloitte & Touche 16, 31, 151, 154, 159, 165, 166, 171, 206(n113, n115)

Deloitte & Touche (Milan) xi, 21

Deloitte and Touche Sport 146

Demsetz, H. 134

Denmark 2, 54, 77, 100, **101–14, 201–2**

broadcasting revenues 15n

culture 102, 110, 201(n71)

culture and society 130–1, 204(n90)

politics 102, 201(n68)

sports associations 103

structure of Danish football 102–4

Denmark: constitution (1849) 102

Denmark: Ministry of Business 102

Deportivo la Coruña 10t, 25t

Derby County 64t, 68, 81t, 148t, 162t

Desmond, D. 204(n89)

Deutsche Fussball Bund (DFB) 203(n85)

dialogue 138, 140, 182

directors 19, 22, 28, 32, 69, 78, 85–8, 95, 98, 100, 109, 111, 112–13, 119, 120, 123, 127, 129–31, 138–40, 151, 161, 178, 183

directors' box 86

disabled people 51, 144e

disclosure **142–4**, 161, 172, 183

disinvestment 134

distance learning 197(n35)

dividends 80, 106, 130e, 168e, 169e

Dobson, S. 5, 7, 17, 32

Dreier, P. 170

Dublin 40, 68–9

Duke, V. 49

Dundee 6t, 64t, 149t, 163t

Dundee United x, 22, 64t, 81t, 81n, 149t, 163t, 174t, 190, 195(n14)

Dunfermline Athletic 81t, 149t, 163t

Dutch Civil Code 200(n59–60)

Dutch Eredivise 99

Dynamo Kiev 25t

East Fife 174t, 189

economic downturn 28

Edwards, M. 204(n89, n95)

Eindhovense Voetbal Vereniging PSV (EVV) 93, 95, 97, 97f

Elliot, L. 198(n39)

Ellis, D. 83

employees 77, 139

enabling development 69

Endemol (Dutch television company) 204(n89)

England 7, **8–9**, 77, 153

concentrated sporting success 8t

large television market 16

taxation 123

television rights fees 14t

UEFA country coefficient 22

yo-yos, parachutes, trampolines **17–22**

English National Investment Company (ENIC) 82–4, 87, 132t, 200(n58)

minority stake/dominant shareholder in Tottenham Hotspur 135–6

Enron 138

entertainment 111, 112–13, 202(n72), 206(n111)

environmental issues 150

Équipe, L' 167

Estudi Estadio 29t

ethnicity 92

Euronext Exchange 91

Europa newsletter 40

European Championships (2008) 173, 176

European Commission 42, 44, 69, 84, 153

European Court of Arbitration for Sport 84

European Court of Justice 37, 40

European Union (EU) 206(n105)

law/regulations **36–9**, **39–41**, 84, 197(n33)

single market 100

European University Football
League 201(n64)
Everton FC
annual reports (electronic
access) 150
community initiatives 66
disclosure 64t
financial information (electronic
availability) 148t
investment in training and
development 164
ownership 81t
social involvement 60e
youth development narrative
disclosure 162t
Excelsior Mouscron 40

FA Cup 197(n25)
FA Premier League/FA Premiership
(1992–) **8–9**, 13–21, 30, 33, 61–2,
79, 90, 150, 156, 158–9, 168e,
198(n42), 200(n53)
broadcasting income as percentage
of turnover 15t
charitable donations 63t
distribution of television income
earnings gap 15t, 15n, 15–16
Old Firm participation **34–6**
survivability of promotion 17, 18t
'top–heavy financial rewards' 20
FA Premier League Annual Charter
Reports 142
family 76, 115–16, 117, 125, 126,
128, 132, 135
Faulkener, R. 70
Fayed, M.A. 17
FC København (FCK, 1992–) xi, 5,
66–7, **104–14**, 131, 136, 137, 139,
201–2
business 109–10
'close to bankruptcy' (1997) 105–6
corporate governance and
communication 113–14
diversified ownership 132t
economic diversification 27

fan culture 110–13, 114
listed company (1997) 105, 113,
114, 202(n73)
origins 104–5
ownership and structure 106–9,
202(n73)
part of Parken Sport and
Entertainment 104
FC København Fan Club 105
FC Internazionale Milano see
Internazionale Milano
Fenerbahce 25t
Ferdinand, R. 130, 130e
Ferguson, Sir Alex 182, 204(n89)
Fever Pitch (Hornby) 47–8
Feyenoord 12t, 12, 25t, 92,
201(n63, n67), 201(n61)
Fiat 115, 118, 202(n76)
Field of Dreams (charity) 62
Figo, L. 126
financial difficulties 4, 160, 172
financial information 2
borrowing and
securitization 155–9
content analysis 173–7
deferred income 155, 156e
electronic availability 148–9t
inside knowledge 206(n114)
interpreting an
interpretation **151–65, 205–6**
interpreting interpreter's
interpretation **166–81, 206–7**
narrative communication 161–5
objectivity 166
press 166–7
professionals 165–6
quality 177–81
quantity 172–7, 207(n126)
reporting business 167, 170
reporting business of
football 171–2
sale and leaseback of
players 159–60,
206(n113–14)
summary reports 152, 206(n106)

financial institutions   1, 76, 132
financial journalism   **167, 170,**
   207(n120–1)
Financial Licensing Documentation
   (FLD)   152
financial reporting   77, 82, 200(n55)
Financial Reporting Standards
   FRS 5 (*Off balance sheet*
      transactions, 1994)   160
   FRS 10 (*Goodwill and intangible*
      assets, 1997)   152, 154,
      206(n107)
financial statements   146, 147, 154,
   206(n109)
   historical cost convention   154
   notes   155, 159e
   post-balance sheet events   159e
   true and fair view   160
financial sustainability   96, 100
Financial Times   167, 171
Fininvest   117
Fiorentina   9, 9t, 124
First Division (old), England   2,
   200(n53)
FIFA   xi, 44, 69, 153, 202(n77)
   Regulations for Status and Transfer
      of Players (2001)   153
   World Cup (2002)   1, 201(n64),
      202(n77)
flâneurs   50f, 51, 85, 85f
Flemming Østergaard
   Management A/S   107t
Foosen, P.   xi, 33–4, 39, 97f, 98–9
football
   aim of book   3
   'can remain people's game'   184
   central argument of book   56
   changing channels   **27–30**
   country culture and history   126
   economic characteristics
      'peculiar'   5, 124
   economics   **4–42, 194–7**
   representational sport   55, 92,
      201(n62)
   social dimension   2, 183

social significance   176
television dependency   **12–16**
Football Aid   **61–2**, 63, 66
Football Association, 41, 69, 146, 160,
   198(n38), 199(n49)
   Rule thirty-four   79–80
football club management   78, 90
football clubs
   'always up for sale'   129
   business and social
      organizations   **128–44, 203–5**
   businesses   2, **43–73, 197–9**
   central argument of book   56
   code of good governance   142
   common good   56–60
   concentrated control   135
   concentrated ownership   80
   disclosure index   64t
   economic diversification
      difficult   27–8, 196(n20)
   'effectively monopolistic'   137, 138
   expectations 'no longer of purely
      sporting nature'   145
   few sources of income   27
   financial difficulties   45, 52, 53, 56,
      172, 198(n40)
   'financial information not
      conveniently available'   146
   geographical immobility   53
   German classification   203(n85)
   help to popularize capitalism   177
   inclusivity   **138–44**
   incorporated as companies   1, 74
   integration (horizontal/vertical)   31
   Italian   135, 146
   listed companies   57–8, 64, 75, 77,
      79–82, 84–5, 103, 103t, 113, 125,
      128–9, 132, 135, 141,
   market control   129, 203–4(n88)
   market principles and business
      ethos   **136–8**
   'mature businesses'   31
   objectives   **74–5**
   organizational forms   **72–127**, 138,
      200–3

ownership   76, 123, 131, 132t
'primarily social institutions'   137
rationale for flotation   129
relocation   66, 67, 72
social dimension   2, **55–73**, 85, 86, 176, **197–9**
taxation   122–3
'trans–national organizations'   33, 197(n25)
turnover   171
Football in the Community (FIC)   61
Football Expo   34
Football Fans Census   199(n47, n49)
Football Governance Research Centre (FGRC)   139, 141, 142, 205(n100)
Football League   69, 192, 198(n38)
football managers   21, 127, 183
football pools   122
Football Task Force   49, 51–2, 61–2, 143e
football–television nexus   1, 111–12, 116–17, 120
Football's Going Down (Banks, 2002b)   207(n125)
Fort, R. D.   71
foundation (*stichting*)   92, 200(n92)
Foy, G.   x
France   7, **11–12**, 13, 15t, 79, 121, 167
concentrated sporting success   11t
declining television audience for football   29t
domestic licensing system   22
taxation   122
television rights fees   14t
UEFA Champions League (television market share)   30t
franchising   31, 71–2, 199(n49)
UK meaning   199(n48)
US meaning   67, 199(n48)
FTSE 100 index   171
Fulham   17, 155

G14 clubs   21, 26, 27, 33, 92, 195(n11–12), 197(n24)
website   196(n17)

Galatasaray   25t
Gallhofer, S.   170
gate receipts   27, 101, 120, 121, 155, 157, 158, 169e, 196(n16), 206(n112)
Gazetta dello Sport   167
GDP   78, 90, 101, 114, 202(n75)
German Civil Code   203(n85)
Germany   7, **10–11**, 77, 79, 90, 141, 151
accounting practices (World War I)   170
concentrated sporting success   10t
declining television audience for football   29t
lack of specialist sports newspapers   207(n118)
survivability of promotion   18t
taxation   122
television rights fees   14t
Gerrard, B.   155, 194(n8)
Gesellschaft mit beschränkter Haftung (GmbH)   203(n85)
GildhoCentret   104
Giulianotti, R.   48, 50–1, 85, 201(n62)
Giuseppe Meazza Stadium (San Siro district, Milan)   1, 119, 121–2
Gjelsten, Rune   69
Glasgow   1, 182
Glazer, M.   204(n89)
globalization   76, 77, 102
Goddard, J.   5, 7, 17, 32
Gold, L.   34
Goldring, J.   127
Graham, G.   136
Granada   18
Greece   83, 84, 92
Green Bay Packers   71
Griggs, M.   67, 192
Guardian   180, 189, 190, 191, 193
Gullit, R.   99–100

Haas, B.   168e
Hamburg SV   10t

Hamil, S.   xi, 57, 140, 203(n88)
  et al. (2001a) 140, 214
  et al. (2001b) 203(n88), 214
Hammam, S.   68–9, 199(n46)
Hammer, D.   xi, 105–6, 109–13, 136,
  202(n73)
Hampden Park debentures   175t,
  192
Hand, D.   207(n117)
handball   108
Harding, J.   197(n34)
Hartford Whalers   67
Haslam, J.   170
Haynes, R.   48
Heart of Midlothian   6t, 6
  disclosure   64t
  financial information (electronic
    availability)   149t
  financial information (website
    availability)   150
  ownership   81t
  youth development narrative
    disclosure   164t
Heerenveen   12t
Hellwig, M.   203(n86)
Helsinki: European Council
  (1999)   37, 38
Herald, 173t, 180, 185, 187, 190, 191,
  193
hermetic leagues   21, 32
Herrera, H.   119
Hertha Berlin   10t
Hibernian   6t, 6, 194(n2)
  disclosure   64t
  financial information (electronic
    availability)   149t
  ownership   81t
  private football companies (receipt
    of public money)   173, 176
  youth development narrative
    disclosure   164t
Hill Zimmer, M.   44
HM Customs
  challenge and opportunity   182
  disclosure   142–4

Independent (newspaper)   47, 172,
  173t, 185, 189, 191, 192, 193
Independent Football Commission
  (2001)   41
industrial and provident
  societies   205(n100)
inflation   158, 170
influence   88, 89
Inland Revenue   198(n38)
'Inside Football' (Conn)   172
Inter-Active   xi, 120, 198(n44)
interest rates   157
International Accounting Standards
  Board   200(n55), 205–6(n105)
Internazionale Milano ('Inter Milan';
  'Inter'; 1908–)   xi, 9, 9t, 29, 115,
  117, **119–20**, 127, 134, 135, 137,
  139, 194(n5), 198(n44), 202(n80)
  concentrated ownership   132t
  G14 club   195(n12)
  ownership structure, 123
  player salaries, 203(n83)
Internet   49, 59, 67, 100, 147, 150,
  167, 197(n35), 201(n66–7)
Inverness Caledonian Thistle (ICT,
  1994–)   67, 72, 178
investment   87, 97, 204(n92)
  long-term   157, 169e
  medium-term   157, 158
  in players   16, 19
  short-term   157, 158
  training and development
    activities   164–5
investor confidence   77
investors   75, 90, 105, 130, 130e
  conflict with supporters   79
  diversification   158
  investment rationale   132
Ipswich Town   8t, 16, 17, 195(n9)
  cost of relegation   19t, 195(n10)
  financial information (electronic
    availability)   148t
  yo-yo club   18, 19t
  youth development narrative
    disclosure   162t

IRAP (Italian local tax) 123
Istituto Finanziario Industriale
(IFI) 117, 118
Italian Cup (*Coppa Italia*) 14t, 122f
Italy 3, 7, 21, 77, **114–27**, 167,
202–3
accountability 123–7
accounting policies 152
concentrated sporting success 9t
declining television audience for
football 29t
earnings 46
football finances 120–3
football structure 116–19
large television market 16
Lega Calcio 118f, 122, 122f
ownership structure 115–16, 117,
123–6
structural rationale 128–9
taxation 122–3
television rights fees 14t
UEFA Champions League
(television market share) 30t
UEFA country coefficient 22
ITV Digital 18, 28, 46, 111, 158

Jones, I. 48
journalists
City 179
lack of financial expertise 178–81
sports 178–9
Juventus FC 9, 9t, 29, 114, 117, 118,
135, 146, 194(n5), 202(n76, n80–1)
G14 club 195(n12)
Initial Public Offering (IPO) 118,
118f, 121, 203(n87)
profitable 118
shareholder structure 118f
UEFA Champions League market
pool league table 25t

Kaiserslautern 10t
KBs Fodbold Fund 107t
Keevins, H. 179

Kelly, G. x
Kerr, J. 177
Kilmarnock 6t, 27, 64t, 81t, 149t,
164t
King, A. 49
KirchMedia 14n, 28, 111
ProSieben SAT 1 14t
Kirkcaldy: Raith Rovers **55–6**, 81t
Kjaer, M. 107t
KNVB *see* Royal Netherlands
Football Association
Københavns Boldklub (KB) 66,
104–5, 110
Kommanditgesellschaft auf Aktien
(KgaA) 203(n85)
Komplementär 203(n85)
Kondar Limited 200(n58)
Koppel, C. 69, 199(n47)
KPMG 165, 201(n65)
Kuypers, T. 16, 203(n82)

Larsen, A. xi, 105, 113–14,
202(n74)
Lavoie, D. 151
law **36–9**, **39–41**, 42, 69, 197(n33)
Lazio (SS Lazio) 9t, 117, 126, 135,
157, 202(n80)
Pay–TV deal 29, 196(n21)
UEFA Champions League market
pool league table 25t
Leeds United 8t, 9, 61, 63, 157, 159,
171
disclosure 64t
financial information (electronic
availability) 148t
investment in training and
development 164
ownership 81t
sell-on-value of playing squad 155
youth development narrative
disclosure 162t
Leeds United plc 130, 130e, 158,
195(n13)
Leegte, W. van der 97f
Lehn, K. 134

Leicester City   63
  disclosure   64t, 65t
  financial information (electronic
    availability)   148t
  ownership   81t
  placed into administration (October
    2002),   159
  securitization disclosure   158, 159t
  youth development narrative
    disclosure   162t
Leicester City plc   58e
Leighton, Alan   195(n13)
Lens   11t
Letza, S.   137, 141
Levy, D.   xi, 83–4, 86–9, 135,
  200(n58)
Leyton Orient Fans' Trust   61
Liberal Party (Denmark)   102
licensing systems   78
Lille   11t, 12, 25t
limited liability companies   78, 79,
  146, 147,   196(n19)
  separation of ownership and
    control   80
  sporting versus financial
    objectives   79–80
listed companies   161
live action   198(n36)
Liverpool FC   8, 8t, 48, 56, 194(n5)
  annual reports (electronic
    access)   150
  disclosure   64t
  financial information (electronic
    availabil
  G14 club   195(n12)
  ownership   81t
  UEFA Champions League market
    pool league table   25t
  youth development narrative
    disclosure   163t
Livingston   6t, 6
local authorities   121
Locomotiv Moscow   25t
Loftus Road (company)   81t
Lomax, B.   xi, 52, 54

London Stock Exchange   79, 80
  listing requirements   88
Lønmodtagernes Dyrtidsfond
  (employees capital pension
    fund)   106, 107t
Lopez, F.   126
Los Angeles   71
lower divisions   17, 18
Lucifora, C.   46
Luton Town   48
Lyon (Olympique Lyonnais)   11, 11t,
  25t, 195(n12)

McAlpine, H.   x
McCann, F.   106, 177–8
McConnel, J.   186–7
McDonaldization/Disneyization   49
McLean, J.   174t, 190
McManus, J.P.   204(n89)
McNeill, B.   178
Mafia   121
Magnier, J.   204(n89)
Mahony, D.F.   35, 147
Mail on Sunday   173t, 193
Major League Baseball   32
Malcolm, D.   48, 49, 53
  et al. (2000)   48, 49, 53, 216
Mallorca   10t, 25t
management   78, 95, 141,
  204(n91–2)
management board (*raad van
  Bestuur*)   96, 97f, 98
Manchester   1, 182
Manchester City   17, 148t, 157, 163t
Manchester United   1, 8, 8t, 17, 63,
  182, 194(n5)
  BSkyB takeover bid (1999)   31, 176
  disclosure   64t, 65t
  financial information (electronic
    availability)   148t
  financial information (website
    availability)   150
  G14 club   195(n12)
  helps to popularize capitalism   177
  merchandising   197(n32)

ownership 81t
participation in World Club
    Championship
    (2000) 197(n25)
share float (1991) 178–9
UEFA Champions League market
    pool league table 25t
website (www.ManUtd.com) 147,
    150
Manchester United plc 130, 130e, 15
claims about community
    status 58e
diversified ownership 132t
investment in training and
    development 164
potential takeover bids 129,
    204(n89)
stock market capitalization 171,
    207(n122–4)
takeover target 204(n95)
youth development narrative
    disclosure 163t
Manders, T. 197(n33)
Marca 167
market forces 16, 26, 43, 45, 49, 76, 77,
    89, 106, 110, 129, **136–8**
marketing 49
Marra, M. x, xii
Marseille (Olympique Marseille) 56,
    11t, 195(n12)
mass communication 170
match scheduling 112
Match of the Day 29t
Mayer, C. 116, 133–4
Meazza, G. 119
media 1, 34, 44, 127, 129, 167, 178,
    203(n86)
interactive 100, 201(n66)
see also BBC; newspapers; radio;
    television
media contracts: UEFA Champions
    League 196(n16)
Media Partners 27, 33
media studies 170
Mediobanca 202(n76)

merchandise/merchandising 16, 49,
    59, 86, 120–1, 143e, 168e, 169e,
    197(n32)
counterfeiting 121
UEFA Champions
    League 196(n16)
Merchesi, A. xi, 21, 121–2, 125–6
mergers 28, 66, 105
Merrill Lynch 28
Merton (London borough) 69,
    199(n47)
Metz 11t
Middlesbrough FC 60e, 63, 64t, 81t,
    148t, 163t
Milan (AC Milan) 9t, 29, 117, 127,
    194(n5), 195(n12), 202(n80)
Milan City Council 121
Milan FC (later AC Milan) 119
Milan Stock Exchange (*Borsa
    Italiana*) 115–18
Milton Keynes 68–71, 199(n49)
Mitrano, J.R. 67
mobile phones 201(n67)
Modernising Company Law (DTI
    white paper, 2002) 60, 205(n102)
Monaco 11t
monitoring 141
Monopolies and Mergers
    Commission 31
Montedison 202(n76)
Moorhouse, H.F. 48
Moratti family 117, 132t
    Angelo 119
    Massimo 119–20, 123, 124, 127,
        134–5, 136
Morrow, S. 57, 130, 152
Motherwell 6t, 6, 64t, 81t, 81n, 149t,
    164t
Motson, J. 12–13
Mundo Deportivo 167
Murdoch, R. 28
Murphy, P. 9, 194(n1), 218
Murray, D. 36, 125, 180–1
mutuality (*Lega Calcio*) 122
mutuality (ownership) 204(n89)

Naamloze Vennootschap (NV)
(public limited company) 90–1,
92
Nantes FC 11t, 25t
narrative communication **161–5**
National Insurance 122
Nationwide Building Society 51
Nationwide League 8, 17, 18–19, 21,
28, 30, 35, 46, 62, 156, 158,
195(n11)
Netherlands 3, 33, 54, 77, **90–101**,
131, 141, 196(n18)
broadcasting revenues 15n
business organizations 90–1
concentrated sporting success 12t
declining television audience for
football 29t
small television market 16
structure of Dutch football 91–2
New Business of Football (Morrow,
1999) 152
'New Financial Journalism' 170
New Statesman 171
New York Giants 71
Newcastle United 8t
attendance records 206(n112)
disclosure 64t, 65t
financial information (electronic
availability) 148t
financial information (website
availability) 150
helps to popularize
capitalism 177
ownership 81t
securitization 157, 206(n112)
youth development narrative
disclosure 163t
Newcastle United plc 58e
News of the World 172
newspapers/press 86, 146, **166–7**,
204(n89)
broadsheet 173t, 174–5t, 176, 179,
181, 185–93
content analysis **173–7**
misinterpretation 206(n110)

sections 174–5t, 176, 185–92
survey (2002) **172–3**, 173t, **185–93**,
207(n126)
tabloid 170, 173t, 174–5t, 176,
179–81, 186–91, 193
see also media
Nice: European Council (2000) 37
Nørby Committee, 102, 200(n56)
North Atlantic Cup 34
Norway 33, 54
notes to the accounts 147
Nottingham Forest 81t
Novantesimo 29t

O'Malley, T. 71
O'Neill, M. 191
Obelic (Serbia) 114
Observer 173t, 186, 192, 193
OECD (author) 77–8, 139
off balance sheet finance 159, 160
Office of Fair Trading
(OFT) 194(n6)
OFR *see* Operating and Financial
Review
Old Firm (Celtic/Rangers) 5–8, 41,
194(n1–2)
attempt to take part in an English
league **34–6**
league matches lost to other SPL
clubs 7t
rivalry 7, 194(n3)
see also Celtic; Rangers
Olympiakos 25t
Olympique Lyonnais 11, 11t, 25t,
195(n12)
Olympique Marseille 56, 11t,
195(n12)
ondernemingsraad (works council) 91
Oosterwijk, F. 92, 94
Operating and Financial Review
(OFR, 1993–) 142, 147, 161,
162–4t, 205(n102)
organizational forms **75–8**
Østergaard, F. xi, 105–6, 111, 114,
136, 202(n72)

overseas aid 201(n68)

ownership 203(n88)

concentrated 80, 133, 134, 135, 150

and control 128, **131–6**

diversified 132t, 133, 150

dominant 125, 133, 134–5

family 115–16, 117, 125, 126, 128, 133, 137

types 132t

El País 167

Palestine, 198(n44)

Panathinaikos 25t

PAOK Thessaloni 201(n66)

parachute payments 15t, 15n, 17–18, 20, 158

Pareto-optimality 41, 72, 199(n50–1)

lesser standard 41, 184

Paris St Germain (PSG) 11t, 195(n12)

Parken National Stadium 108, 111–12

Parken Sport and Entertainment (1999–; previously FCK) 103t, 104, 105, **106–9**, 113

balance sheet 107t

leisure and entertainment company 108

listed company 108

objectives 109

ownership 106, 107t

revenues 109

share issues 108

share price 106, 108f

turnover and profits 106, 107t

Parliament (Italy) 117

Parma 9t, 29, 117, 196(n21), 202(n79–80)

Parmalat Finanziaria company 117, 202(n79)

Parsons, W. 170

partnerships 200(n57)

Pay TV 14t, 28–9, 49

Pellegrino, E. 119

performance–related pay (PRP) 21–2, 195(n14)

Perkins, S. 49

personality 136, 205(n97)

PFA 45, 46, 198(n38)

Philips 91, 201(n65)

PSV's main sponsor 201(n64)

see also PSV Eindhoven

Philips Stadium (Eindhoven) 100

Pirelli 115, 119

PKF 157, 165

player contracts 153

player finance techniques 166

players 2, **44–7**, 93, 96, 127

average wage (FA Premiership) 44

employment rights 37

estimated sales value 164

job insecurity 46

sale and leaseback **159–60**, 206(n113–14)

status and rights 39

playing merit 17

population 26, 41

Porto (FC Porto) 25t, 195(n12)

Portugal 34, 77, 92, 100

power imbalance (clubs/ supporters) 140

Premiere World 14t

Preston North End 81t

Pricewaterhouse Coopers (PWC) 146, 152, 165, 171

Principles of Corporate Governance (OECD, 1999) 77–8

private corporations 77

private sector: Denmark 101

privatization 137, 141, 177

Professional Footballers' Association (PFA) 44

profit and loss account 152, 155

profits 62, 96, 106, 107t, 118, 169e, 171, 203(n82)

losses 62, 125

PSG (Paris St Germain) 11t, 195(n12)

PSV (*Philips Sport Vereniging*)
Eindhoven xi, 12t, 12, 33–4, 39,
92–101, 131, 136, 139, 196(n18)
corporate governance 96–8
G14 club 195(n12)
operational issues 99–101,
201(n65–6)
ownership and structure 94–6
pricing policy (affordability) 101
turnover 99t
UEFA Champions League market
pool league table 25t
PSV Football Foundation 95
PSV *Naamloze Vennootschap*
(1999–) 94–6, 97f
PSV plaza 201(n67)
public limited companies (plcs) 51
PWC (Pricewaterhouse
Coopers) 146, 152, 165, 171
pyramidal structures 128

Queen's Park Rangers 81t
Quinn, N. 174t, 191
Quirk, J. 71

raad van commissarissen (supervisory
board) 91
racism 51, 55, 142
radio 166–7
RAI 14t, 29, 202(n77)
Raleigh (North Carolina) 67
Ran–Bundesliga 29t
Rangers 6t, 6, 83, 125, 196(n18)
community initiatives 66
concentrated ownership 132t
disclosure 64t
financial information (electronic
availability) 149t
ownership 81t
youth development narrative
disclosure 164t
see also Old Firm
Rangers plc
not a listed company 180

proposed rights issue
(2000) 179–81
Real Madrid 1, 10t, 10, 157, 194(n5)
G14 club 195(n12)
membership organization 126
television deal with Canal Satellite
Digital 194(n7)
UEFA Champions League market
pool league table 25t
Real Sociedad 10t
Reboca 203(n83)
Reclaim the Game (Reid) 48, 171
redistribution 38, 122
Reel Radio 166
Reggina 196(n21)
relegation 20–1, 158, 195(n10)
Rennes 11t
rent (economic) 44, 197(n35)
research **41–2**
restraint on trade 32
Restrictive Practices Court 194(n6)
Ridsdale, P. 130e
rights issues 207(n127)
risk 106, 166
Rivaldo 206(n108)
Roda JC 12t
Rokke, K.I. 69
Roma (AS Roma) 9, 9t, 126, 135,
202(n80)
financial performance (2001) 125t
listed company (2000–) 118, 125
Pay-TV deal 29, 196(n21)
UEFA Champions League market
pool
Roma 2000 (company) 118
Romario 100
Ronaldo 100, 120, 203(n83)
Rosen, S. 19, 46, 197(n35)
Rosenborg 25t
Rosner, D. 35
Rotterdam 92
Rowbottom, N. 206(n107)
Royal Netherlands Football
Association (KNVB) 91–2, 93,
95, 146

rugby league 33
Rushden and Diamonds (1992–) 67,
175t, 192

SAFCommunity 63, 64t, 65t
St Johnstone 6t, 64t, 149t, 164t
St Mirren 149t, 164t
salotto buono 116, 126, 202(n76)
Sampdoria (1946–) 67
Sanderson, A. 19, 197(n35)
Saras (Sardinian oil refineries) 119
satellite television 28, 49, 166
Schalke 04 10t, 25t, 203(n85)
Schroders 130e
Schuitema, F. 97f
Scotland 5–8, 23, 34, 77, 92, 100
  broadcasting revenues 15n
  certainty of outcome 5
  concentrated sporting success 6t
  link between resources and
      performance 194(n1)
  'minimum efficient scale'
      problem 7
  proposed bid to host 2008 European
      Championships 173, 174t,
      185–7
  television rights fees 14t
Scotland on Sunday 173t, 180, 181,
  188, 192, 193
Scotsman 13, 173t, 178, 185, 186,
  187, 189, 190, 191, 193
Scottish Cup 178
Scottish Executive 53–4
Scottish Football Association
  (SFA) 79, 146
Scottish Parliament Official Report
  (2001) 54
Scottish Premier League (SPL) 5–6,
  14t, 22, 30, 33, 36, 62, 150, 154,
  156, 196(n18)
  charitable donations 63t
  lack of competitive balance 8,
      194(n4)
  points differential 6t, 6n

proposed establishment of
    television station 173, 174t, 176,
    187–9
  table minus 'Old Firm' 194(n2)
Scudetto, the 124, 134
Seagrave Haulage Combined Counties
  League 70
season tickets 86, 155, 157
securitization 155–9, 166, 206(n111)
Sedan 11t
Selhurst Park 70
Sensi, F. 83, 118, 125, 135
Sensi, R. 118
Serie A 9–10, 21, 29, 118–22, 122f,
  202(n80)
  attendances 116
  broadcasting income as percentage
      of turnover 15t
  club finances 121t
Serie B 116, 118f, 122f
Serie C 9
service sector 78, 90
Shankly, B. 182
share prices 178, 207(n127)
share register 205(n99)
shareholder trusts 205(n100)
  see also supporters' trusts
shareholder value 137
shareholders 32, 60, 74, 76–7, 80,
    86–7, 89, 91, 106, 129, 131–6, 140,
    146, 147, 150–1, 200(n54),
    204(n92, n95), 207(n127)
  controlling 126
  cross–holdings 115, 128, 131
  diversified 133
  dominant 80, 134, 136
  minority 115, 134, 177
  small 134
  utility preferences 134
shares
  golden 95
  preference 95
  trading volumes 204(n93)
  voting 80
Sheffield United 81t

Sheffield Wednesday FC   60e, 63, 64t, 81t
Shleifer, A.   204(n92)
Shore, H.   83t, 83n
Silver Shield   81t
Simmons, R.   46
Simpson, S.   198(n39)
Sinclair, A.   126
SIF Fodbold
   Support   103t, 201(n69)
Sir Norman Chester Centre for
   Football Research   69,196(n22)
Slack, J.   xi, 120, 127, 198(n44)
Slavia Prague   83
small and medium–sized
   enterprises   101, 115
Smallman, C.   137, 141
Snijders, D.   97f
Soccer Investor   121–3, 146, 166, 194(n4), 204(n93), 207(n116)
social capital   53, 183
social class   48, 92
social cohesion   42, 47, 71; *see also* inclusivity
Social Democratic Party
   (Denmark)   102
social market model   90
Social Security contributions   122
social welfare   **41–2**
Sogecable   28
Southampton   64t, 68, 81t, 149t, 163t
Southampton Leisure Holdings
   plc   58e, 81t
Spain   7, 153, 167
   accounting policies   152
   concentrated sporting success   10t
   individual television deals   15, 194(n7)
   survivability of promotion   18t
   taxation   122
   television audience for football   29t
Sparta Prague   25t, 26
Spartak Moscow   25t
special purpose vehicle (SPV)   157
Spiers, G.   180

SPL   *see* Scottish Premier League
sponsorship   27, 93, 99, 100, 143e, 155, 169e, 201(n64–5)
Spooren, F.   xi, 94, 97f, 98, 101, 201(n66)
sport   38, 102
Sport (Spanish national daily newspaper)   167
SportBusiness   34, 166
sporting competition   31, 158
sporting merit   21, 26, 42
sports clubs: freedom to establish in another EU Member–State   40
sports newspapers   116, 127, 167
sportswear   82, 196(n20)
SS Lazio   *see* Lazio
stadiums   4, 68, 70, 71, 93, 157, 158, 159e, 204(n94)
   Italy   121
   live action   198(n36)
   Plough Lane (Wimbledon)   69, 199(n47)
   safety requirements (Taylor Report)   129
stakeholder concept   43
stakeholder involvement   144
stakeholder representatives   141
stakeholders   2, 4, 5, 58, 59, 60, 73, 75, 89, 96, 98, 105, 129, 133–5, 137–9, 147, 150, 151, 172, 181, 183, 203(n86)
   incumbency bias   72
   prospective   72, 73
STAR market   118–19
status   205(n97)
Stein, J.   47, 182
Stichting PSV Voetbal (PSV Foundation)   93, 97f
stock markets   47, 76, 79, 95, 96, 129, 142
   capital markets   102
Stream   14t, 29, 196(n21)
structural change   **31–42**
   agenda for change   41–2
   change and the law   39–41

economics of change 31–6
policy for change 36–9
social welfare, consultation,
  research 41–2
structure NV (*structuurregeling*) 91,
  96
Studio Sport 29t
Stuttgart 10t
Sugar, Sir Alan 82–3, 83t, 135–6,
  204(n96)
Sun 173t, 187, 188, 190, 191, 193
Sunday Herald 172, 173t, 186, 188,
  193, 194(n2)
Sunday Mail 173t, 179, 187, 188,
  193
Sunday Times 173t, 188–9, 191, 193
Sunderland AFC 63, 68
  disclosure 64t, 65t
  financial information (electronic
    availability) 149t
  financial information (website
    availability) 150
  investment in training and
    development 164
  ownership 81t
  profits and losses 169e
  social involvement 60e
  turnover 169e
  youth development narrative
    disclosure 163t
Sunderland plc 57, 58e, 166, **168–9e**
super clubs (elite clubs) 16, 17, 31,
  33, 30, 39, 41, 136
super creditors 46, 160, 198(n38)
Super League 32, 33, 38, 196(n23)
Superliga (Denmark) 5, 104, 105,
  111, 113
superstars 45, 197(n36)
  Rosen's theory (1981) 46
supervisory board (*raad van
  commissarissen*) 91, 96–7, 97f,
  98
supporter groups 143e
  code of good governance 142
supporter-directors 141–2, 205(n101)

supporter-investors/
  supporter-shareholders 113–14,
    125–6, 132–5, 172, 202(n73),
    204(n94), 204–5(n96)
supporters/fans 1, 5, **47–55**, 62, 80,
  85–9, 98, 101, 129, 135–8, 140,
  172, 182–4, 197–8(n36), 198(n40),
  201(n67), 204(n89)
  categories (Giulianotti) 50f, 50–1,
    85–6, 133
  challenges 183
  conflict with investors 79
  expectations 131
  'free-market conversion into
    customers' 85, 89
  FCK **110–13**
  Inter Milan 119, 120
  involvement initiatives 139,
    205(n98)
  'moral owners of the team' 127
  priced out 49
  social composition 48
  unvarying loyalties 2, 137
Supporters Direct (government
  initiative, 2000–) xi, 52, 86, 89,
  141, 203(n88), 205(n100)
supporters' associations 203–4(n88)
supporters' representatives 78, 141
supporters' trusts **51–5**, 89–90,
  141–2, 205(n100)
Survey of Football Club Accounts
  (Touche Ross, 1993–) 165
Swansea City 81t
Sweden 34, 54
Szymanski, S. 8, 16, 32, 203(n82)

Tampa Bay Buccaneers 204(n89)
Tannadice Park x
Tanzi family 117 202(n79)
tax liability 160
taxation **122–3**, 202(n81)
Taylor, R. 48
Taylor Brothers x
Taylor Report 43, 67–8, 129
teachers 197(n35)

Teachers Insurance and Annuity
  Association 159e
technology 1, 45, 197(n35)
Telefoot 29t
Telepiu 14t, 29
television 111, 166
  changing channels **27–30**
  football's dependency **12–16**
  highlights 14t, 29t
  live action 14t, 29t, 198(n36)
  saturation coverage of football 29,
    196(n22)
television audience 26, 35, 36, 45,
    197(n31)
  declining 7, 29, 29t
  highlights programmes 29t
  market share (UEFA Champions
    League) 30t
television deals 26, 30, 155, 168e,
    196(n18)
television income/revenues 2, 4,
    35–6, 99, 112, 120, 122, 158, 159e,
    169e, 197(n32), 200(n53),
    202(n80)
  distribution 14–15, 18, 30, 183
  dwindling 7
  search for alternatives 175t, 192
television markets 33
  audience size 24
  domestic 24
  minor/small 16, 33
television rights 11, 44
  fees 14t
tennis 105
Thatcher Government 177
THST *see* Tottenham Hotspur
  Supporters' Trust
Thynne, I. 127
ticketing/tickets 49, 55, 59, 82, 122,
    143e, 196(n20)
Times, The 170, 173t, 185, 187, 189,
    192, 193
Timmer, J.D. 96, 97f
Torino: television deal with
    Telepiu 196(n21)

Tottenham Hotspur (1882–) **82–90**,
    129, 135–7, 142, 204–5(n96)
  annual charter report
    (2001–02) 143–4e
  business 84–7
  disclosure 64t
  diversification 82, 196(n20)
  diversified ownership/concentrated
    control 132t
  financial information (electronic
    availability) 149t
  financial information (website
    availability) 150
  governance and
    accountability 88–90
  listed on stock exchange (1983) 80,
    82, 83
  ownership 81t, 82–4, 132t,
    200(n58)
  youth development narrative
    disclosure 163t
Tottenham Hotspur plc
Tottenham Hotspur Supporters' Trust
    (THST) xi, 70, **86–90**, 139, 140,
    143e
Touche Ross 165
TPS 14t
trade union membership 54
transfer fees 100, 110, 125, 126, 160
  accounting **152–5**, 206(n107)
  in-contract 153
  unpaid 22, 147
transfer windows 46
transfers 37, 46, 93, 130, 130e, 158,
    168e, 172
transparency/openness 84, 88, 116,
    119, 126, 128, 131, 145, 147, 181
Tricker, R.I. 141
Turkey 77, 92
Tutto Sport 167

Udinese 9t, 196(n21)
UEFA 16, 32, 37, 42, 44, 69, 147, 153
  accounting principles 151
  big five countries 7

club licensing system
(proposed) 22
EU protection 39
national associations 33, 34, 69,
205(n103)
UEFA (author) 145
UEFA: European Cup–Winners'
Cup 202(n78)
UEFA: European Cup 13, 22, 119,
182, 195(n15), 201(n61), 202(n78)
UEFA Champions' League
(1992–) 13, 16, 38, 87, 154, 175t,
182
country coefficients 22–3,
195–6(n15)
commercial rights 196(n16)
five largest leagues 196(n17)
inequality **22–7**
licensing rights 196(n16)
market pool system 24, 25t, 26
objectives 26e
regulations 26
revenue distribution 23t, 24t, 26–7,
183, 196(n17–18)
see also 'UEFA: European Cup'
UEFA Club Licensing System 78,
144–6, 151–2, 154, 165, 183
financial criteria 145
'five areas' 145
implementation (2004–,
forthcoming) 145, 205(n103)
UEFA competitions 1, 7, 16, 84, 110,
183
English clubs banned
from 194(n5)
implications of Old Firm
participation in FA
Premiership 36
Italian success 117, 119, 202(n78)
places won 8, 194(n5)
UEFA Cup 104, 114, 119, 201(n61,
n66)
five largest leagues 196(n17)
Italian success 119, 202(n78)
'unitary supervisory board' 98

United Kingdom 3, 52, **78–90**, 140,
151, 197
corporate structure 129
declining television audience for
football 29t
demography 72
football companies (ownership type,
1997) 81t
lack of specialist sports
newspapers 207(n118)
structure of football **79–82**
UEFA Champions League
(television market share) 30t
United States of America 44, 67,
205(n104)
Unlocking the Potential (credit union
action plan, 2001) 54
Utrecht 12t

Valencia 10t, 195(n12)
van der Coolwijk, H.C.R. 97f
van der Peol, A.P.M. 97, 97f
van Raaij, H. xi, 93, 96–8, 100
Vance, C. 206(n109)
Verkerk, R. 97f
Veron, J.S. 154
Via Digital 28, 194(n7)
Vicenza 83
Vienot Report (M. Vienot) 200(n56),
222
Vieri, C. 119–20, 203(n83)
Vishny, R.W. 204(n92)
Vitesse 12t
volunteering 54
voting rights 115, 136, 204(n91)

Waddington, I. 48
et al. (1998) 48, 222
wage expenditure 195(n8)
wage restraint 21, 195(n11)
wages (salaries/earnings) 4, 18,
19–20, **44–7**, 79, 100, 120, 122,
126, 158, 168e, 180, 197(n35)
correlation with league
performance 124–5, 203(n82)

wages (salaries/earnings) (*cont.*)
  earnings gap 30
  entertainer analogy 45, 197(n36)
  'personal scale of operations'
      effect 45
  unpaid 22, 147
  unsustainability 124, 203(n83)
wages to turnover ratio 28
Walfrid, Brother 59e
Walker, J. 8, 17, 125
Wark, K. 188
water industry 137, 141
Watford 64t
Watford Supporters' Trust 52–3
websites 57, 59, 69, 70, 86–7, 97,
    144e, 146, 167, 196(n17), 198(n42)
  disclosure index 64t
  social involvement 60e
  www.ManUtd.com 147, 150
Wembley Stadium 1, 174t, 189
Werder Bremen 194(n5)
West Bromwich Albion 81t
West Ham United 8t, 64
  claims about community status 58e
  disclosure 64t, 65t
  financial information (electronic
      availability) 149t
  investment in training and
      development 164

not a listed company 57
ownership 81t
youth development narrative
    disclosure 163t
Wetzels, M. 133, 204(n94)
Wild, J. xi, 87–8, 135
Wilkesman, U. 203(n85)
Willem II 12t
Williams, J. 48, 49
  et al. (2001) 48, 223ó"ó
Wimbledon 40, 64t, **68–70**, 81t,
    199(n49)
Wimbledon Independent Supporters'
    Association (WISA) 69, 70
Winkelman, P. 199(n49)
works' councils 98
World Club Championship
    (2000) 197(n25)
Worldcom 138
Wright, A. 178

yo-yo clubs 17–18, 20
York City 175t, 191
Yorkhill Children's Hospital 63n
Yorkshire Water 137

Zaragoza 10t
Zimmer, M. 44